TRAVELS OF THE CRIMINAL QUESTION

'The criminal question' draws attention to the specific location and constitution of a given field of forces, and the themes, issues, dilemmas and debates that compose it. At the same time it enables connections to be made between these embedded realities and the wider, conceivably global, contours of influence and flows of power with which it connects. This in turn raises many questions. How far do the responses to crime and punishment internationally flow from and owe their contemporary shape to the cultural and economic transformations now widely known as 'globalisation'? How can something that is in significant ways embedded, situated, and locally produced also travel? What is not in doubt is that it does travel – and travel with serious consequences. The international circulation of discourses and practices has become a pressing issue for scholars who try to understand their operation in their own particular cultural contexts. This collection of essays seeks a constructive comparative view of these tendencies to convergence and divergence.

Oñati International Series in Law and Society

A SERIES PUBLISHED FOR THE OÑATI INSTITUTE
FOR THE SOCIOLOGY OF LAW

General Editors
Judy Fudge   David Nelken

Founding Editors
William L F Felstiner   Eve Darian-Smith

Board of General Editors
Rosemary Hunter, University of Kent, United Kingdom
Carlos Lugo, Hostos Law School, Puerto Rico
Jacek Kurczewski, Warsaw University, Poland
Marie-Claire Foblets, Leuven University, Belgium
Roderick Macdonald, McGill University, Canada

Titles in this Series

Social Dynamics of Crime and Control: New Theories for a World in Transition edited by Susanne Karstedt and Kai Bussmann

Criminal Policy in Transition edited by Andrew Rutherford and Penny Green

Making Law for Families edited by Mavis Maclean

Poverty and the Law edited by Peter Robson and Asbjørn Kjønstad

Adapting Legal Cultures edited by Johannes Feest and David Nelken

Rethinking Law, Society and Governance: Foucault's Bequest edited by Gary Wickham and George Pavlich

Rules and Networks edited by Richard Appelbaum, Bill Felstiner and Volkmar Gessner

Women in the World's Legal Professions edited by Ulrike Schultz and Gisela Shaw

Healing the Wounds edited by Marie-Claire Foblets and Trutz von Trotha

Imaginary Boundaries of Justice edited by Ronnie Lippens

Family Law and Family Values edited by Mavis Maclean

Contemporary Issues in the Semiotics of Law edited by Anne Wagner, Tracey Summerfield and Farid Benavides Vanegas

The Geography of Law: Landscapes, Identity and Regulation edited by Bill Taylor

Theory and Method in Socio-Legal Research edited by Reza Banakar and Max Travers

Luhmann on Law and Politics edited by Michael King and Chris Thornhill

Precarious Work, Women and the New Economy: The Challenge to Legal Norms edited by Judy Fudge and Rosemary Owens

Juvenile Law Violators, Human Rights, and the Development of New Juvenile Justice Systems edited by Eric L Jensen and Jørgen Jepsen

The Language Question in Europe and Diverse Societies: Political, Legal and Social Perspectives edited by Dario Castiglione and Chris Longman

European Ways of Law: Towards A European Sociology of Law edited by Volkmar Gessner and David Nelken

Crafting Transnational Policing: Police Capacity-Building and Global Policing Reform edited by Andrew Goldsmith and James Sheptycki

Constitutional Politics in the Middle East: With Special Reference to Turkey, Iraq, Iran and Afghanistan edited by Saïd Amir Arjomand

Parenting after Partnering: Containing Conflict after Separation edited by Mavis Maclean

Fighting for Political Freedom: Comparative Studies of the Legal Complex and Political Liberalism edited by Terence C Halliday, Lucien Karpik and Malcolm M Feeley

Responsible Business: Self-Governance and Law in Transnational Economic Transactions edited by Olaf Dilling, Martin Herberg and Gerd Winter

Rethinking Equality Projects in Law edited by Rosemary Hunter

Regulating Deviance: The Redirection of Criminalisation and the Futures of Criminal Law edited by Bernadette McSherry, Alan Norrie and Simon Bronitt

Living Law: Reconsidering Eugen Ehrlich edited by Marc Hertogh

Contractual Certainty in International Trade: Empirical Studies and Theoretical Debates on Institutional Support for Global Economic Exchanges edited by Volkmar Gessner

Multicultural Jurisprudence: Comparative Perspectives on the Cultural Defense edited Marie-Claire Foblets and Alison Dundes Renteln

Legal Institutions and Collective Memories edited by Susanne Karstedt

Changing Contours of Domestic Life, Family and Law: Caring and Sharing edited by Anne Bottomley and Simone Wong

Criminology and Archaeology: Studies in Looted Antiquities edited by Simon Mackenzie and Penny Green

The Legal Tender of Gender: Welfare Law and the Regulation of Women's Poverty edited by Shelley Gavigan and Dorothy Chunn

Human Rights at Work edited by Colin Fenwick and Tonia Novitz

Travels of the Criminal Question

Cultural Embeddedness and Diffusion

Edited by
Dario Melossi
Máximo Sozzo
and
Richard Sparks

Oñati International Series in Law and Society

A SERIES PUBLISHED FOR THE OÑATI INSTITUTE
FOR THE SOCIOLOGY OF LAW

·HART·
PUBLISHING

OXFORD AND PORTLAND OREGON
2011

Published in the United Kingdom
by Hart Publishing Ltd
16C Worcester Place, Oxford, OX1 2JW
Telephone: +44 (0)1865 517530
Fax: +44 (0)1865 510710
E-mail: mail@hartpub.co.uk
Website: http://www.hartpub.co.uk

Published in North America (US and Canada)
by Hart Publishing
c/o International Specialized Book Services
920 NE 58th Avenue, Suite 300
Portland, OR 97213-3786
USA
Tel: +1 503 287 3093 or toll-free: (1) 800 944 6190
Fax: +1 503 280 8832
E-mail: orders@isbs.com
Website: http://www.isbs.com

© Oñati IISL 2011

British Library Cataloguing in Publication Data
Data Available

ISBN: 978-1-84946-076-7 (hbk)
ISBN: 978-1-84946-077-4 (pbk)

Typeset by Criteria International
Printed and bound in Great Britain by
CPI Anthony Rowe, Chippenham, Wiltshire

Contents

List of Contributors

Alesssandro de Giorgi is Assistant Professor of Justice Studies, San Jose University, USA.

David Garland is Arthur T Vanderbilt Professor of Law and Professor of Sociology, New York University.

Dario Melossi is Professor of Criminology in the Faculty of Law at the University of Bologna.

David Nelken is Distinguished Professor of Sociology at the University of Macerata, Italy, and Distinguished Research Professor of Law at the University of Cardiff, Wales. He also teaches a course on comparative criminal justice as Visiting Professor at the Centre of Criminology at Oxford.

Nicole Rafter is Professor and Senior Research Fellow at the School of Criminology and Criminal Justice, Northeastern University.

Iñaki Rivera Beiras is Professor of Criminology and Penal Law at the University of Barcelona and the Director of the Observatory of the Penal System and Human Rights of the same university.

Rossella Selmini is Professor of Sociology of Law, Deviance, and Social Change at the University of Modena and Reggio Emilia.

Máximo Sozzo is Professor of Sociology and Criminology in the Faculty of Social and Juridical Sciences at the National University of Litoral.

Richard Sparks is Professor of Criminology in the School of Law at the University of Edinburgh.

1

Introduction. Criminal Questions: Cultural Embeddedness and Global Mobilities

DARIO MELOSSI, MÁXIMO SOZZO AND RICHARD SPARKS

I N THE PROCESS of bringing together this book we spent a certain amount of time wondering about an appropriate title, as editors and authors are inclined to do. Finding a form of words that in some way encapsulates a theme, or an ambition, or which at any rate does not misrepresent the content of individual contributions too grievously, is one of the perils and privileges of editorship.

We concluded that a good way to express what the various papers were about,[1] and at the same time to name the underlying and emergent project that we hope to advance, was with reference to the 'the criminal question', and to the duality that we see as inherent to it between mobility and embeddedness. We are well aware that the expression 'the criminal question' does not at present have much currency in English-language criminology and that in consequence our title might appear slightly stilted. One of the hopes that animate this volume is that meaning may be *discovered*, as well as 'lost' in translation. The term 'the criminal question', as we use it here, has been carried across from the Italian

---

[1] This book is the product of the discussion developed at the International Institute for the Sociology of Law of Oñati in the context of the Workshop 'Discourses and Practices of Crime and Punishment: The Question of Cultural Embeddedness and Travels', that took place on 19–20 June 2003 and was convened by the editors of this volume. We are grateful to the IISL for providing financial support for this workshop and a wonderful environment in which to hold it; and to the participants who made possible the emergence of the 'international-conversation-in-action' that this volume attempts to record and develop. We are only too well aware that much time has elapsed and can only apologise to our long-suffering contributors. There are many reasons for this, among them that genuine international collaboration, even in our hot, wired times is just not as simple as it seems.

language and is a resonant one in the context of the intellectual and political debates surrounding the orientations of criminological work in Italy in recent decades.

In the mid-1970s the journal called *La questione criminale*, the criminal question, was founded in Bologna. At least in Italy, it came to embody the meaning and research agenda of what was at that time coming to be called critical criminology. A few years later, in *Limited Responsibilities*, Tamar Pitch, one of the main participants and contributors to that act of foundation, and a key figure in the development of critical criminology in Italy, had this to say about what the criminal question is:

> To study the criminal question is different from studying crime. It means that crime is not considered independently from the procedures by which it is defined, the instruments deployed in its administration and control and the politics and debates around criminal justice and public order. The criminal question can therefore be provisionally defined as an area constituted by actions, institutions, policies and discourses whose boundaries shift [...] (Pitch, 1995:52)

Pitch went on to call attention to the need to 'be aware of the fact that the sociologist and the criminologist themselves contribute to the construction of the criminal question through their analyses, discourses, political interventions and debates' (ibid: 54), a point to which we return in a moment. She also noted that 'what "the public" think of as crime and what, according to the "public" should be considered crime, or what cultural and symbolic significance is carried by law and criminal justice, is an integral aspect of the criminal question' (loc cit).

It should be clear that in this perspective the criminal question is, by definition, one steeped within a specific historical and more especially a *cultural* situation. Despite a degree of contemporary popularity of 'culturalist' approaches to law, crime and justice (the widely touted notion of 'cultural criminology', for example) it remains the case that even to float the idea of 'the cultural' as a mode of analysis or explanatory resource is to court theoretical controversy and perhaps to beg many of the most knotty questions. Nevertheless, the production and circulation of ideas, representations and symbols around these matters continues with ever-greater intensity and through ever-more diverse channels and networks. This is true, we suggest, both for official and quasi-official governmental discourses (whether these originate 'within' the state as such or in commercial or nonstatutory 'centres of calculation' (Rose, 2000) and for the multiform channels of news and entertainment media, campaigning and interest groups, internet blogs and chat-rooms and the rest of our bewildering contemporary conversations.

As Garland made clear in his paper at Oñati Seminar (which appears in this volume in somewhat revised and extended form), the boundary between analyses that foreground questions of culture and those that emphasise material interests and functional imperatives has always been an artificial and problematic one:

'culture encodes and is encoded by economic and political forces, and [that] the analysis of culture is not a distraction from the study of penal power's controlling effects but is, on the contrary, a vital component of such study'. Moreover, Garland continues:

> Cultural categories, habits and sensibilities are embedded in, and constitutive of, our political and economic institutions. The study of culture does not begin where the study of power and economics leaves off — it is a constituent part of any political or economic analysis.
>
> In studying social relations, we can, and do, make rough demarcations between the domains of the economic, the political, the legal, the scientific, and the cultural — and these distinctions serve a useful purpose, up to a point. But unless we want to confine 'culture' to the world of leisure, art and entertainment (and, in so doing, artificially restrict the study of meaning and sensibility as it relates to social action) it turns out that the generic category of 'culture' envelops all of the other, more specific social categories. If the distinctive stuff of culture is meaning, perception, feeling, sentiment, value, belief and the various forms of their expression, then, in the social world, it is not particularly distinctive at all. Culture is suffused through all social relations, institutions and practices, and abstracting it away from these forms necessarily does violence to the true relationship between meaning and action.

Seen in this light the notion of 'the criminal question' does useful work in drawing attention on the one hand to the specific temporal and geographical location and constitution of a given field of forces, and the themes, issues, dilemmas and debates that compose it; and on the other it encourages us also to see the connections between these embedded realities and the wider, conceivably global, contours of influence and flows of power with which it connects. We should therefore expect each instance of 'the criminal question' to carry the weight of its history and to display the obdurate legal, institutional, linguistic particularities of the political culture of which it is an intrinsic component. There will be in every case conflicts, enmities and affiliations that we can expect only initiates to grasp, at least without some fairly effortful induction for the newcomer. Conversely, no individual case-in-point will really be entirely hermetic, immune to external influence, or lacking common features with others. In this sense the theoretical and methodological difficulties that have always attended comparative social scientific analysis are magnified, but not superseded, in conditions of late modernity.

Formulations of the criminal question get around. They are passed on through various media and networks. Some of these now make images and ideas almost globally available, almost immediately. Others, like academic and professional journals, conferences, congresses and so on, are less obvious channels of influence which, though they may well have expanded and intensified recently, have longer histories. How far do the many ways of circulating images of and responses to crime and punishment internationally flow from and owe their contemporary shape to the cultural and economic transformations now widely known as 'globalisation'? Giddens has influentially argued that globalisation can be defined as 'the intensification of worldwide social relations which link distant localities in such a way that local happenings are shaped by events occurring many miles away and vice versa' (1990: 64). Similarly Beck speaks of 'the processes through which sovereign national states are criss-crossed and undermined by transnational actors with varying prospects of power, orientations, identities and networks' (2000:11). Globalisation produces, he suggests, 'multiplicity without unity'. For us, the question at issue concerns how such conditions bear upon the construction of the criminal question in any given place and time. We believe that there is ample evidence that there is much more at stake than simply pressure towards homogeneity, though that exists too.

One of the editors of this book has written elsewhere, developing this issue, of a 'historical embeddedness' of social control and punishment (and, more implicitly, of deviance and crime) (Melossi, 2001). This term in turn raises some substantial definitional problems. What precisely is meant by *embeddedness*, and how can something that is in significant ways embedded, situated, and locally produced also *travel*?

Some years ago, a celebrated article by Mark Granovetter helped to introduce the notion of embeddedness into sociological parlance. There, embeddedness was defined as 'the argument that the behaviours and institutions to be analysed are so constrained by ongoing social relations that to construe them as independent is a grievous misunderstanding' (Granovetter, 1985, 481–2). Granovetter referred to 'embeddedness' *tout court*, in yet another twist on the century-long sociologists' attempt at rescuing *homo oeconomicus* from his indenture to economics. Melossi subsequently directed his attention to the *cultural* embeddedness of historical institutions, such as the institutions of social control and punishment. For Melossi the implication is 'that such institutions cannot be conceived separately from the historical evolution and development of the larger setting of social action within which they have emerged — a setting constituted also through given cultural traditions' (Melossi, 2001).

Indeed, all sociological explanation, in whatever mode, is contextual and perhaps, in the parlance of the ethnomethodologists, 'indexical' (Heritage, 1984). The very purpose of the 'descriptive metalanguages' deployed in sociological analysis is 'the explication and mediation of divergent forms of life' (Giddens, 1979: 162). For example, this might have a distinct bearing on the ways in which we reflect upon the history of criminological thinking, and the differences between its histories in different national settings. Methodologically speaking, such historical inquiry might stand closer to the 'historical hermeneutics' defended by Quentin Skinner (in many publications, for example, 2002) — an influential position in the wider history of social and political ideas but one only lightly explored by criminologists to date (cf Loader & Sparks, 2004).

We remain persuaded that embeddedness in the senses outlined here continues to be a crucial feature of the criminal question wherever we encounter it, and that this imposes certain fairly stringent conceptual and methodological demands in the ways in which it is proper to theorise and study it or feasible to intervene in practice. At the same time part of the *raison d'être* of this book is precisely that the criminal question also travels. The phenomena of crime and crime control are in a strong sense historically constituted and culturally located and they circulate. Moreover, some social theorists argue that *disembedding* is a characteristic feature of contemporary social systems (Giddens, 1990: 21; see also Nelken, this volume). Giddens defines disembedding as 'the "lifting out" of social relations from local contexts of interaction and their restructuring across indefinite spans of time-space' (loc cit). Among the disembedding mechanisms that Giddens sees as intrinsically involved in the development of modern social systems he numbers the establishment of 'expert systems' (1990: 22). It may well be true to say that criminology as an academic discourse and crime control as an arena of practice display quite weakly developed forms of expertise by comparison with some of Giddens's favoured examples, such as the aerospace industry. Nevertheless, from the invention of penitentiary imprisonment to the creation of new 'moral inventions' (O'Malley, 1992), such as zero-tolerance policing or situational crime prevention, these fields have generated institutions, techniques and quasi-technical vocabularies that have achieved widespread, though not necessarily universal or uniform, application.

The example of the penitentiary is instructive here, as well as historically central. From its inception in the religious and ideological contexts of the 18th century the penitentiary was a model — or strictly speaking a range of competing models — that was understood by its proponents as capable of being transported to and replicated in new settings (Melossi & Pavarini, 1981). Bentham, for example, explicitly viewed the Panopticon as a device that he could actively market to potential purchasers, even if it never made him the fortune he hoped for. John Howard's influence gained greatly from the authority associated with his epic journeys through Europe and the precision of his first-hand observations. De Tocqueville's place in this story also derives from an experience of travel, and hence a role in mediating between the intellectual worlds of Europe and the new American republic.[2] As Scharff Smith (2004) has shown, throughout much of the nineteenth century there was a complex series of voyages, missions, exchanges that led to penal ideas crossing and recrossing the Atlantic and increasingly to the reimportation of penitentiary standards and innovations from the New World back to the Old. Moreover, these patterns of circulation would eventually also transport the penitentiary *savoir* much further afield, to South America (Salvatore & Aguirre, 1996) and beyond. It is instructive to see these patterns of circulation not just as the precursors of the great penological congresses of the early twentieth century (latterly recalled by Radzinowicz, 1999) but as the ancestors — remote perhaps but nonetheless direct — of today's entrepreneurial think-tanks, manuals, distance-learning programmes, and private prison industries.

---

[2] It may be worth recalling here that the official history of the Eastern State Penitentiary in Philadelphia, opened in 1829, characterises it as 'the first modern building in the United States', www.easternstate.org/history/sixpage.php.

All contemporary fields of knowledge production[3] entail an infrastructure of publication, dissemination and exchange — courses, conferences, citation indices, meetings, networks, newsletters, e-mails, websites. Of course, it has not entirely escaped us that our own activities, and specifically occasions such as the workshop from which the present volume originally arose, are a small instance of this general process. The networks through which academic exchanges are conducted may initially be formed in some sense accidentally, but they also develop most easily along lines of linguistic and cultural affinity. For example, throughout the modern era criminological and other scientific discourse has travelled relatively easily between, for example, Italy, Spain and Latin America. Remarkably, the 1930 Penal Code of Fascist Italy, so-called 'Codice Rocco', became a 'model penal code' for many democratic countries also because it incorporated, albeit in a conservative way, some of the precepts of the Positive School, another true international phenomenon in itself (Marques & Pires, 2007). Latin America's criminology has certainly owed quite a bit to its connections with the Southern and Latin part of Europe (del Olmo, 1981). At the beginning, one century ago, such connections may have been with the Italian Positive School but, more recently, they developed in unison with the teachings of Alessandro Baratta, a sort of 'liberation criminology' (Sozzo, 2006). Despite all this, English-language criminology has in the main remained blissfully unaware of the content, scope, and even of the existence, of scholarly communities working in Italian, German, Spanish, French, Dutch, Japanese and other languages. Meanwhile, and crucially, discourse travels exceptionally easily from an English-language point of production to other sites (see further the contributions by Melossi, Selmini and Sozzo, in this volume).

Only latterly have such well-trodden pathways been supplemented and complicated by the more unpredictable, multidirectional flows facilitated and accelerated by the general availability of electronic communication (see further Sozzo, this volume).[4] We are acutely conscious that for just such reasons the examples and cases of criminological travel that are outlined in this book constitute a minute and somewhat arbitrary selection, both thematically and geographically, of those that might have been mentioned with equal interest. Similarly, our curiosity is engaged here in the first place by issues of embeddedness (and disembedding), translation, translocation and diffusion even if, as we willingly accept, this is only one way of responding to the notion of *travel*. A number of contributors in this volume are concerned to discuss a somewhat different possibility, namely the diffusion of *common* models and

---

[3] We avoid for the present the potentially endless discussion associated with the term 'discipline' in this context, let alone the labyrinths of inter- and multi-disciplinarity.

[4] It may be the case that the creation in 1999 of a European Society of Criminology, now hosting a lively and well-attended annual conference and publishing a significant scholarly journal, and the promotion of networks, such as the International Society of Criminology and various more specialised groups provide opportunities to redress the historic situation that we describe here.

practices, or at least seemingly very similar ones (see in particular the papers by de Giorgi and Rivera), especially under the pressure of a certain dominant, even hegemonic, economic and cultural position. Some travellers — the point hardly needs labouring but is nevertheless somewhat central — are more powerful than others. Their 'cargo' carries more weight, authority and capacity to effect change than does the freight of other, less privileged wanderers (Wacquant, 1999b; Bourdieu & Wacquant, 2001).

One of the strongest and most prominent arguments that constructions of the criminal question travel — and travel with serious consequences — is presented in the recent work of Loïc Wacquant. In Wacquant's view convergences between the language and practice of criminal justice systems around the world do not result simply from common responses to similar problems, nor yet from the pragmatic adoption or emulation of lessons or techniques. Rather, Wacquant detects the dominance of a certain set of models and slogans — 'broken windows', 'zero tolerance', 'no-frills prisons' and so on — that are, in his view, integral to the ways in which 'hegemonic neo-liberalism' (2009 b: 5) superintends the insecurities and fears that it itself engenders. These developments, on this account, come as a package and are actively and energetically exported by think-tanks, consultants and other evangelists for neoliberalism and for its penological and policing solutions. In these ways, Wacquant argues, 'the dissemination of 'zero tolerance' partakes of a broader international traffic in policy formulae that binds together market rule, social retrenchment, and penal enlargement' (Wacquant, 2009b: 171).

For Wacquant this set of conditions is not adequately approached via theoretical perspectives that postulate an evolutionary transition between societal stages or eras (from modernity to late- or post- or reflexive-modernities, for example). The issue on this view is not *succession* but *diffusion* — the diffusion of an actively promulgated orthodoxy. Thus:

> The punitive turn of public policy, applying to *both social welfare and criminal justice*, partakes of a *political project* that responds to rising *social* insecurity and its destabilizing effects in the *lower rungs* of the social and spatial order. This project involves the *retooling and redeployment of the state* to buttress market-like mechanisms and discipline the new post-industrial proletariat while restraining the internal disruptions generated by the fragmentation of labor, the retrenchment of social protection schemes, and the correlative shake-up of the established ethnic hierarchy (ethnoracial in the United States, ethnonational in Western Europe, and a mix of the two in Latin America). But the crafting of the new Leviathan also registers the external influences of political operators and intellectual entrepreneurs engaged in a multilayered campaign of ideological marketing across national boundaries in matters of capital/labor, welfare, and law enforcement. Even as neoliberalism is from its inception a multisited, polycentric and geographically uneven formation, at century's turn this campaign to revamp the triadic nexus of state, market, and citizenship from above had a nerve center located in the United States, an inner ring of collaborating countries acting as relay stations (such as the England in Western Europe and Chile in South America), and an outer band of societies targeted for infiltration and conquest (Wacquant, 2009b: 172).

It is not our primary task here to evaluate Wacquant's strong diffusionist thesis. It is worth noting that while Wacquant clearly believes that the proponents of the new consensus exercise powerful influence, he interprets the eager reception of his own work, especially in Latin America (and its multiple, rapid translations into various languages) as signals of resistance, and the search — often by state officials themselves — for other pathways and for 'civic firebreakers' with which to hold back the sway of what Bourdieu & Wacquant (2001) earlier termed the 'new planetary vulgate'.

One of our concerns here, and one that we feel has been less fully examined in recent debates, is with the *reception* side of the dynamics of policy mobility and transfer. How are new theories, concepts and ideas, or new gadgets, slogans and policy instruments imported? How (if at all) are they naturalised, adapted or changed in that process? For similar reasons, we have much less to say here than some of our contemporaries about the significance of contemporary moves towards specifically transnational or supranational agencies and institutions, although we freely acknowledge these to be crucially significant aspects of the contemporary scene, and ones that link strongly with the more particular issues that are our current focus (see, eg Huggins, 1998; Sheptycki, 2000; Sheptycki & Wardak, 2004; Franko Aas, 2007).

For now we feel there is a good deal still to be explored about how discourses and practices move around, sometimes gain ground and influence in previously 'alien' contexts, and pass across boundaries between states and regions. We also take the view that there are some quite tricky conceptual and terminological problems involved when talking about the international and intercontinental mobility of representation, policies, practices and so on. What happens to these cultural objects when they arrive at intersocietal 'edges' (Giddens, 1984)? How are they enabled to circulate? Who facilitates that circulation and why? For some cultural objects the peculiarities that go along with their 'embedded' character may render movement difficult, or mean that the transformations that they undergo in the process are especially marked (Nelken, 2009; Nelken, this volume). Others, perhaps increasingly, seem designed to be generic, to move around lightly and rapidly, for commercial or political reasons, so that anyone with the necessary know-how could institute a programme, set up a franchise, replicate a study and so on. In these instances research and policy guidance are produced in such a way as to encourage a degree of transcultural standardisation, via the use of validated questionnaires, risk-assessment protocols, best-practice guidelines, performance indicators, and so on. One influential example might be the approach pioneered by the International Centre for the Prevention of Crime in Montreal (www.crime-prevention-intl.org). Another could be the widely adopted five-point scale for the robustness of evaluation measures devised by criminologists at the University of Maryland (Sherman *et al*, 1997). It is not our objective here to dispute the effectivity of these endeavours, nor the often heroically entrepreneurial efforts of their authors. We merely raise the question of whether the possibility of complexity arising in translation may be denied or overlooked in some models of research and intervention, perhaps making it harder to identify or acknowledge when it occurs. Another issue, taken up here most explicitly by Sozzo, concerns the diverse possible sources of criminological knowledge and practice. In many cases, the most readily transportable knowledges are those that come packaged-for-use by local elites. In this sense it is unsurprising if the most 'international' criminology turns out to be one of a rather technocratic orientation.

Conversely, pausing to reflect on the difficulties of translatability and on the networks of influence and affinity that effect some kinds of circulation rather than others, highlights for attention such issues as the ways in which cultural capitals are accumulated and exchanged; the peculiar position of the criminal question in the preferred narratives and self-images of particular nation-states; the part played by criminal justice in the struggles for political mastery and self-definition that attend processes of transformation from autocracy to democracy, and so on. In this regard, which criminologies, techniques or practices travel best and come to be canvassed or adopted in new locations is a politically significant question.

The very questions of translation and translocation raise obdurate and challenging conceptual issues. When something that is 'embedded' moves around, is it simply 'translated' – carried across or lifted over – from one 'embeddedness' to another? A number of contributions in this volume are involved in trying to understand processes and experiences of 'translocation', in the sense that something — discourses and practices around crime —has been moved from 'there' to 'here'. Conventional accounts of 'policy transfer' do not generally problematise the ways in which the object being transferred may also be *transformed*, to a greater or lesser extent, in the process of moving across space and between contexts. Neither do they seriously countenance the possibility that some versions of 'transfer' are engaged in expounding and exporting a 'concentric', metropolitan world-view at the expense of local knowledges, commitments and democratic preferences.

Perhaps indeed we should consider the travels of the criminal question as a special case of the question of *translation* as a general issue. No one has put more forcefully than Alfred Schutz — in his famous essay 'The Stranger' — just why questions of translation are of central significance for social theory. Translation here is both a literal, technical problem (the problem of moving between languages without sacrifice of meaning or force) and a metaphor for mobility and the mediation of cultural frames of reference:

> The discovery that things in his surroundings look quite different from what he expected them to be at home is frequently the first shock to the stranger's confidence in the validity of his habitual 'thinking as usual'. Not only the picture which the stranger has brought along of the cultural pattern of the approached group but the whole hitherto unquestioned scheme of interpretation current within the home group becomes invalidated. It cannot be used as a scheme of orientation within the new social surroundings. For the members of the approached group their cultural pattern

fulfils the functions of such a scheme. But the approaching stranger can neither use it simply as it is nor establish a general formula of transformation between both cultural patterns permitting him, so to speak, to convert all the coordinates within one scheme of orientation into those valid within the other (Schutz (1944), 503/4).

Indeed, the question of translation is one of the most complex that sociologists and other social observers have to deal with. At the most general level all attempts at sociological explanation — not to mention sociological understanding (*Verstehen*) — involve translation, at least in Giddens's senses of explication and mediation noted above. We do not intend to involve ourselves here (and are not qualified to do so) in the deep and protracted debates on translatability, incommensurability, indeterminacy (Van Quine & Orman, 1960; Davidson, 1984) and interpretation (McCarthy, 2002) that have provided such a *leitmotif* of twentieth century philosophy. Neither, on the other hand, do we think that students of criminology and the sociology of social control can properly conclude that such matters have nothing at all to do with their topics and simply ignore the issue. In our view the working premise for researchers on crime and crime control, especially but not only in a comparative or transnational framework, must be that these practices are necessarily generated within, in Putnam's terms, a 'certain framework of pre-understandings' (1992: 209). This carries some substantial implications for grasping what is at stake in the criminological conversations of diverse times and places and for how one goes about historical, comparative and cross-cultural research.

We may very well assume, for instance, following Rusche & Kirchheimer (1968 [1939]) that there is a historical and statistically evidenced connection between periods of economic slowdown and change in the use of prisons (a change for the worse). Specific studies will however have to show that there are reasons actors give to themselves (whether these actors are criminals, police officers, judges, media people, policy makers, or whatever) that make them act, under specific economic circumstances, in the direction predicted by Rusche and Kirchheimer. In this sense, in respect of the *meanings* that social actors attach to what they do, there is no social action that is not 'culturally embedded'.

Translocation as a species of translation always implies some degree of creativity, of innovation. Walter Benjamin argued that translation in literature involves 'transformation and renewal' such that 'the original undergoes a change' (1969: 73). The 'object' which moves across space is always likely to undergo some sort of alteration. The local actors who take on the work of translating a discourse or technique into their own historical and cultural context have to adapt it to the local problems and vocabularies. In so doing they produce its 'metamorphosis', acting as 'traduttori traditori' (Sozzo, 2006; Sozzo, this volume). It may well be that those who experience working in more than one culture often show a keen and special sensitivity towards these issues, if only because the experience of being a foreigner and working with another language brings this point home in a way that all the other types of 'translations' we are involved with, both in our everyday life and in our scientific endeavours, do not (see further Melossi, 2000).

Perhaps the notion of elective affinity famously employed by Max Weber in *The Protestant Ethic* (Weber (1958 [1904–05], 91–92) provides a more useful analogy for thinking about the translocation of crime control discourse than Giddens's image of disembedding as 'lifting out'. When any cultural product or institution of consequence travels abroad it alters the context in which it arrives, and is itself altered to some extent. Its 'elective affinity' with certain cultural-historical elements in the context of its origin gives way to a different 'reaction' with other historical-cultural elements. However, the movement from one mode of elective affinity to another will produce patterns that have a great deal in common. To give an example, the affinity of the early workhouses, the 'Ur-prisons' so to speak, with something called 'manufactures', in England or Holland in the sixteenth-century, finds echoes in other parts of the world, for instance southern Europe or Latin America or, more recently Asia or Africa, even if neither term — 'workhouse' and 'manufacture' — fully captures what certain sites of coerced production are, and are called, in Brazil, Thailand or Ghana now. Furthermore, all of this will happen in a situation of deep conflict and competition, within which different courses of action, different discourses, venues, blueprints and practices will be tried out and find their development (see Melossi, this volume).

Travels of discourses and practices around crime have been a recurrent feature of modernity — see the examples outlined by Rafter in this volume and Sozzo (2006). Nevertheless, these processes have arguably become significantly more intense in the last quarter century or so, and their pace has accelerated sharply. New mechanisms and new vectors for enabling the diffusion and mobility of discourses and practices have emerged. The fact that there is a good deal at stake in that mobilisation — financially, politically and culturally — has become more expressly recognised. At the same time, and notwithstanding the massive cultural power of the North Atlantic sphere, there is a diversification and increased complexity of the directions of travelling, as in the case of restorative justice (Karstedt, 2001, 2002). By extension, there is a multiplication of the actors that made discourses and practices travel, from the experts and political 'authorities' of the XIX century to the many new 'experts' of our own time (consultants, representatives of nongovernmental organisations and foundations, etc) and international and supranational organisations (International Development Bank, World Bank, European Union, United Nations, etc) (Wacquant, 1999; Haggerty, 2004).

The diffusion and circulation of discourses and practices around crime seems to have reached another level of prominence in our present. That is why the international circulation of these discourses and practices becomes a pressing issue for scholars who try to understand their operation in their own particular cultural contexts (Newburn & Sparks, 2004: 10). But this evidence does not simply mean that there is some sort of uniform picture that is increasingly 'going global' in this field (O'Malley, 2002). We need to challenge the premature and frequently misleading premise that everything everywhere is flooded by sameness — a claim that is frequently combined with a dystopian and pessimistic view about our present and its political potentialities. We may thus be able to engage afresh in an encounter with the empirical moment, *here* and *there* (Nelken, 2000), constructing a comparative gaze that entertains the possibility of distinguishing tendencies to convergence and to divergence, addressing the 'tense and contradictory intersection between "the space of flows" and the "space of places"' (Newburn & Sparks, 2004: 3, citing Castells (1996); see also Sparks, 2001; Jones & Newburn, 2002; 2006).

This is an intellectual endeavour that is forbiddingly difficult for the individual author. But for an international scholarly community — with its networks for dialogue and exchange — as a whole, it seems achievable. This book — and the workshop from which it emerges — represents an attempt to construct these kinds of bridges for an international pluralist conversation, putting together scholars working from different sociological and criminological perspectives and from diverse cultural horizons around this problem.

REFERENCES

Aas, K & Franko (2007) *Crime and Globalization* (London, Sage).

Beck, U (2000)*What Is Globalization?* (Cambridge, Polity Press).

Benjamin, W (1969) 'The Task of the Translator' in W Benjamin (ed) *Illuminations* (New York, Schocken Books).

Bourdieu, P & Wacquant, L (2001) 'Neoliberal Newspeak: Notes on the New Planetary Vulgate' *Radical Philosophy*, 108.Castel, R (1995) *Les Metamorphoses de la question sociale* (Paris, Fayard).

Castells, M (1996) *The Rise of The Network Society* (Oxford, Blackwells).

Davidson, D (1984) *Inquiries into Truth and Interpretation* (Oxford, Clarendon Press).

Del Olmo, R (1981) *América Latina y su criminología* (Mexico City, Siglo Veintiuno Editores).

Giddens, A (1979) *New Rules of Sociological Method* (London, Hutchinson).

—— (1984) *The Constitution of Society* (Cambridge, Polity Press).

—— (1990) *The Consequences of Modernity* (Cambridge, Polity Press).

Granovetter, M (1985) 'Economic Action and Social Structure: a Theory of Embeddedness' *American Journal of Sociology*, 91, 481–510 [DOI: 10.1086/228311].

Haggerty, K (2004) 'Displaced Expertise: Three Constraints on the Policy-Relevance of Criminological Thought' *Theoretical Criminology*, 8, 211–231 [DOI: 10.1177/1362480604042244].

Heritage, J (1984) *Garfinkel and Ethnomethodology* (Cambridge, Polity Press).

Huggins, M (1998) *Political Policing: The United States and Latin America* (Duke University Press).

Jones, T & Newburn, T (2002) 'Atlantic Crossings: "Policy Transfer" and Crime Control in the USA and Britain' *Punishment and Society*, 4, 165–194 [DOI: 10.1177/14624740222228536].

—— (2006) *Policy Transfer and Criminal Justice* (Buckingham, Open University Press).

Karstedt, S (2001) 'Comparing Cultures, Comparing Crime: Challenges, Prospects and Problems for a Global Criminology' *Crime, Law, and Social Change*, 36, 285–308 [DOI: 10.1023/A:1012223323445].

—— (2002) 'Durkheim, Tarde and Beyond: The Global Travel of Crime Policies' *Criminal Justice*, 2, 111–123.

Loader, I & Sparks, R (2004) 'For an Historical Sociology of Crime Policy in England and Wales Since 1968' *Critical Reviews of International Social and Political Philosophy*, 7, 5–32 [DOI: 10.1080/1369823042000266495].

McCarthy, T *Radical Interpretation and Indeterminacy* (New York, Oxford University Press, 2002).

Marques, TP (2007) '*Mussolini's Nose: A Transnational History of the Penal Code of Fascism*', PhD Thesis (Florence, European University Institute).

Melossi, D (2000) 'Translating Social Control: Reflections on the Comparison of Italian and North-American Cultures Concerning Crime Control' in S Karstedt & KD Bussman (eds) *Social Dynamics of Crime and Control* (Oxford, Hart).

—— (2001) 'The Cultural Embeddedness of Social Control: Reflections on the Comparison of Italian and North-American Cultures Concerning Punishment' *Theoretical Criminology*, 4, 403–424 [DOI: 10.1177/1362480601005004001].

Melossi, D & Pavarini, M (2000) *The Prison and the Factory* (London, Macmillan).

Nelken, D (2000) *Contrasting Criminal Justice: Getting from Here to There* (Aldershot, Ashgate).

—— (2009) 'Comparative Criminal Justice: Beyond Ethnocentrism and Relativism' *European Journal of Criminology*, 6, 291–313 [DOI: 10.1177/1477370809104684].

Newburn, T & Jones, T (2002) 'Policy Convergence and Crime Control in the USA and the UK: Streams of Influence and Levels of Impact' *Criminal Justice*, 2, 173–203 [DOI: 10.1177/1466802502002002718].

Newburn, T & Sparks, R (2004) 'Criminal Justice and Political Cultures' in T Newburn & R Sparks (eds) *Criminal Justice and Political Cultures. National and International Dimensions of Crime Control* (Cullompton, Willan Publishing).

O'Malley, P (1992) 'Risk, Power and Crime Prevention' *Economy and Society*, 21, 252–275 [DOI: 10.1080/03085149200000013].

—— (2002) 'Globalizing Risk? Distinguishing Styles of Neoliberal Criminal Justice in Australia and the USA' *Criminal Justice*, 2, 205–222.

Pitch, T (1995) *Limited Responsibilities* (London, Routledge).

Putnam, H (1992) *Renewing Philosophy* (Cambridge, Harvard University Press).

Van Orman Quine, W (1960) *Word and Object* (Cambridge, MIT Press).

Rose, N (2000) 'Government and Control' in D Garland & R Sparks (eds) *Criminology and Social Theory* (Oxford, Oxford University Press).

Rusche, G, Kirchheimer, O & Melossi D, *Punishment and Social Structure* (New York, Russell and Russell).

Salvatore, R & Aguirre, C (editors) (1996) 'The Birth of the Penitentiary in Latin America: Essays on Criminology, Prison Reform, and Social Control, 1830–1940' (Austin, University of Texas Press).

Scharff Smith, P (2004) 'A Religious Technology of the Self: Rationality and Religion in the Rise of the Modern Penitentiary' *Punishment and Society*, 6, 195–220 [DOI: 10.1177/1462474504041265].

Schutz, A (1944) 'The Stranger: an Essay in Social Psychology' *American Journal of Sociology*, 499–507 [DOI: 10.1086/219472].

Sheptycki, J (editor) (2000) *Issues in Transnational Criminology* (London, Routledge).

Sheptycki, J & Wardak, A (2004) *Transnational and Comparative Criminology* (London, Cavendish).

Skinner, Q (2002) *Visions of Politics. Volume One: Regarding Method* (Cambridge, Cambridge University Press).

Sozzo, M '"Traduttore Traditore".Importación cultural, traducción e historia del presente de la criminología en América Latina' in M Sozzo (ed) *Reconstruyendo las criminologías críticas*. Buenos Aires: Ad-Hoc.

Sparks, R (2001) 'Degrees of Estrangement: The Cultural Theory of Risk and Comparative Penology' *Theoretical Criminology*, 5, 159–176 [DOI: 10.1177/1362480601005002002].

Wacquant, L (1999a) *Les prisons de la misère* (Paris, Editions Raisons d'Agir).

—— (1999b) 'How Penal Common Sense Comes to Europeans: Notes on the Transatlantic Diffusion of Neoliberal Doxa' *European Societies*, 1–3, 319–352.

—— (2009a) *Punishing the Poor: The Neoliberal Government of Social Insecurity* (Durham, Duke University Press).

—— (2009b) *Prisons of Poverty* (University of Minnesota Press).

Weber, M (1958) [1904] *The Protestant Ethic and the Spirit of Capitalism* (New York, Oxford University Press).

Part I

Cultural Embeddedness of Punishment

2

Concepts of Culture in the Sociology of Punishment

INTRODUCTION

Contemporary work in the sociology of punishment gives a prominent place to the concept of culture and to cultural analysis (Garland 1991; Savelsberg 1999; Smith et al 2000; Tonry 2001; Strange 2001; Lynch 2002; Vaughan 2002; Smith 2003a; Penfold 2004; Valier 2004; Crawley 2004; Gray and Salole 2005; Piacentini 2004, 2005). Indeed, it has become conventional wisdom that penal institutions have important cultural dimensions and consequences (Sarat 1999, 2001; Garland 2002; Sarat and Boulanger 2005) and that 'cultural factors' are prominent in the causal determinants that shape penal policies and practices (Melossi 2001; Simon 2001; Vaughan 2002a; Whitman 2003; Zimring 2003). A parallel emphasis on 'the cultural' is also apparent in contemporary criminology (Ferrell 1999; Presdee 2000; Hayward and Young 2004; Ferrell et al 2004). In these respects, the sociology of crime and punishment is aligning itself with an intellectual trend that has occurred all across the humanities and social sciences – a cultural turn (Bonnell and Hunt 1999) that seems altogether appropriate in our mass-mediated, image-saturated, late-modern world.

But this embrace of 'culture', however timely and appropriate, threatens to introduce a degree of conceptual confusion into the field, not least because the notion of 'culture' is notoriously multivalent, both as a theoretical concept

---

* This paper began as a presentation to a conference on 'Discourses and Practices of Crime and Punishment: The Question of Cultural Embeddedness and Travels', organised by Dario Melossi, Máximo Sozzo and Richard Sparks in Onati, Spain in 2003. The author is grateful to the conference organisers and participants and also to Lynn Chancer and two anonymous referees for their comments and criticisms. An earlier version appeared in 10 *Theoretical Criminology* (2006) 4, 419–47. The author and editors are grateful to the editors of that journal for permission to reprint the article here.

and as an object of analysis. The intensified interest in culture and cultural analysis is also liable to promote analyses that regard culture as an independent analytical domain rather than an integral aspect of social relations and to privilege description and explication as the primary purposes of research, thereby diverting the sociology of punishment away from the more ambitious project of social explanation.[1] In this essay, I undertake an analysis of the various ways in which the concept of 'culture' is currently deployed in the sociology of punishment, offer a clarification of the theoretical and conceptual issues involved, and argue for the integration of cultural analysis into the explanatory project of a multi-dimensional sociology.

THE CHANGING PLACE OF 'CULTURE' IN THE SOCIOLOGY OF PUNISHMENT

Until quite recently, sociologists of punishment tended to neglect culture in their efforts to identify the social determinants and functions of penal institutions. In the 1970s and 80s, the Marx-and-Foucault-inspired focus of the field was on class control and disciplinary domination rather than on cultural meanings and sensibilities. In those days, if 'culture' showed up at all, it was usually in the guise of power-knowledge discourses embedded in the apparatus of penal power, or else as systems of ideology that mystified economic exploitation and reproduced the dominance of the ruling class. And the point of studying these narrowly conceived cultural forms – for that is what they are – was not to trace their various meanings and cultural connotations but more narrowly to trace their instrumental effects in organising or legitimating penal control.

The idea that penal institutions were grounded in cultural values and perceptions; that they drew upon specific sensibilities and expressed particular emotions; that they were sites of ritual performance and cultural production; and that they produced diffuse cultural effects as well as crime control – these were not prominent considerations at that time. Despite the legacy of Emile Durkheim (1983, 1984), and the subsequent analyses of writers such as Mead (1918), Sorokin (1937), and Sutherland (1939), the cultural and expressive characteristics of penal practice were moved out of the limelight to make way for a more single-minded focus on the political and instrumental aspects of the phenomenon.[2] The interpretive search for meaning and the excavation of

[1] This tendency is exacerbated where the impetus for research grows out of 'cultural studies' rather than 'cultural sociology'. Work in the sociology of punishment that situates itself within the traditions of Durkheim, Elias, or Douglas tends to integrate the cultural and the social and to combine explication and explanation.

[2] The tradition of prison ethnography which studied the cultural worlds that inmates created for themselves – exemplified by works such as Clemmer (1940), Sykes (1958) and Goffman (1961) – tended to dry up in this period. Jacobs' book *Stateville* (1977) was

cultural significance were displaced by more functionalist accounts of penal control.

That time now seems long gone. Today, culturalist analysis is a prominent feature of writing in this field. Writers pay close attention to the role of culture in the shaping of punishment, and to the cultural consequences of penal practices. Not the least reason for this shift was the realisation that culture encodes and is encoded by economic and political forces, and that the analysis of culture is not a distraction from the study of penal power's controlling effects but is, on the contrary, a vital component of such study (Garland, 1990).

Lest I seem too quick to point out the faults of others, I should note that the trajectory of my own work is no exception to the general pattern I am describing here – indeed its development illustrates quite well the intellectual shift that the field has undergone over the last few decades. Thus the theoretical and historical analyses of the early 1980s (Garland and Young 1983; Garland 1985) do not explicitly discuss 'culture' at all, despite the fact that a close reading of specific ideologies and forms of knowledge – together with their institutional effects[3] – was a central feature of these studies. *Punishment and Modern Society*, published in 1990, argued for the importance of a specifically cultural dimension in social theories of punishment and directed attention to penality's cultural consequences as well as its causes. More recently, *The Culture of Control* (Garland 2001), developed a history of the present in which cultural phenomena stand centre stage in an argument claiming that recent changes in the social organisation of everyday life have given rise to a new collective experience of crime and a new 'culture of control' that is expressed and embodied in the conduct of governmental and non-governmental actors.

Perhaps, like Monsieur Jourdain, we had been speaking about culture all along. But it seems to me that the explicit acknowledgement of this cultural dimension – when it was eventually identified and discussed – changed the research agenda of the sociology of punishment in significant respects. A new self-consciousness about cultural issues directed attention to aspects of the phenomenon that had previously been ignored. New sources of theoretical inspiration emerged – above all Elias, Geertz, and Bourdieu. New methods of inquiry were developed and new kinds of explanation began to appear. The result is a field that looks rather different from the one that existed twenty years ago.

the last major work in this tradition for some 20 years, and already it was moving away from the study of culture to scrutinise the relation of prison dynamics to the regulatory controls of mass society.

[3] A 'culturalist' framework might suggest that what Marxists term 'ideology' is nothing other than 'culture' viewed in terms of its political and economic effects. Indeed, from Gramsci (1971) onwards, neo-Marxists such as Stuart Hall and Ernesto Laclau have been quite explicitly applying the methods and concepts of cultural analysis to the problem of ideology. Similarly, the 'knowledges' addressed by Foucauldian studies are formalised systems of cultural meaning and a product of scientific culture.

This pursuit of cultural themes and the use of culture concepts has taken many forms and produced many fine analyses. Some sense of their range and variety might be had by reading Dario Melossi (2001) on the cultural embeddedness of social control and the complex relation between religious ethos and punitive practice[4]; Martin Wiener (1990) on the cultural frameworks that shaped crime policy in Victorian and Edwardian England; Martha Grace Duncan (1996) on the unconscious images and literary figures that shape the cultural meanings of imprisonment; Ryan King and Joachim Savelsberg (2003) on the importance of collective memory and cultural trauma in the penal policy of Germany and the USA; Pieter Spierenberg (1984), John Pratt (2002) and Barry Vaughan (2000) on the impact of changing manners and sensibilities in the 'civilising' of punishment; Philip Smith (2003) on cultural myths and symbolic meanings surrounding penal technologies; or Vic Gatrell (1994) on the changing emotional responses to public hangings in 18th century England.

The new prominence of the concept of culture in contemporary studies of punishment makes it opportune to explore the ways in which 'culture' is now being understood in the sociology of punishment literature and to point to some of the conceptual and analytical problems that may be involved. In developing its understandings of culture, the sociology of punishment has drawn upon prior work in sociology, anthropology, and cultural studies, taking over concepts and lines of inquiry that were first developed elsewhere. Conceptions of culture in the sociology of punishment will therefore tend to reproduce the assumptions, arguments and conceptual patterns that appear in these other disciplines – and, in doing so, will introduce some of the tensions and ambiguities that have become apparent there. A discussion of these conceptual patterns and the various problems with which they are associated may therefore be useful for the further development of the field.[5]

TWO CONCEPTIONS OF 'CULTURE'

When the idea of 'culture' is invoked in sociological or historical analysis it is typically used in one of two rather different senses (Sewell 1999, 2005: ch 5). In the first sense, the analysis asserts the importance of distinctly cultural factors as a causal force in shaping penal institutions (*culture* as opposed to *not culture*) while in the second, the analysis points to different cultures (*this* culture as opposed to *that* culture) and seeks to show that contrasting cultures produce different patterns of penality.

[4] For a different analysis of the influence of religion on punishment, see Savelsberg (2004).

[5] My discussion of the concepts of culture and the problems of cultural analysis draws particularly upon the following discussions: Sewell (1999); Swidler (2001); Kuper (1999); Brightman (1995); and Ortner (1984).

In the first usage, the intention is to isolate specifically 'cultural' forces (or ideas, or symbols, or values, or meanings, or sentiments – the ontological stuff of which culture is composed has a number of aspects and is understood in a variety of ways); to distinguish them from other kinds of entity (such as social, political, economic, or criminological factors); and to show that these cultural isolates have a distinct determinative force of their own.[6] An example of this approach is to be found in Gatrell's book, *The Hanging Tree* (1994) which describes how the refined sensibilities cultivated by nineteenth century English elites eventually led many of them to express revulsion at the sight of judicial hangings. (Whether they actually felt revulsion, or felt they ought to feel it, and expressed themselves accordingly, is one of the issues Gatrell leaves hanging.) Whether as genuine motivation or as a rhetorical form that glossed other more material interests, these expressions of refinement and affront played a prominent part in the campaign that led to the abolition of public hanging in 1867. Gatrell argues that this new sensibility (he regards it as 'squeamishness' rather than true humanitarianism – it was, after all, public hangings, rather than hangings as such, that were being abolished) exerted its own causative force in bringing about the abolition of the public spectacle. '[C]ulture generated its own momentums as well as its own resistances' (Gatrell 1994: 25). He is quick to add, however, that this causal force was at its strongest when it corresponded to, or ran in the same direction as, interests of a more material kind. 'Only rash historians would privilege material or political or cultural causes without interrelating all three' (Gatrell 1994:25).

In the second kind of usage, the analytical distinction being made is not between different aspects of the social whole or different types of social relations, but instead between different social wholes, each of which is understood as a distinctive 'culture'. Understood in this way, a culture is a more-or-less bounded, more-or-less unified, set of customs, habits, values and beliefs. It is a distinctive universe of meaning, a distinctive form of life, or a distinctive 'world' in the sense that Nelson Goodman (1978) gave to the term. Such cultures are usually associated with particular communities, such as an ethnic group, a social class or a nation – so that we might talk of Jewish culture, working-class culture, or American culture – and the forms of life that these particular groups embody and enact.

Here the term 'culture' operates as a totalising term, standing for all of the distinctive traditions, folkways, institutions and values associated with a specific social group or society and a particular historical moment. Weiner (1990 ch1) invokes it in this sense when he talks about 'Victorianism' as the cultural

[6] One sees a similar conceptual move in some Marxist analyses, where ideological practices form a distinct 'level' of the social formation, and are accorded a degree of independent effectiveness (or 'relative autonomy') in a context where the fundamental causal force is exerted by the 'economic' level, to which ideological practices ultimately refer.

setting out of which nineteenth century English penal policy emerged. Analysis typically proceeds by means of empirical comparison – this culture compared to that – and this is the implicit basis upon which arguments about 'American Exceptionalism' or 'bourgeois penality' usually rest.

In this usage, 'culture' is not so sharply contrasted to 'politics' or 'economics' – indeed, in the hands of some early anthropologists, the 'culture' of a people is assumed to include its social roles, political structures, and material artifacts. Thus, for example, the early twentieth century anthropologist Franz Boas (1966:159) defined culture as 'the totality of the mental and physical reactions and activities that characterise the behaviour of the individuals composing a social group...' If there is a conceptual opposition that defines 'culture' here it is the idea of 'biology' – culture being the distinctive social world that human beings have actively (and variously) created for themselves, the learned social forms that shape group life and individual identity and which are transmitted by social rather than biological processes. Most modern writers use the terms 'culture' and 'subculture' to describe a group's distinctive values, meanings and dispositions – a collective consciousness or *habitus* that may correspond to, but is not identical with, the economic position or political orientation of the group in question. In this respect they follow Clifford Geertz who distinguishes sharply between 'cultural systems' and 'social systems' rather than Boas.

Deployed in this way by sociologists of punishment, the concept of culture may be used to explain differences (or similarities) in the penal practices of different societies by showing that the practices in question are the product of specific cultural traditions or frameworks of values. As Melossi (2001:407) puts it 'Punishment is deeply embedded in the national/cultural specificity of the environment which produces it.' Thus the Dutch 'culture of tolerance' may be contrasted to the more punitive penal culture of England and Wales (Downes 1988) or the national culture of Italy may be opposed to that of the USA (Melossi 2001) as an explanation for continuing differences at the level of national penal practices. The specificity of particular cultures, together with their tendency to shape the sense of action and events, also has consequences for 'penal transplants'(c/f Watson 1974). Penal institutions, legal terms, or criminological conceptions that are transferred from one culture to another will tend to change their character and connotations as they become embedded in the new cultural setting (Melossi 2001:404).

PROBLEMS IN THE ANALYSIS OF 'CULTURE' AS MEANING

Both of these usages have their uses, so to speak, and authors succeed in using them to good effect. And, in fact, one can point to instances where both usages are condensed in a single idea – as with the concept of 'subculture', which is used to highlight the *cultural* characteristics of a specific group (the style, dress, taste, attitude, argot, etc. of group members, as distinct from their economic class position, or political orientation) *and* to differentiate *this specific culture* from the culture of 'the mainstream' or from other subcultures. But it is also the case that each distinct usage raises certain problems that ought to be borne in mind whenever they are deployed. It is these problems that I wish to highlight here, without at all implying that these always or necessarily show up in the work of scholars who use these terms.

With regard to the first usage – *culture* as opposed to *not culture* – there is an operational (and ultimately a conceptual) difficulty in isolating the distinctively 'cultural' components of social relations from the other, presumably 'non-cultural', aspects with which they are typically bundled. One might suppose, for example, that it would be an easy matter to abstract the cultural aspects of a penal practice from its control aspects but in practice it is often impossible to draw such a distinction. Penal control can be achieved though the manipulation of meaning. A sentencing judge may choose merely to reprimand an offender and refrain from imposing any restrictive penalty. But this official attribution of negative legal meaning to the person and his conduct – his act is adjudged to be criminal, he is stigmatised as an offender – may have control effects by shaping the offender's subsequent conduct and, more importantly, the conduct of others towards him. Correspondingly, direct forms of control – the restriction of liberty, the infliction of pain, or the deprivation of resources – often depend for some of their control effects upon the meaning and value that groups and individuals attribute to these measures. The same penalty will be regarded and experienced differently – and will exert greater or lesser control – depending on the cultural context in which it is deployed and the ways in which its meaning is 'read' or interpreted by its various audiences. A monetary fine imposed in civil proceedings may be folded into the offender's routine costs of doing business. The same fine, imposed in a criminal case, may cause the offender to desist from the behaviour in question.

Similarly, one might suppose that the cultural aspects of a penal institution can be distinguished from its economic aspects – when one is talking of the institution's resources, its sources of support, the interests it serves, or the effects that it produces. But even 'purely economic' phenomena are always also cultural phenomena in so far as they depend on cultural understandings of what is to count as valuable or useful, as well as cultural understandings of what are effective and acceptable means to pursue these values. The exchange of goods, the pursuit of profits, the accumulation of wealth, the marshalling of resources, the interaction of supply and demand – these are the defining features of economic activity and economic interests. But each of these entails cultural commitments of a definite kind: as Max Weber (1904–05) argued a century ago, economic action may be predominantly instrumental and technical in character, but it always embodies cultural, spiritual and moral values.[7]

---

[7] EP Thompson (1978:264) made the same point in the language of Marxism: 'I am calling in question ...the notion that it is possible to describe a mode of production

Weber's argument refers to the ends of economic action but it is no less true of the means by which these ends are pursued: cultural forms are embodied in legal rules and manufacturing technologies, in purchase and sale, and in the specific modes of accounting and allocation that we use to organise these activities. When we say that a penal institution serves economic interests, or reproduces economic arrangements, we are not bracketing off culture and talking about something else – we are invoking a familiar and convenient aspect of culture: the economic domain with its distinctive forms and characteristics. Rigidly distinguishing the 'cultural' from the 'economic' aspects of punishment as if they were entirely different things involves something of a category mistake, in much the same way that distinguishing 'culture' and 'power' does. Cultural categories, habits and sensibilities are embedded in, and constitutive of, our political and economic institutions. The study of culture does not begin where the study of power and economics leaves off – it is a constituent part of any political or economic analysis (Geertz 1981; Haskell and Teichgraeber 1996).

In studying social relations, we can, and do, make rough demarcations between the domains of the economic, the political, the legal, the scientific, and the cultural – and these distinctions serve a useful purpose, up to a point. The cultural domain can, for example, be narrowly construed to refer to leisure time activities and the products of 'the culture industry' – fashion, style, film, art, literature, museums, sport, media representations, etc. Cultural criminology has its primary focus here (Ferrell 1996; Hayward and Young 2004), as does the sociology of culture (Wolff 1981). But scholars in both fields frequently slide over into a broader conception of what 'culture' entails, going beyond the study of subcultures, styles, and artistic works to study the production of social meaning more generally (See Ferrell 1999:400 on 'criminological *verstehen*' and Crane 1994 on the shift from the sociology of culture to a cultural sociology) . The tension here, once again, is between the two different conceptions of what culture is.

The object of cultural analysis can be a determinate '*culture*' (eg the revenge culture of the Norse sagas; the Dutch 'culture of tolerance'; an inmate subculture, etc) by which is meant a more or less integrated system of meaning, learned and sustained through recurring use, grounded in the collective activities and understandings of a specific group. 'Cultures' in this sense are the 'webs' of meaning that men have collectively spun. But the object of cultural analysis can also be 'cultural *meaning*'[8], which refers not to a collective entity ('a culture') but instead to the specific sense that social actors bring to their actions, or which their actions appear to entail, or which they attribute to the actions of others.

---

in 'economic' terms; leaving aside as secondary (less 'real') the norms, the culture, the critical concepts around which this mode of production is organised.'

[8] Strictly speaking, the modifier 'culture' is redundant here – all meaning, however subjective and individual, derives its sense and communicative possibility from its relation to a culture and to the language and shared understandings that culture makes available.

Here the concern is not exactly with the webs of culture but instead with the individual threads of 'meaning' that are a culture's raw materials (and out of which cultural webs are spun).

The focus upon subjective meaning, and its semiotic, intentional and emotional aspects, is clearly one aspect of any study of 'a culture'. But it is also, and more generally, a necessary aspect of any study of social action that seeks to acknowledge the mental (or semiotic) aspect of an actor's conduct. Weberian interpretive sociology, for example, insists that a concern with such meaning is an essential component of the study of social action and that it is, moreover, a defining feature of the 'cultural' as opposed to the 'natural' sciences. Given this overlap and intertwining between 'culture' as a collective entity and 'the cultural' as the dimension of meaning, it is hardly surprising to find that writers who urge us to study culture also urge us to attend to meaning (Geertz 1973; Ferrell 1999; Alexander 2003; Hayward and Young 2004). But for all their relatedness, we should notice that the two objects of analysis ('a culture' and 'a meaning') are not quite the same thing.

If we follow the trajectory of current social theory and refuse to restrict 'culture' to the world of leisure, art and entertainment (and, in so doing, resist the still-active assumption that while culture may shape the soft margins of social life, it has little effect upon hard-edged political and economic institutions, where power and interest prevail) it turns out that the generic category of 'culture' envelops all of the other, more specific social categories. If the stuff of culture is meaning, perception, feeling, sentiment, value, belief and the various forms of their expression, then, in the social world, it is not particularly distinctive stuff. Culture (in that broad sense) is suffused through all social relations, institutions and practices, and abstracting it away from these forms necessarily does violence to the true relationship between (cultural) meaning and (social) action.

This point has methodological consequences. It is often assumed that the quintessential cultural materials are texts, images, signs and symbols, and that a cultural analysis of an institution is an analysis of these aspects of its operation. On the basis of this understanding, cultural analyses of penal phenomenon typically focus their attention upon punishment's discursive texts (government reports, judicial opinions, sentencing laws, hanging day broadsheets, literary and theatrical representations, artistic images, etc) or else its ceremonial scenes and symbols (the scaffold ritual, the courtroom drama, the prison design). As a matter of practical convenience, this makes good sense – the best clues to the perceptions or beliefs or feelings that support a practice are often found in the elaborated discourses or depictions associated with it. But methodological convenience should not produce a restrictive definition of the phenomenon under study.

Culture can be most easily 'read' in texts, images and rituals but it is also embedded in non-discursive, non-ceremonial practices – such as technologies, spatial arrangements, bodily postures, habitual behaviour, and specific performances. For example, as Megan Comfort (forthcoming) shows in her study of prison visiting at San Quentin, the 'uncertain waiting periods, punitive architecture, and strict regulation of apparel and belongings that women endure at the gates of the correctional institution' may represent themselves as security measures but they also function as a means of mortification and abasement that stigmatises visitors and inducts them into a culture of 'secondary prisonisation'.

Where social action and institutions are concerned, the study of culture (in the broader sense of cultural *meaning*) cannot easily be cabined or confined. The analytical separation of meaning from action, symbol from substance, form from function, cultural from non-cultural, is only ever a pragmatic effort to tame real-world complexity by a wilful act of artificial abstraction. Such distinctions are altogether necessary for the purpose of analysis – and we should notice that every major tradition of cultural sociology offers some version of this elemental division, whether it is the separation of ideological relations from material ones, knowledge from power, social categories from forms of life, cultural sensibilities from figurational relations, or cultural capital from position in the social field. But however necessary these abstractions may be, they are never quite satisfactory. Culture/not-culture distinctions – at least in the study of social action and institutions – can rarely withstand close scrutiny precisely because they *are* artificial, separating out aspects of human action and social practice that are, in fact, inseparably intermeshed and integrated. This is why theorists so often invent seemingly paradoxical terms designed to suggest the fusion rather than the separation of elements of action – think of Louis Althusser's insistence that 'ideology has a material existence', (Althusser 1971:155); or Weber's representation of religious beliefs as 'ideal interests' (Weber 1904–05); or Foucault's concept of 'power-knowledge' (1980).

The point to draw from this is not that a focus on 'the cultural' or on 'meaning' in the sociology of punishment is misplaced or mistaken. The point is that we need to bear in mind that such a focus does not deal with a distinct, *sui generis* object in the world but rather with a specific aspect of social practices. That 'aspect' is only ever isolated by the act of analytical abstraction and, if its significance is to be properly understood, it must always be re-integrated into the practice in which it is operative. It follows that, in the sociology of punishment, the study of 'the cultural' and of 'meaning' should not, and ultimately cannot, be separated from the hard-edged, 'material', aspects of penal practice, such as penal technologies, penal economics, penal politics, and penal violence. Paying attention to culture, using the tools of cultural analysis (close reading, discourse analysis, hermeneutics, iconography, ritual analysis, etc), focusing on meaning and sensibility, thinking about audience and interpretation – these should enhance our understanding of penal power, penal violence, penal techniques and penal resources, not inhibit or displace it.

The creation and communication of meaning in penal practice is an ongoing and inevitable aspect of the activity. Scholars of culture are typically drawn to the ritualised aspects of punishment (the hanging day ceremony, the pronouncement of sentence, the prison induction process) since these practices are explicitly concerned to craft and communicate meaning in a serious, deliberate manner. Scholars are also drawn to moments of penal change and penal drama – instances of penal excess (Garland 2005a), or enactments of penal reform (Wiener 1990) – where the messages communicated by punishment appear to take on new meanings or to become more emphatic precisely because they break with established patterns and conventional expectations. It is equally important, however, to analyse penal routines and standardised arrangements, since these also enact meaning, value, and sensibility, even if their audience is a more restricted one and their communications less vivid. Indeed, the cultural meanings of routine practices are often more revealing for being 'offstage' and understated. The modern American execution protocol, with its behind-the-scenes staging, blank imagery, bureaucratic process, and low-key public announcements, embodies a symbolism and sensibility of a very definite kind, however much its stagers seek to suppress communication and down-play the event's ritual character (Lofland 1977, Johnson 1998, Garland forthcoming).

PROBLEMS WITH THE ANALYSIS OF 'CULTURE' AS COLLECTIVE ENTITY

If the first usage of the culture concept is problematic because 'the cultural' (and its meanings) cannot easily be separated from the other aspects of social relations, the second usage is troublesome for rather different reasons. The notion of a cohesive, shared culture that is unified and bounded, totalising in its comprehensiveness, deeply imbued in group members, and distinctive of a particular people or a particular place is problematic today not because it is conceptually incoherent – it is not – but because it tends to overstate the force and unity of dominant value systems, misrepresents the relationship of individuals to cultural norms (Abu-Lughod 1991), and is increasingly at odds with the reality of modern social life (Geertz 2006).

In anthropology, where 'culture' (variously conceived) has always been the central object of study, the theoretical debates of the last few decades have ceased to argue over how to conceptualise culture (culture as structure of binary oppositions; culture as system of symbols and meanings; culture as practice; culture as performance) and have, instead, argued about the worth of the concept itself. Robert Brightman sums up a wide-ranging and complex debate (inspired by feminist, post-colonial, post-structuralist, post-modern and historical scholarship, largely in reaction to the dominance of the Geertzian paradigm in the 1970s and 80s) by pointing to a series of intellectual problems associated with the concept of culture. These 'defects of culture' include 'holism, localism, totalisation, coherence, homogeneity, primordialism, idealism, ahistoricism, objectivism, foundationalism, discreteness, and divisive effects' (Brightman 1995: 512) – characteristics that downplay the importance of individual action and events, the extent of intracultural variability and fragmentation, and the inevitability of disorder, contradiction and contestation. Critics of the concept (notably James Clifford, Lila Abu-Lughod and Pierre Bourdieu) emphasise instead more agonistic concepts such as *habitus*, hegemony and discourse, and stress the importance of particularity, contestation and historicity.

These debates are not much referenced in the sociology of crime and punishment but their underlying themes are relevant and familiar. More than 40 years ago, David Matza (1964) mounted a critique of the dominant conception of 'the delinquent subculture', observing that this conception overstated the subculture's autonomy, its difference from the mainstream, its unity, and above all its place in the beliefs and behaviour of gang members. More recently, there has been much debate about the extent to which generalised cultural claims about 'popular punitiveness' or a 'culture of control' accurately capture the specificity of thought and action about crime control in particular social settings (Hutton 2005; Girling et al 2000; Savelsberg 2002). To highlight these problems is not to argue against the importance of generalising analyses – whether of 'culture' or of any other social form – but rather to stress the importance of an ongoing dialectic of argument between studies of general and particular, abstract and concrete, system and practice, script and performance (Garland 2001: vii).

Part of the current problem with 'culture' is, as Brightman (1995:509) points out, that older conceptions 'can no longer engage a world in which social identities, practices and ideologies are increasingly incongruent and volatile.' As a consequence of colonisation, global trade, ethnic intermarriage, cultural exchange and commercial interdependence, there are very few social groups whose culture is altogether distinctive and unmixed with that of others. This is true even of the relatively isolated and underdeveloped peoples that formed the traditional focus of anthropological study – cultural anthropologists have long since given up on the quest for the untouched aboriginal culture. Something approaching pure indigenous cultures may have once existed, but international exchange and local diversification have put an end to that.

This is all the more true of modern western societies, which are the product of centuries of commercial and communicative interaction[9] – a state of affairs that is reflected in recent scholarly concern with the phenomena of cultural 'crossings' and 'hybridity' (Pieterse 1995; Young 1996; Anthias 2001). Cultures overlap and intermingle, just as social and ethnic groups do, and individual lives are lived out in complex relations to multiple groups and mixed identities. 'Movement between ways of being in the world defines our times as much as do contrast and tension between them. The confusion of forms of life is, increasingly, the common state of things' (Geertz, 2006). Modern commerce and communication give rise to a constant exchange of ideas and technologies, the co-mingling of customs, and the convergence of tastes and habits – despite the effort of social groups to maintain distinctions and conserve traditions. Modernising social forces such as capitalist markets, mass production, consumerism,

---

[9] Natalie Zemon Davis's book *Trickster Travels: A 16th Century Muslim Between Worlds*, shows that cultural hybridity and boundary crossing have a long history.

democratisation, and technology may not have produced 'Americanisation' on a global scale, as some sociologists have claimed, but they have contributed to the emergence of ways of life (automobiles, suburbs, shopping malls, 'flexible working') and forms of politics (neo-liberalism, deregulation, 'welfare reform') that have become established to some degree in most advanced societies. The result is that contrasts between national cultures (or between local cultures within a nation) are now mostly a matter of degree and emphasis rather than mutually exclusive difference. Particular cultural traits – values, perceptions, sensibilities, traditions, representational forms – exist in different mixes in different places, and thus give each group and each place some degree of specificity and distinctiveness. But increasingly it is a difference of mix rather than a difference of type.

Cultural differences can thus be legitimately invoked as factors in the explanation of penal variation, but these differences must be carefully explicated and substantiated. Comparative scholarship cannot rely upon totalising national contrasts as an unproblematic explanatory resource. Nor can it be assumed that the specification of a culture's dominant themes and general figures will unproblematically explain specific practices in that society. Thus when Whitman (2003) invokes American culture in contradistinction to European culture, pointing to long-standing contrasts in attitudes towards matters of status and individual dignity as an explanation for contemporary contrasts in the intensity of punishment, he runs up against the problems of cultural pluralism, intracultural contestation, and historical change. Similarly, when Melossi (2001:407) talks of 'cultural traditions of punishment' the phrasing is helpful only if one bears in mind that national traditions are various and internally contested and that the historical trajectories of national penal systems exhibit major changes and discontinuities. There is no single 'American' culture for these purposes any more than there is a separate and singular 'European' one with which it can contrasted. For most explanatory purposes, the analyst is obliged to deal with cultural differences at a level of specificity that is much more fine-grained than that of the nation. Which is, in fact, what most sensitive scholars proceed to do: Melossi (2001), for instance, conceives of national cultural traditions not as fixed frameworks of a singular character but as more flexible 'vocabularies of motive' that provide a distinctive repertoire of values and meanings within which penal policies are forged.[10] Whitman (2003) qualifies his most sweeping America-Europe comparisons by noting the cultural and historical specificities of France and Germany, his primary points of reference.

The 'cultural toolboxes' of specific groups and societies – embedded in social institutions and connected to the interests of political elites – are distinctive in the same way that national languages are distinctive: they may encode the same reality, and enable similar forms of action, but they impart

---

[10] See, more generally, Rogers Smith (1993) on 'multiple traditions' in American culture.

a distinctive inflection and idiom, invoke a different ethos, entail different emphases and connotations. In that sense, they exert a force that helps to shape policy and practice and to sustain differences across time and place. But this 'force' becomes operative only when it is *enacted*, which is to say, folded into the practices of individuals, groups and organisations – practices that are always overdetermined and whose relationship to the dominant cultural forms are rarely simple or straightforward.

Finally, if the problem of internal complexity and historical change takes the edge off sharp cultural contrasts, and limits the explanatory power of cultural commitments, the growing importance of policy transfer and penal transplants dulls them even further (Wacquant 1999, Newburn 2002). The international exchange of penological ideas and technologies has been a fact of life since the late nineteenth century, a fact that has led to a growing convergence of professional cultures and the rapid transfer of policy prescriptions and institutional ideologies.

THE AIMS AND OBJECTS OF CULTURAL ANALYSIS

Cultural analysis is not a singular kind of thing. Culture is studied in different ways and for different purposes. One major source of this variation is the nature of the questions that motivate the research. A scholar may study 'culture' as an independent variable in an attempt to explain a dependent variable, such as a rate of imprisonment or the retention of the death penalty. Attempts to explain penal variation across places or penal change across time may turn to 'culture' as a possible cause. In this kind of study, 'culture' is being distinguished from other candidates for causal efficacy, such as 'economic factors', 'political regimes' or 'crime rates'. As Douglas (1992: 167) notes, rather wearily, 'In social theory the word 'culture' becomes an extra resource to be wheeled in after other explanations are defeated.' Such analyses are typically reductive in their conceptions of culture, and necessarily rely on rather thin descriptions of what that culture is.

A study that sets out to inquire about the meanings of a penal practice, or about the ways a penal ritual engages in symbolic communication with its various audiences will put more emphasis on the detailed explication of meaning and the close analysis of the symbolic conventions and interpretive practices involved (Hay 1975; McGowen 1987; Meranze 1996; Garland 2005a). Similarly, inquiries that seek to understand the affective aspects of penal practice (Miller 2000), or the ways in which expressive punishments convey emotional energy (Pratt 2000), or the specific sensibilities that tolerate some forms of penal violence but are repelled or embarrassed by others (Gatrell 1994), will tend to focus upon affective rather then cognitive aspects of culture, narrowing in on the structures of feeling that shape penal practice and the range of emotions that certain punishments typically evoke.

When writers in the sociology of punishment choose to study culture they often have different understandings of what it is that they are studying and how they should organise their study. Some scholars study culture as it is expressed in images and pictorial representations, examining artistic artifacts in order to reveal the cultural understandings and sensibilities that shaped the experience of punishment in specific places and periods (Edgerton 1984, Merback 1999). Others train their attention on the ideas and conceptions that shape understandings of punishment – focusing on what one might term the formalised aspects of penal culture, as manifested in programmatic documents, scientific reports, and official classification systems (See Foucault (1977); Cohen (1985); Garland (1985)). The study of ideas and conceptions has also been pursued in a broader manner, to include the study of cosmological ideas – as in McGowen's study of the changing metaphor of 'the body' in early modern English penality (McGowen 1987) – and also literary and fictional forms, as in Wiener's study of 'the intellective dimensions [that] have given meaning to the social activity of dealing with crime' (Wiener 1990:3).

Some writers study the representation of punishment in literature, examining the tropes and metaphors that depict the penal experience and integrate it into the cultural imagination. In this mode, Duncan (1996) explores literary images, cultural archetypes, and unconscious fantasies of the prison and the outlaw, arguing that our cultural relationship to crime and punishment is more complex and ambivalent than is usually assumed and that an 'unconscious mythological universe' influences the acts of offenders and those who punish them. Bender (1987) develops the literary analysis of penal forms into an historical argument about cultural causation when he argues that the eighteenth century realist novel 'enabled' the emergence of reformed penitentiaries because these novels created in their readers a certain 'texture of attitudes' and a 'structure of feeling' that had an elective affinity with the 'penitentiary idea'. He argues that each of these 'social texts' – the realist novel and the reformed penitentiary – is 'structured by a kind of narrative form that treats the material world, character, consciousness, personality, authority and causation itself in a distinctive [realist] manner' (Bender 1987: 4–5). The causal claim is that the prior existence of the realist novel was one of the historical conditions that made possible the subsequent popularity of the penitentiary.

Other writers investigate the characteristic emotional responses elicited by punishment by studying the evidence of broadsheets, eye-witness accounts and reformers' discourse, focusing especially upon the ways in which these have changed over time, or varied between social classes. Writers such as Spierenburg (1984), Sharpe (1985) and Gatrell (1994) have sought to uncover changing structures of feeling and sensibility in so far as these can be inferred from historical evidence. In a rather different vein, contemporary students of public opinion analyse opinion poll data in order to trace shifting public attitudes and understandings of penal phenomena (Beckett 1997; Gross and Ellsworth 2003).

An alternative approach is to address culture not in its intellectual or aesthetic dimensions but instead in its behavioural aspects. Culture, in this perspective, becomes a matter of habits and routines, of everyday patterns of activity and interaction, of taken-for-granted orientations and recipes for action. This aspect of culture refers to the embedded and embodied habits of social actors who have been 'acculturated' to the norms of life in specific settings. It refers to the common sense understandings that these actors have acquired, and to the perceptions, judgements and evaluations that they habitually make as a consequence of this acculturation. Culture, in this sense, is a matter of *habitus*, a concept that focuses on the point of convergence between the behavioural orientations of individual actors and the norms, constraints and power relations of the social field in which they act (Bourdieu 1990). It is this dimension of culture that is examined in Garland (2001) when it refers to the new routines of everyday life and the new dispositions of penal actors that have recently emerged in certain late modern societies. Similarly, Carlen's classic study of women's imprisonment (Carlen 1983) reveals the cultural assumptions that are embedded in sentencing decisions, the organisation of prison space, and the patterns of inmate-guard interaction, and demonstrates how these practices embody, enact and reproduce specific understandings of gender.

The scope and purpose of cultural study also vary. Sometimes the aim is to study culture 'in its own terms'– explicating signs and symbols, identifying recurring tropes and cultural connotations, and tracing the ways in which a penal institution is conventionally interpreted and understood (Duncan 1999). Such studies are typically synchronic, examining penal culture at one point in time, linking cultural understandings of punishment to the broader cultural universe of which they form a part. Other scholars take a historical approach, showing the ways in which punishment has been encoded by different cultural frameworks at different historical periods. These cultural frameworks may be examined as distinct and contrasting contexts, separated in time (Foucault 1977; Wiener 1990), or the scholar may trace the processes of historical transformation that led from one to the other (McGowen 1987). Sometimes the aim of the study is more fully sociological, aiming not just to identify patterns of penal culture but also to locate these patterns within the larger social formation of which they form a part. Thus developments in penal culture (such as the emergence of reform ideas, the refinement of sensibilities, movements in philosophy, changes in penal symbolism, shifts in public opinion, etc) are linked to changes in other social relations and shown to be interacting elements in a complex social structure (Durkheim 1902/1983; Spierenburg 1984; Bender 1987; Garland 1985, 2001).

The cultural phenomena discussed in these studies also vary in their ontological character – their substance, depth, temporality and durability. The cultural elements analysed may be transient social currents such as public opinion (Beckett 1997; Ellsworth and Gross 2003), semi-institutionalised cultural formations of a relatively short-term nature, such as 'the crime complex' of the

1980s and 1990s (Garland 2001); institutionalised modes of thought and action, such as 'liberalism' or 'penal-welfarism' (Garland 1985); or else embedded cultural values – such as individualism, Catholicism, egalitarianism, or localism – that have a long-standing character and are grounded in confessional practices, regional traditions or national identities (King and Savelsberg 2003; Zimring 2003; Whitman 2003). Distinguishing between these rather different kinds of phenomena – between constitutive cultural bedrock and transient cultural currents – is important here, not least because their rather different temporalities and durations are often indicative of their role in social organisation.[11] And in the historical study of cultural symbols or practices, one needs to attend to shifts in the connotations or behavioural consequences of the phenomenon in question. Cultural elements are often transformed over time, so that the same symbols come to be interpreted differently and get associated with new interests (think of the changing resonance of 'the victim') and old values come to lose their grip over individual attitude and social action (think of the decline of 'rehabilitation' as a mobilising idea in the 1970s) .

The longevity and depth of these phenomena are only two of the dimensions on which they vary. Penal ethnographies (eg Girling, Loader and Sparks 2000) have shown that cultural forms that are sometimes assumed to be more or less universal and undifferentiated – such as the contemporary control culture, the fear of crime, public attitudes towards delinquent youth – are, in fact, quite variegated in their local meanings and specific uses, depending for their sense on subjective orientations and the effects of time, place and circumstance. Thus Girling et al (2000) suggest that generic crime-control cultures and abstract symbols are the stuff of mass media discourse and academic generalisation: in actual use, these cultural attitudes and perceptions become much more inflected and differentiated in their meaning.

Most importantly, we need to bear in mind that there is no such thing as 'the' cultural meaning of a symbol, or practice, or institution – cultural meanings always exists in the plural, particularly where the symbol or practice in question has a high degree of social importance or visibility. The social meaning of any

[11] Two characteristics of the 'cultural dimension' of social practice that testify to its (relative) autonomy are its differential temporality and generality. Values, ideas, beliefs, and sentiments may endure for more or less time than the practices to which they are initially attached – thus a practice may endure even though the beliefs that initially supported it have disappeared (eg benefit of clergy in the 18th century; the swearing of an oath in court today) and a belief system may persist long after its material basis has disappeared (eg the persistence of a crime complex a decade after crime rates have substantially declined Garland 2001.) And specific cultural elements that are present in one institution or practice may simultaneously appear in several others (eg the managerialist ideas which came to shape prison administration in the 1980s were also present in many other organisations.) These differential aspects are what make cultural analysis feasible. For further arguments for the autonomy of the cultural, see Sewell (1999:48–52).

significant symbol, practice or institution will typically be layered and contested, subject to heteroglossic variation rather than tightly contained singularity of reference (Laqueur 1989; Smith 2003). The immediate connotations of a particular practice may be widely shared and self-evident to most people, but this broad significance is not the same as the meanings it has for those most closely affected, or for experts, or for those who sense in the practice the echoes of previous practices and politics. Different audiences will read the phenomenon differently, often in competing ways. To many conservatives, today's American death penalty is an example of super-due process, wasteful expenditure and unnecessary delay, a system that too often hesitates to deliver the legal punishment that murderers richly deserve (Kosinski and Gallacher 1995). To many liberals and African Americans, the same system communicates a very different message – conveying unacceptable echoes of racial violence and lynching (Jackson, Jackson and Shapiro 2001). The meanings that officials use to characterise a practice (the prison as correctional; the death penalty as a deterrent; visiting arrangements as merely practical) may be hotly resisted by those opposed the practice, and by those upon whom it is imposed.

Some penal institutions become the stuff of myths and legend – the guillotine is an example (Arasse 1989; Gerould 1992; Smith 2003) – or of standard depictions in popular culture and entertainment – think of images of the prison in film, literature, blues songs and rap lyrics (Duncan 1996). Others are known only to the cognoscenti and mean little to the general public. Even with respect to high profile penal practices – the death penalty, supermax prisons, victim impact statements, ASBOs – the public is often surprisingly ill-informed. At any given time, a majority of the population may have only a superficial engagement with penal institutions, deriving their information and understandings from news stories or folk prejudices. An issue may have profundity and symbolic depth for some, while being regarded by the majority of people as a matter of indifference or little practical importance.

INTEGRATING CULTURAL MEANING AND SOCIAL ACTION, EXPLICATION AND EXPLANATION

By way of conclusion I want to argue against an over-reliance upon cultural analysis as a framework for understanding punishment and penal change and to emphasise the importance of multi-dimensional analysis and explanatory ambition. In particular I want to argue that we should isolate and analyse the 'cultural' elements of punishment only as a preliminary to more integrated analyses that fold cultural elements into multi-dimensional accounts of the causes and consequences of penal practices.[12]

---

[12] Philip Smith (2003a) makes a related point when he says 'What is needed is a two stage approach to analysis and writing. We first need a thick description of what the...

Since my work is often seen as being sympathetic to a 'culturalist' approach, I ought perhaps to explain why I think it necessary to draw back from theoretical tendencies that are beginning to emerge in this field.[13] A concern of my past work – developed in the wake of Foucault and the power-and-control analyses he inspired – has certainly been to bring culture back in (see Garland 1990, 1990a and 1991). But my intention has always been to study culture (or, more precisely, specific cultural forms) in the context of a multi-dimensional social theory and to use the explication of punishment's cultural meanings to assist in the development of explanatory accounts of specific practices of punishment and specific processes of penal change. In this approach, the interpretation of cultural meaning is viewed not as an alternative to the development of sociological or historical explanation but as a necessary component of it. This, essentially Weberian, approach has definite ramifications for our conceptualisation of culture and its role in the development of explanatory accounts.

In a multi-dimensional social analysis (see Garland 1990) 'culture' is no more a self-standing and self-contained area of social life than is 'power' or 'law' or 'economics'. To talk of 'culture' is to talk of those aspects of social action or social artifacts that are ideational, affective or aesthetic – categories and classifications, styles of thought and ways of seeing, structures of feeling and psychological dispositions, values and sensibilities, bodily comportment and spatial arrangements – and which can be studied by attending to the signs, symbols, and performances through which these otherwise nebulous phenomena are publicly represented (Geertz 1983). But, as I have argued here, the cultural aspects of action are only ever that – *aspects*. They are one dimension among others – one of the several elements that typically converge to motivate and instantiate social practices.

In this conception, every individual action, every collective practice, every social institution, has its cultural elements. Sometimes these cultural elements are foregrounded, as they are in art, or leisure, or fashion, or entertainment – the discourse and display involved in penal rituals foreground symbolic meaning in this way (Smith 2003) as does the stylised deviance studied by cultural criminologists such as Ferrell (1996)). Sometimes they are further back in the mix – as in the ideas and values that are embedded in classification practices, legal procedures or penal technologies. But cultural elements are always present, and are always admixed with other aspects of action that are more commonly understood as economic or political. As Mary Douglas notes somewhere, the symbols and aesthetics and attitudes of culture are not separable from the hard-headed world of material interest: they are the vehicles through which these interests are pursued. For example, the phenomenon of racism in contemporary

punishment, law or policy at hand actually *means*... We can then go on to see how this intersects with institutional and political realities.'

[13] For critical discussions of recent books that offer 'culturalist' interpretations of penal institutions, see Garland (2002), (2005b) and (2005c).

western societies is often understood as a cultural one – a matter of cultural stereotypes and mental prejudices. But racism flourishes and is reproduced in institutional practices and social divisions where it meshes with the economic and political interests of particular social groups to the detriment of others. In its real social life it is an aspect of power structures, economic stratifications, social and spatial segregation, and sometimes of legal doctrine (Frederickson 2002). To study racism as culture without also seeing it as a set of social, political and economic interests would be as partial and misleading as it would be to study racism as a matter of social division without reference to the cultural meanings and legitimations that keep these conflicts in place. It is precisely this idea that Bourdieu seeks to capture when he defines race as 'a social principle of vision and division'(Wacquant 2001: 113).

The cultural analyses I have developed in my work are not self-standing or an end in themselves. The analysis of *The Culture of Control* (Garland 2001), for example, aims to show that the ways of thinking and feeling that have grown up around crime and insecurity – what I call the 'crime complex' or the 'culture of high crime society' – are cultural adaptations to predicaments that are, in turn, conditioned by the field of social forces in which the relevant actors are operating. Economic interests, political projects, intra-group dynamics, dominant ideologies, professional claims, experienced insecurities, psycho-dynamic processes – all of these are implicated in the emergence of that cultural formation. And it is these motivations and interests, with their different structural sources and political resources, and their various forms of cultural representation and resonance – not just some disembodied, self-generating 'culture' – that converge to produce the popular and political discourses, habitual practices, legislative enactments, judicial decision-making, penal practices and social institutions that make up the distinct 'cultures of control' exhibited by the USA and the UK at the end of the 20th century.

The term 'culture' marks an analytical abstraction, artificially separated from the other motivations and constraints that shape social action. The point of abstracting in this way – its heuristic function – is to isolate the languages and symbols through which attitudes are cultivated, aims formulated, and practices legitimated and to attend to the structures of meaning that they invoke and sustain. These symbols – the meanings of which are structured by their relation to other symbols and grounded in specific practices and ways of life – have a logic and a rhetorical force of their own which may be explicated, thus revealing a specific dynamic through which motivations are formed and actions are prompted. The interpretive analysis of culture's texts and symbols is an important step towards social explanation, as Weber, Geertz, and Bourdieu have shown. But in order for it to contribute to that end the analyst must show more than just a correlation, or even an elective affinity, between culture and conduct – he or she must show *how* the meanings in question come to relate to action. In order to move from the analysis of culture to an explanation of action we have to show how culture relates to conduct, how specific symbols, values or ideas come to be a motivational force or operational basis for action. Between *culture* understood as a symbol system and *action* understood as an embodiment of culture in the shape of conduct and practices, there are specific processes of enactment (Geertz) and embodiment (Bourdieu) that need to be identified and understood.

If the analysis of culture is to inform the explanation of conduct we need an account of the processes and mechanisms that translate (or enact, perform, inflect, express, and rework) culture into action (Archer, 1996; Swidler 2001). If a 'cultural tradition' is to be accorded causal efficacy in explaining present-day penal action, we need an account of the mechanisms that transmit this cultural attitude through time, and reproduce it in the present. Thus Zimring's claim that a 'culture of vigilantism' can explain the empirical correlation between the distribution of lynching events in the 1890s and the distribution of executions in the 1990s remains a speculative one because he is unable to identify the mechanisms by which that 'tradition' has been transmitted over time and is translated into the decision-making of legal actors in the present (Zimring 2003; Garland 2005a). As King and Savelsberg (2003) show in their comparative study of cultural trauma and punishment, what matters most for present purposes is not that a historical event or past experience has occurred but rather that it has been institutionalised (in law, in law enforcement, in socialisation practices, in rituals of commemoration, etc) in a manner that creates and sustains a collective memory capable of shaping action in the present.

In any concrete social analysis, we should see 'cultural' elements operating together with interests and actions that obey a (psychological, or economic, or political, or legal, or criminological) logic of a somewhat different kind. A multi-dimensional analysis strives to depict a process in which all of these things are operating at once, in the complex motivations and overdetermined forms of action that make up any institutional practice. Cultural forms – languages, symbols, texts, architectures, the ideational and aesthetic and emotional aspects of social life – can be isolated for the purposes of study, and the 'thick description' of these forms and their meanings is an important task for research. But while the task of explicating meaning, tracing symbolic reference, or mapping out mythologies is an important and necessary one, it ought not to mark the limits of our ambition. The same might be said of the now popular project of identifying emerging trends in penal and social control. Such analyses are important and valuable in their own right, but the task of sociology is explanatory as well as descriptive. One wants to know how to *explain* penal transformations, not just how to document and classify them.

For the discipline, if not necessarily for the individual researcher, cultural explication ought to be a preliminary to the social explanation of the phenomenon in question. Cultural forms never exist outside their social context of use and the practices of interpretation that are brought to bear upon them. And it is to these uses, contexts, and practices that social explanation ought finally to return. The classic works of cultural sociology – Weber's *Protestant Ethic and the Spirit of*

Capitalism, Durkheim's *Elementary Forms of the Religious Life*, Thompson's *Making of the English Working Class*, Elias's *Civilizing Process* and *Court Society* , Bourdieu's *Distinction*, and Geertz's 'Deep Play: Notes on the Balinese Cockfight' prominent among them – are classic precisely because they pursue this ambition and succeed in developing compelling analyses, both at the level of cultural meaning and at the level of social causation. The collective ambition of the sociology of punishment should be to aim for nothing less.

REFERENCES

Abu-Lughod, L (1991) 'Writing Against Culture' in R Fox (ed), *Recapturing Anthropology* (Santa Fe, University of New Mexico Press) 137–62.
Alexander, JC (2003) *The Meanings of Social Life: A Cultural Sociology* (Oxford, Oxford University Press).
Althusser, L (1971) 'Ideology and Ideological State Apparatuses' in *Lenin and Philosophy and Other Essays* (London, New Left Books).
Anthias, F (2001) 'New Hybridities, Old Concepts: The Limits of 'Culture'', 4 *Ethnic and Racial Studies* 1, 610–41.
Arasse, D (1989) *The Guillotine and the Terror* (London, Allen Lane).
Archer, MS (1996) *Culture and Agency: The Place of Culture in Social Theory* (Cambridge, Cambridge University Press).
Beckett, K (1997) *Making Crime Pay: Law and Order in Contemporary American Politics* (New York, Oxford University Press).
Bender, J (1987) *Imagining the Penitentiary: Fiction and the Architecture of Mind in Eighteenth Century England* (Chicago, University of Chicago Press).
Boas, F. (1966) *The Mind of Primitive Man* (New York, Free Press).
Brightman, R (1995) 'Forget Culture: Replacement, Transcendence, Relexification' *Cultural Anthropology* 4, 509–46.
Bonnell, VE and Hunt, L (eds) (1999) *Beyond the Cultural Turn: New Directions in the Study of Society and Culture* (Berkeley, CA, University of California Press).
Bourdieu, P (1990) *The Logic of Practice* (Palo Alto, Stanford University Press).
Brightman, R (1995) 'Forget Culture: Replacement, Transcendence, Reflexification' *Cultural Anthropology* 4, 509–46.
Carlen, P (1983) *Women's Imprisonment: A Study in Social Control* (London, Routledge).
Clemmer, D (1940) *The Prison Community* (New York, Holt, Rinehart and Winston).
Cohen, S (1985) *Visions of Social Control* (Oxford, Polity Press).
Comfort, M (forthcoming) *Doing Time Together: Forging Love and Family in the Shadow of the Prison* (Chicago, University of Chicago Press).

Crane, D (1994) *The Sociology of Culture: Emerging Theoretical Perspectives* (Oxford, Blackwell).

Crawley, EM (2004) 'Emotion and performance: Prison officers and the presentation of self in prisons' *Punishment & Society* 4, 411–27.

Douglas, M (1992) *Risk and Blame: Essays in Cultural Theory* (London, Routledge).

Downes, D (1988) *Contrasts in Tolerance: Post-war Penal Policy in the Netherlands and England and Wales* (Oxford, Oxford University Press).

Duncan, MG (1996) *Romantic Outlaws, Beloved Prisons: The Unconscious Meanings of Crime and Punishment* (New York, NYU Press).

Durkheim, E (1902/1983) 'The Evolution of Punishment' in S Lukes and A Scull (eds), *Durkheim and the Law* (Oxford, Martin Robertson).

—— (1984) *The Division of Labour in Society* (London, MacMillan).

Edgerton, SY (1985) *Pictures and Punishment: Art and Criminal Prosecution during the Florentine Renaissance* (Ithaca, Cornell University Press).

Ferrell, J (1996) *Crimes of Style: Urban Graffiti and the Politics of Criminality* (Boston, Northeastern University Press).

—— (1999) 'Cultural Criminology' *Annual Review of Sociology* 25, 395–418

Ferrell, J, Hayward, K, Morrison, W and Presdee, M (eds) (2004) *Cultural Criminology Unleashed* (London, Glasshouse Press).

Foucault, M (1977) *Discipline and Punish: The Birth of the Prison* (London, Allen Lane).

—— (1980) *Power/Knowledge: Selected Interviews and Other Writings* (New York, Pantheon).

Frederickson, G (2002) *Racism: A Short History* (Princeton, Princeton University Press).

Garland, D (1985) *Punishment and Welfare: A History of Penal Strategies* (Aldershot, Gower).

—— (1990) *Punishment and Modern Society: A Study in Social Theory* (Oxford, Oxford University Press).

—— (1990a) 'Frameworks of Inquiry in the Sociology of Punishment' *British Journal of Sociology* 1,1–15.

—— (1991) 'Punishment and Culture: The Symbolic Dimensions of Criminal Justice' in A Sarat and S Silbey (eds) *Studies in Law, Politics and Society Vol 11* (London, JAI Press) 191 – 224.

—— (2001) *The Culture of Control: Crime and Social Order in Contemporary Society* (Oxford, Oxford University Press).

—— (2002) 'The Cultural Uses of Capital Punishment' *Punishment & Society* 4, 459–88.

—— (2005a) 'Penal Excess and Surplus Meaning: Public Torture Lynchings in 20th Century America' 19 *Law & Society Review* 4, 793–834.

—— (2005b) 'Capital punishment and American culture' *Punishment & Society* 4, 347–76.

—— (2005c) 'Review of Jarvis, "Cruel and Unusual: Punishment and US Culture"' 14 *Social and Legal Studies* 299–302.

—— (2007) 'Rethinking the Symbolic-Instrumental distinction: Meanings and Motives in American Capital Punishment', in A Brannigan and G Pavlich (eds) *Critical Studies in Social Control: The Carson Paradigm and Governmentality* (London, Cavendish Publishing).

Garland, D and Young, P (1983) *The Power to Punish* (Aldershot, Gower).

Gatrell, VAG (1994) *The Hanging Tree: Execution and the English People, 1770-1868* (Oxford, Oxford University Press).

Geertz, C (1973) 'Deep Play: Notes on the Balinese Cockfight' in C Geertz *The Interpretation of Cultures* (New York, Basic Books).

—— (1973) *The Interpretation of Cultures* (New York, Basic Books).

—— (1981) *Negara: The Theater State* (Princeton, Princeton University Press).

—— (2006) 'Among the Infidels' *New York Review of Books* 53(5) 23 March.

Gerould, D (1992) *Guillotine: Its Legend and Lore* (New York, Blast Books).

Girling, E, Loader, I and Sparks, R (2000) *Crime and Social Change in Middle England* (London, Routledge).

Goffman, E (1961) *Asylums: Essays on the Social Situation of Mental Patients and Other Inmates* (Harmondsworth, Penguin).

Goodman, N (1978) *Ways of Worldmaking* (Indiana, Hackett Pub Co).

Gramsci, A (1971) *Selections from the Prison Notebooks* (London, Lawrence and Wishart).

Gray, G and Salole, A (2005) 'The Local Culture of Punishment' *The British Journal of Criminology* Advance Access, June 17, 2005; doi:10.1093/bjc/azi057

Gross, SE and Ellsworth, PC (2003) 'Second Thoughts: Americans' Views on the Death Penalty at the Turn of the Century' in SP Garvey (ed) *Beyond Repair: America's Death Penalty* (Durham, Duke University Press).

Haskell, TL and Teichgraeber, RF (eds) (1996) *The Culture of the Market: Historical Essays* (New York, Cambridge University Press).

Hay, D (1975) 'Property, Authority and the Criminal Law' in D Hay et al, *Albion's Fatal Tree: Crime and Society in Eighteenth Century England* 17–63.

Hayward, KJ and Young, J (2004) 'Cultural Criminology: Some Notes on the Script' *Theoretical Criminology* 3, 259–74.

Hutton, N (2005) 'Beyond Popular Punitiveness', *Punishment & Society* 3, 243–58.

Jacobs, JB (1977) *Stateville: The Penitentiary in Mass Society* (Chicago, University of Chicago Press).

Jackson, Rev JL, Jackson, JL and Shapiro, B (2001) *Legal Lynching: The Death Penalty and America's Future* (New York, New Press).

Johnson, R (1998) *Deathwork: A Study of the Modern Execution Process* 2nd edn (New York, Wadsworth).

King, RD and Savelsberg, JJ (2003) 'Collective Memory, Institutions and Cultures of Punishment' Paper delivered at the 2003 Annual Meeting of the ASA, Atlanta.

Kosinski, A and Gallacher, S (1995) 'Death: The Ultimate Run-On Sentence' 46 *Case Western Reserve Law Review* 1.

Kuper, A (1999) *Culture: The Anthropologists Account* (Cambridge, Harvard University Press).

Laqueur, T (1989) 'Crowds, Carnival and Death' in Beier (ed) *The First Modern Society* (Cambridge, Cambridge University Press).

Lofland, J (1977) 'The Dramaturgy of State Executions' in *State Executions Viewed Historically and Sociologically: The Hangmen of England and the Dramaturgy of State Executions* (New Jersey, Paterson Smith).

Lynch, M. (2002) 'Capital Punishment as Moral Imperative: Pro-Death-Penalty Discourse on the Internet' *Punishment & Society* 2, 213–36.

Matza, D (1964) *Delinquency and Drift* (New York, Wiley and Sons).

McGowen, R (1987) 'The Body and Punishment in 18th Century England', *Journal of Modern History* 59, 6511–79.

Mead, GH (1918) 'The Psychology of Punitive Justice' *American Journal of Sociology* 23, 577–602.

Melossi, D (2001) 'The Cultural Embeddedness of Social Control: Reflections on the comparison of Italian and North-American cultures concerning punishment' *Theoretical Criminology* 4, 203–224.

Meranze, M (1996) *Laboratories of Virtue: Punishment, Revolution and Authority in Philadelphia, 1760–1835* (Chapel Hill, University of North Carolina Press).

Merback, MB (1999) *The Thief, the Cross and the Wheel: Pain and the Spectacle of Punishment in Medieval and Renaissance Europe* (Chicago, University of Chicago Press).

Miller, WI. (2000) 'Clint Eastwood and Equity: The Virtues of Revenge' in A Sarat and T Kearns (eds) *Law in the Domains of Culture* 161–202.

Newburn, T (2002) 'Atlantic Crossings: Policy Transfer and Crime Control in England and Wales' *Punishment and Society* 2, 165–94.

Ortner, S (1984) 'Theory in Anthropology since the Sixties' *Comparative Studies in Society and History* 1, 126–66.

Penfold, R (2004) 'The Star's Image, Victimization and Celebrity Culture' *Punishment & Society* 3, 289–302.

Piacentini, L (2004) 'Penal Identities in Russian Prisons' *Punishment & Society* 2, 131–47.

—— (2005) 'Cultural Talk and other Intimate Acquaintances with Russian Prisons' *Crime, Media, Culture* 2, 189–208.

Pieterse, N (1995) 'Globalization as Hybridization' in M Featherstone et al (eds) *Global Modernities* (London, Sage).

Pratt, J (2000) 'Emotive and Ostentatious Punishment' 2 *Punishment & Society* 4, 417–39.

—— (2002) *Punishment and Civilization* (London, Sage).

Sarat, A (2001) *When the State Kills: Capital Punishment and the American Condition* (Princeton, Princeton University Press.

Sarat, A and Boulanger, C (eds) (2005) *The Cultural Lives of Capital Punishment* (Palo Alto, Stanford University Press).

Savelsberg, JJ (1999) 'Cultures of Punishment: USA-Germany' Paper presented at the 1999 Annual Meeting of the American Society of Criminology, Toronto.

—— (2002) 'Cultures of Control in Modern Societies' 27 *Law and Social Inquiry* 3, 685–710.

—— (2004) 'Religion, Historical Contingencies, and Cultures of Punishment: The German Case and Beyond' *Law and Social Inquiry*, 29.

Sewell, WH Jr (1999) 'The Concept(s) of Culture' in VE Bonnell and L Hunt (eds) *Beyond the Cultural Turn* (Berkeley, University of California Press).

—— (2005) *Logics of History: Social Theory and Social Transformation* (Chicago, University of Chicago Press).

Sharpe, JA (1985) 'Last Dying Speeches: Religion, Ideology and Public Execution in Seventeenth Century England 107 *Past and Present* 1, 144–67.

Simon, J (2001) 'Fear and Loathing in Late Modernity: Reflections on the Cultural Sources of Mass Imprisonment in the United States'*Punishment & Society* 1, 21–33.

Smith, M, Sparks, R and Girling, E (2000) 'Educating Sensibilities: The Image of 'the Lesson' in Children's Talk about Punishment;, *Punishment & Society* 4, 395–415.

Smith, P (2003) 'Narrating the Guillotine: Punishment Technology as Myth and Symbol' 20 *Theory, Culture and Society* 5, 27–51.

—— (2003a) 'Culture and Punishment: Report on a Thematic Session at American Sociology Association Conference, Atlanta' (on file with the author).

Smith, RM (1993) 'Beyond Tocqueville, Myrdal, and Hartz: The Multiple Traditions in America' *American Political Science Review* 87, 549–566.

Sorokin, PA (1937) *Social and Cultural Dynamics* (New York, American Book Co).

Spierenburg (1984) *The Spectacle of Suffering: Executions and the Evolution of Repression* (Cambridge, Cambridge University Press).

Strange, C (2001) 'The Undercurrents of Penal Culture: Punishment of the Body in Mid-19th century Canada' *Law and History Review* 2, 343–86.

Sutherland, EH (1939) *Principles of Criminology* (Philadelphia, Lippencott).

Swidler, A (2001) *Talk of Love: How Culture Matters* (Chicago, University of Chicago Press).

Sykes, G (1958) *Society of Captives* (Princeton, NJ, Princeton University Press).

Thompson EP (1978) 'Folklore, Anthropology, and Social History' *Indian Historical Review* 2, 247–66.

Tonry, M (2001) 'Unthought Thoughts: The Influence of Changing Sensibilities on Penal Practice' *Punishment & Society* 1, 167–81.

Tylor, EB (1924) *Primitive Culture* 7th Edition (New York, Brentano's).

Valier, C (2004) 'The Power to Punish and the Power of the Image' *Punishment & Society* 3, 251–54.

Vaughan, B (2000) 'The Civilizing Process and the Janus-Face of Modern Punishment' *Theoretical Criminology* 1, 71–91.

—— (2002) 'The Punitive Consequences of Consumer Culture'*Punishment & Society* 2, 195–211.

—— (2002a) 'Cultured Punishments: The Promise of Grid-Group Theory' *Theoretical Criminology* 4, 411–31.

Wacquant, L (1999) 'How Penal Common Sense Comes to Europeans: Notes on the Transatlantic Diffusion of Neoliberal Doxa' *European Societies* 1–3 (Fall) 319–52.

—— (2001) 'Deadly Symbiosis: When Ghetto and Prison Meet and Merge' in D Garland (ed) *Mass Imprisonment: Social Causes and Consequences* (London, Sage).

Watson, A (1974) *Legal Transplants: An Approach to Comparative Law* (Edinburgh, Scottish Academic Press).

Weber, M (1904–5/2002) *The Protestant Ethic and the Spirit of Capitalism* (LA, Roxbury Publishing).

Whitman, JQ (2003) *Harsh Justice: Criminal Punishment and the Widening Divide Between America and Europe* (New York, Oxford University Press).

Wiener, MJ (1990) *Reconstructing the Criminal: Culture, Law and Policy in England, 1890–1914* (Cambridge, Cambridge University Press).

Wolff, J (1981) *The Social Production of Art* (London, MacMillan).

Young, R (1996) *Colonial Desire: Hybridity in Theory, Culture and Race* (London, Routledge).

Zimring, FE (2003) *The Contradictions of American Capital Punishment* (New York, Oxford University Press).

3

Neoliberalism's Elective Affinities: Penality, Political Economy and International Relations*

DARIO MELOSSI

In this chapter, I intend to discuss the relationships between two very different ways of conceiving change in penality. On the one hand, I consider a concept derived from the pioneering work by Georg Rusche, the idea that is, of connecting the movement in penality to 'long cycle' change in socio-economic, demographic, and class structures. Such change seems to be roughly effective in orienting the *direction* of the slope in imprisonment rates (as a measure of punishment) but wholly unable to predict the *size* of those rates. To get closer to the reality of punishment in one specific society and epoch, the analyst has to come to terms with the fact that, by contrast, penal institutions seem to be embedded in cultural and institutional traditions that are derived from history and that are therefore specific to individual 'cultures'. In particular, I would like to address the connections between changing 'vocabularies of punishment' and the discourses of religion, political economy, international relations and masculinity. My empirical reference is to the development of penality (especially as represented by imprisonment rates) in the US and Italy/Europe. I intend to show that the discourse of penality is imbricated in a 'moral web' that links all these various discursive practices. Rather than being the 'product' of an assumed socio-structural change, penality seems to encapsulate a way in which dominant cultural trends 'drive' change in the social structure, moving from a specific cultural context to another, and being creatively adapted (and 'translated') under very different social and historical conditions.

* This is a revised version of papers presented first at the June Workshop in Oñati and then at the American Sociological Association meetings in Atlanta (2003). I would like to thank the participants in the Oñati workshop and the discussant in Atlanta, Philip Smith, for their comments. Please direct all correspondence to: dario.melossi@unibo.it.

'QUALITY' AND 'QUANTITY' OF PUNISHMENT

What came to be regarded as the 'Rusche and Kirchheimer's hypothesis' was the idea that there should be a direct positive relationship between changing imprisonment rates and changing unemployment rates. This was one of the outcomes of the efforts, by later commentators, to develop Rusche's original proposal, according to which we can unearth a historical linkage between the conditions of living among the lowest strata of the working-class and the conditions of living in prison, as well as the style of prisons' management (Rusche & Kirchheimer, 1939). However, there is no doubt that — as Sellin and Sutherland stated when they first read Rusche's original manuscript (Melossi, 2003: xiii–xiv) — Rusche's hypothesis has to be negotiated with many other aspects of social reality and especially with the historical specificity of each country's history. Perhaps, following a famous distinction by Durkheim (1900), one could distinguish between the 'quality' and 'quantity' of punishment. One could hypothesise that, whereas the 'quality' of punishment — ie the specific historical forms that punishment assumes — tends to move in similar ways through the development of the modern world, albeit through unavoidable 'gaps' in time, the 'quantity' of punishment can hardly be predicted in ways which are independent from rather idiosyncratic cultural traditions and political contingencies. Specific religious traditions, forms of government, the sense of one country's role in the world, will hardly be uninfluent on the unfolding of punishment (Savelsberg, 2000; Melossi, 2001). There is indeed a 'cultural' dimension that has to be articulated with Rusche and Kirchheimer's type of explanation but that is autonomous from that, a dimension that in a sense has something to do with the old issue of the relationship between 'structure' and 'superstructure', whether we want to think of it as a linear influence, in the Marxian mode, or as a reciprocal influence, as in Weber's image, derived from Goethe, of *Wahlverwandschaften*, or 'elective affinities' (Howe, 1978).

I intend to follow the latter's orientation in claiming that not only penal practices but also discourses on crime — whether by a 'lay' public or criminologists — are articulated with and indeed an essential aspect of, social and economic policies, as well as of the general political climate of a society and epoch. They constitute, in a sense, the *trait d'union* between a changing social structure and a changing management of punishment (Melossi, 2000a). In this regard, I would endorse David Garland's essential contribution in *Punishment and Modern Society* (1990:243–76) according to which not only does the general culture of a society shape penality but the reverse is also the case: penality is part and parcel of the creation and maintenance of a hegemonic culture — if I may 'translate' Garland's language into my own. Such an orientation is, among other things, better able to welcome Antonio Gramsci's lasting invitation to consider the historical detail of a specific society's culture instead of levelling all kinds of societies as 'stages' in a more general model, the development of which was forever portrayed in Marx's *Capital* — a perennial vice of Marxist (and, in the background, Hegelian) analyses.

'Long Cycles' of Punishment?

Elsewhere I claimed that the research tradition initiated by Georg Rusche might be developed by probing deeply in the direction of what has been called a 'long cycle' or 'long wave' perspective, according to which what is most significant in international socio-economic development, whether this is considered in terms of technological innovation and/or class conflicts, has been happening in long cycles of roughly 50 years (Melossi, 2003). This would be a historical-economic concept more readily connected and employed in order to understand phenomena of an essentially cultural nature, like those of penality, characterised by a slower and more viscous movement than straightforward 'economic' movements.[1]

This long-cyclical view sees the movements in the cycles as induced by the efforts of the actors in the economic arena — essentially entrepreneurs and workers, with 'the State', ie political actors, as a third party increasingly important in the adjudication of the results of conflict between the first two. According to such view, each one of the actors tries to overcome the limitations imposed on its development and 'freedom', by the adverse activities of the other. 'Innovation', for instance, constitutes a crucial tool by which entrepreneurs undercut the power accrued by labour during prolonged spells of prosperity that usually place workers in a privileged position. The result of innovation — articulated with political-legal power — is to destructure and disorganise the type of economy in which the working-class achieved its dangerous (for the entrepreneurs) power. Later on, adapting to innovation, the 'new' working-class would slowly find a way to reorganise.

But what might all this have to do with Rusche's main hypothesis? Rusche's concept of a connection between punishment — and especially imprisonment — and the labour market, can be framed as one of the slowly moving aspects of that larger picture, where imprisonment rises, and conditions within prisons become harsher, in periods when the entrepreneurial elite is on the attack. Later on, after the reestablishment of entrepreneurial hegemony, when the working-class is slowly reconstructing its power and organisation, imprisonment would again be on the decline and conditions of penality would tend to become more prone to 'reform'. Such connections should not be thought of as an 'infrastructure' determining a 'superstructure' but rather — as Max Weber did — as a network of relations of affinity, where the long-cyclical movements are caused by the autonomous but interactive contributions — economic, political, cultural — of all the actors involved.

In the one effort today to develop such a line of analysis, Charlotte Vanneste identified, on the ground of existing literature, the location of the 'peaks' and

---

[1] Schumpeter, Pareto, Sorokin, Kondratieff, Kalecki, are the names most commonly linked to some kind of cyclical theory of socio-economic development (for a recent review, see Rennstich (2002)). Melossi (1985) and Vanneste (2001) have explored the possibility of applying such views to a Ruschean type of analysis.

'troughs' of such long cycles (Vanneste, 2001, p. 56).[2] If we agree to 'measure' the 'behaviour' of penality by means of the indicator of imprisonment rates — a rather unsatisfactory one, but for the time being the only one we have available — it may represent a useful exercise to compare, if only in a merely suggestive way, the 'slope' prediction of the 'long cycle' model, according to Vanneste, with the actual behaviour of imprisonment rates in two countries, Italy and the United States (Fig 1). According to Vanneste's theoretical reconstruction (represented in Fig 1 by the sinusoid line), the peaks would be located *grosso modo* around 1870, 1920 and 1970, and the troughs around 1850, 1895, the period of World War Two, and 1995. Because, according to hypothesis, the imprisonment rate should 'behave' in a fashion opposite to the behaviour of the long cycles, we would derive the prediction of an increase in imprisonment rates in the three 'downswings', 1870–95, 1920–45, and 1970–95, and a decrease instead in the three 'upswings', 1850–70, 1895–1920, and 1945–70. Today we would find ourselves in the midst of a new decrease.

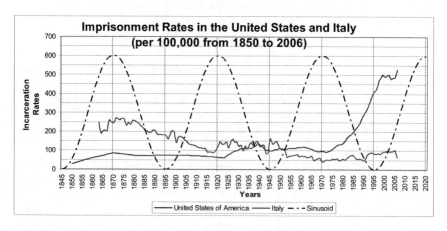

Fig 1. Imprisonment rates per 100 000 in the US and Italy[3]

The axes marked in Fig 1 correspond to the aforementioned 'peaks' and 'troughs'. The behaviour of imprisonment rates seems to — *roughly*! – correspond to the predicted one only for the twentieth-century, ie the last two 'long cycles', but not for the previous one in the nineteenth-century. We can observe in fact an

---

[2] Vanneste goes on to apply this theoretical framework to the case of Belgium.

[3] Italian data are my elaboration of data assembled by the official governmental institute of statistics in Rome (ISTAT). They are equal to the sum of inmates in all adult prison institutions. US data are equal to the sum of inmates in State and Federal prisons. They are based on an update of the data originally collected and elaborated by Cahalan (1979) (the line between 1850 and 1925 is a linear interpolation based on the years for which we have data that is 1850, 1860, 1870, 1880, 1890, 1904, 1910 and 1923). They do not include jail data.

early stage — during which both the US and Italy were in different ways being built—[4] characterised by an effort by the two young nations to 'build' a prison system as part of a modern political and legal order. Under these conditions that lasted until about the 1870s, imprisonment rates were destined to grow, but this would happen under extremely different conditions in the two countries. As Tocqueville stated, the US were characterised by 'a natural equality of conditions' that especially meant an equal possibility of access to the land (for 'the white race'). In Italy, and especially Southern Italy, however, characteristic processes of expulsion of peasants from the countryside were starting to take place that pushed them increasingly toward emigration, while in the North the living conditions of the working-class started slowly to turn for the better. In Italy, very high imprisonment rates during the first two decades after the Unification in 1861, were then followed by a second stage, characterised by a continuous declining trend, common to all of Europe in the period (Sutherland, 1934). In the US at the same time imprisonment rates were quite stable and low (even if these were very low for whites and already characteristically many times higher for those who could not take advantage of the 'natural equality of conditions', ie the Afro-American population).

Since 1895, the slopes of the imprisonment rates have behaved *roughly* as predicted. In the period 1895–1920, we can observe a strong decline in the Italian case and a slight one in the US. The years of the ensuing depression by contrast saw a moderate increase in the US and simply an interruption of the previous downward trend in Italy. These years put a stop to the liberalism and progressivism of the early decades of the century and called for harsher penal policies even if, especially in the US, the general political progressivism of the New Deal made sure that the huge economic hardships never translated into a comparable rise in imprisonment rates (Jankovic, 1977). On the contrary, in Italy the somewhat limited economic impact of the depression on penal policies was exacerbated by the authoritarian political bent of the Fascist regime that, like in contemporary National Socialist Germany, made the fight against crime an essential part of its political and especially rhetorical agenda.

After World War Two, we have again a definite declining trend in Italy and a substantially stable situation in the US, where the well-being of the period did not really translate into a decline of the imprisonment rates (so that, toward the early 1970s, Al Blumstein and colleagues could write of a homeostatic, self-regulating, basically stable imprisonment system (Blumstein & Cohen, 1973)), while by contrast Italy experienced a most decisive fall in her imprisonment rates that around 1970 were among the lowest in the world.

---

[4] Italy became a unified country only in 1861; for the US, an important state like California joined the Union only in 1850 (see Berk *et al* (1981) about the quantitative development of the California penal system), furthermore it seems to me difficult to think of the US as a really unified country before the Civil War.

The early 1970s represented a turning point for both countries: the 'crisis decades' ensued (Horsham, 1994), and 1960s' liberalism started to be rejected. While this happened with a real vengeance in the United States, bringing the imprisonment rates of the country to unparalleled heights and giving birth to the well-known 'great internment' of the last quarter of the twentieth-century, in Italy this simply meant a very slow, oscillating tendency to a moderate increase. It may indeed be worthwhile to focus our attention on this period since the 1970s, a period in which many of the conceptual birds we are here trying to describe seem to have come home to roost. Developments in the US during the period in question are usually mentioned to contradict Rusche and Kirchheimer's hypothesis, because a cyclically oscillating unemployment rate does not seem to have anything in common with a vertically increasing imprisonment rate (one which is exceptional at a global level). That is why, in my analysis of the emergence of the 'great internment' during the crucial period of capitalist reorganisation in the United States between the energy oil crisis in 1973 and the early 1990s — when finally the American economy again took off —[5] I proposed that we should speak not so much in terms of unemployment but in terms of 'pressure to perform' placed on the working-class (Melossi, 1993). In those twenty or so years, in fact, if the unemployment rate was on average higher than in the previous period, what instead changed much more dramatically was the decline in hourly wages (Peterson, 1994), the level of inequality — which increased spectacularly (Kovandzic et al, 1998) — and the participation in the workforce and the total of worked hours, especially by women, which also increased considerably (Schor, 1991). It is in other words as if, sometime in the mid-1970s, the 'social system' started squeezing the working-class for the juice of production, not with only one hand, but with both. The increased level of performance demanded of the American working-class would have as a consequence — according to Rusche's hypothesis — a lowering of the threshold of 'less eligibility' and an increasing pressure to perform also at the general social behavioural level with the consequence that many more infractions of the law, many more punished infractions, and more severely punished would result — all of which happened in the US after the early 1970s.

RELIGION AND PENALITY

Why, however, did this not happen — or, did not happen to the same degree — in Europe, and in particular in Italy, where, after all, 'post-Fordist' transformations

---

[5] This is also the period that many describe as of transition from a 'Fordist' to a 'post-Fordist' economy. For an attempt at connecting the particular version of 'post-Fordist' argument developed by Hardt & Negri (2000) to the question of penal control, see De Giorgi (2002).

also started unfolding, even if at a later stage? In another paper, I had been tempted by the hypothesis that the current very large imprisonment differential between a country characterised by a radical-Protestant tradition, such as the United States and a country characterised by a homogeneous Catholic tradition, such as Italy, may be looked for in the different religious roots of their respective cultures. Such roots would explain the rigorous attitude of severity in one and the indulgent *laissez-faire* attitude in the other, according to stereotypical images that go at least as far back as Luther's polemic against the sins of Rome (Melossi, 2001).

In that very paper, I was however obliged to deeply revise such a hypothesis after having considered the available data more in depth (Melossi, 2001:413–18). On the one hand, van Swaaningen (1997:20–23) pointed out that Holland had both a strong Calvinist background and a strong tradition of tolerance. Even more importantly, however, if we examine the long-historical development of imprisonment rates in Italy and the United States, matters become much more complicated. As we can see in figure 1, American imprisonment rates have been higher than Italian imprisonment rates only since the early 1950s,[6] and the difference appears really huge only after the 1970s, in the period we have called the North American 'great internment'. Now, even if we allow a consideration of the connection of religion to culture of the Weberian type, the idea that a certain kind of culture may be forged within a religious ethic but may later become uprooted from that ethic during the secularisation process, I think we should still ask the question: were religion the explaining factor, would it not be reasonable to assume that, in secularising societies, such as the US and Italy are both deemed to be, the influence of religion should have become less and less relevant? If this were the case, however, and if our hypothesis of an 'elective affinity' between Protestantism and stern punishment were true, then the imprisonment rates of Italy and the US should show behaviour exactly the opposite of the one we can see in Figure 1. If the hold of a strict Protestantism on American culture had somehow been fading, American imprisonment rates should have been declining in the long run and, if an indulgent Catholicism had been doing the same within Italy, Italian imprisonment rates should have been increasing in the long run.[7]

[6] However, in comparing the two curves, one should keep in mind that the US data are somewhat underestimated because we were unable to locate jail data on such a long period.

[7] The 'secularisation' theme, however, should be considered with much caution in the case of the US. The United States is among the most religious societies in the world, in terms of the penetration of religious ideology within their culture, even in the course of the twentieth century (Putnam, 2000: 65-79), to the point that 'one systematic study of the history of religious observance in America estimates that the rate of formal religious adherence grew steadily from 17 percent in 1776 to 62 percent in 1980' (Putnam, 2000:65).

'LEGITIMATION OF VIOLENCE' HYPOTHESIS

Therefore, because it is the diverging trends after 1945 and especially after 1970 that need explanation, I would suggest one last and different, crucial venue of exploration. In the mid-1990s, Dane Archer and Rosemary Gartner, basing themselves on extensive cross-national data, proposed a 'legitimation of violence' hypothesis, according to which 'exemplary' actions by governments, such as the meting out of capital punishment and engaging in wars, would have the effect of presenting their citizens with the message that violence is indeed a way by which differences and conflicts can be resolved, thereby legitimising it. Governments would then act as tried and true 'moral entrepreneurs' and such 'official' forms of legitimation would then translate into higher rates of violent crime, murder, etc (Archer & Gartner, 1984).

In other words, we may want to look at the relationship between crime and punishment, not as linked by the supposedly negative effect of deterrence but rather by a positive correlation: somebody living in a society where violent resolution of conflicts is emphasised will be much more likely to use violence to achieve their own ends than somebody who lives in a society where tolerance and compromise are rewarded. So, it indeed makes sense, in a comparative framework, to try and see whether there has been historically a correlation between governments' official sponsorship of violence (measured by countries' engagements in wars and use of the death penalty), and their violent crime rates (Archer & Gartner, 1984:63–97,118–39). Indeed, Archer and Gartner have found that, with few exceptions, the homicide rates of post-war periods are higher than the homicide rates of pre-war periods, in a way that extends to all age groups and that has nothing to do, therefore, with the so-called 'violent veteran' syndrome (Archer & Gartner, 1984:63–97). Likewise, they found that those societies that abolished the death penalty — Italy being one case in point — tended to have lower homicide rates after the abolition of the death penalty than before. All of this makes sense: if criminal behaviour is connected to the values and lifestyles that are dominant in a given society, the domestic and foreign policy actions of the main agency in society, ie government, are bound to have an exemplary effect throughout society. In Archer and Gartner's own words:

> The term violence conjures up the image of dangerous individuals. We tend to think of violent acts and violent actors in concrete, personalized form. This individualistic bias obscures the very real violence committed by authorities in the pursuit of domestic social control, or by governments in the pursuit of foreign war. Serious violence, including homicide, is produced routinely in the course of law enforcement, crowd and riot control, political subversion and assassination and, of course, war.
>
> While these mortal acts are sometimes politically controversial, they clearly benefit from unique auspices. The private acts of destructive individuals are treated as illegal violence, while official acts of violence are granted the mantle of state authority, and thus shielded from criticism and criminal sanctions... what all wars have in common is the unmistakable lesson that homicide is an acceptable, even praiseworthy, means to certain ends (Archer & Gartner, 1984: 63, 66).

One may ask oneself: what is the message that a child is going to receive about the best way to solve problems when confronted with what he feels to be some limitation on his rights? Is it the use of rational conversation and debate? Is it avoidance? Is it force? Chances are that a child raised in the US will be exposed to a number of recommendations to use force and violence more often than a child raised in Europe, or Japan, or indeed many other countries. Consider the amount of violence he can watch on the media, consider the easy availability of weapons, consider the war rhetoric coming from the upper echelons of society, be these 'drug warriors' or 'Gulf warriors'. Consider, finally, the emphatic positive role that is attributed to violence in a Constitutional Charter where 'the right to keep and bear arms' is one of the fundamental rights of the people!

According to the results of Archer and Gartner's research, there would be a positive, not a negative, relationship between punishment and violence. Could that be, therefore that a more violence-condoning culture — especially in the case of state-sanctioned violence — would also be a culture more easily recommending the use of rigorous, stern punishment? One could then hypothesise that the political institutions of those countries that have found the use of violence and state power 'rewarding', would be much more inclined to recommend the use of violence and stern power, and therefore also severe punishment, than those which have found it 'punishing'. The United States emerged victorious from World War Two and as the only superpower from the confrontation with the Soviet Union at the end of the so-called 'Cold War', would be an example of the former situation. Italy and Germany, for both of which the strong governments of the 1920s and 1930s and then those governments' engagement in war produced disastrous results, would be good examples of the latter case. Certainly, it is a rather common observation in Italy that the experience of fascism powerfully contributed to a lack of confidence in government and 'the State' after World War Two (Pavarini, 1994:50–53). There is no doubt at the same time that such a feeling would articulate quite nicely with an 'indulgentist' tradition that has its roots in a long Italian history and found its logical interpreters in a Catholic party, such as the Christian Democrats — a party that held uninterrupted political power exactly for the time of the so-called 'cold war'.[8] On the contrary, the positive rewards that the United States have seized from the use of violence and power in international relations, engaging in a new war every few years in the course of the twentieth century, would articulate quite nicely with the stern rigour of the most radical varieties of Protestantism. It would also be consistent with the fact that in a small and peaceful country, such as Holland, Calvinism has traditionally shown its more tolerant attitude, as van Swaaningen observed. The personal memories and reflections of Dutch criminologist Louk Hulsman,

---

[8] Developments in Germany have been somewhat similar (Savelsberg, 2000; Graham, 1990).

a leading 'abolitionist' thinker, may very well be applied not only to the case of Holland but more generally to the situation in Western European countries after the experience of the horrors of war, dictatorship, military occupation, and concentration camps:

> There were quite a lot of people involved in making crime policy and doing things in that field who had war experience and some like me who had also had the experience of being imprisoned. I had seen as a kid how unreliable an official system is. I had seen how most of the people in Holland after the German occupation cooperated with the Germans. I had also been arrested by the Dutch police for resistance, and I had seen that you can't trust them. That naturally has an influence, and there were several other people in the Ministry of Justice with comparable experiences (interview in Cayley, 1998: 17).

Likewise, the political culture of a country like Italy — where one of its most popular Presidents (from 1978 to 1985), Alessandro Pertini, was just the most famous among the many Italian politicians who had known long periods of imprisonment under Fascism—[9] would be highly unlikely to express sympathies for imprisonment and stern punishment.

WAHLVERWANDSCHAFTEN: NEOLIBERALISM, INTERNATIONAL RELATIONS, PENALITY

How is it, however, that such different cultural objects as penality, religion, politics and the economy, come together? And, could it be that, within the current process of 'globalisation', some of these relationships, have assumed a different quality? Whereas in fact cultural 'exchanges' and 'travels' — as well as the unending work of 'translation' connected to those activities —[10] have always been with us, the current process of 'globalisation' may have much accelerated such trends, even if finding still robust resistances in their movements. The phenomena that I am referring to and that has been noted by several commentators from different inks, is the increasingly tight connections of globalised cultural processes, such as for instance those in the sphere of economics, in the sphere of international relations and in the sphere of penality. In each of these three areas a common discourse that we may reductively call 'neo-liberal', has advanced in the last 15–20 years showing elements in common, such as a utilitarian philosophy of punishments and rewards, an emphasis on the theme of 'individual responsibility', and also, in a very unstable truce with contemporary 'political correctness', of 'machismo'. All of this was powerfully

---

[9] In a special issue of the journal *Il ponte* in 1949, former political prisoners, who had just become 'founding fathers' of new democratic Italy, wrote about the question of prison reform. As one would expect, the skepticism they expressed about the institution was remarkably high.

[10] See Melossi (2000b, 2001), and Carrabine (2000).

helped by developments where the sense of separateness between internal and external borders has become, especially after 11 September 2001, extremely tenuous. The description of enemy states in terms of the internal enemy, the criminal — as in the expression 'the rogue states' — echoes the use instead of war metaphors to win internal 'wars' against criminality. The reach of the domestic power of some countries, *in primis* the United States in such documents as the so-called 'Patriot Act' (Dworkin, 2002, 2003; Jamieson, 2003; Steinert, 2003), is decreed to extend to the entire globe. In some more specific and different instances, such as in Europe, the process of a European constitution — but something similar has already been announced for *MERCOSUR* — means that the tangle among 'international', 'communitarian' and 'domestic' law has become almost inextricable.

We may think of such developments as an 'Empire' that has come into being as the new environment within which we operate (Hardt & Negri, 2000), or as the intentional worldwide extension, by a radical group of 'Neocons' in the United States (Baker, 2003; Drew, 2003 reviewing Krugman, 2003), of the Weberian principle of the 'monopoly of violence' to become the seedling of a new Global State! In any case, often the same think tanks, and even the same authors, have pushed a connected agenda in the fields of the economy (Bockman & Eyal, 2002), international relations (Drew, 2003) and penality (Wacquant, 1999; Garland, 2001), an agenda which has come to define a certain kind of rationality as the new word to be spread to the furthest flung corners of the globe. This is nothing new in kind. After all, anyone who has studied the spread of economic rationality, penality and 'the white man's burden' in the modern era, has witnessed the spread of a certain kind of rationality, a certain way of thinking about man and society. The supremacy of white, adult, proprietor, preferably Protestant, males has never been recommended as a special privilege to be accorded to that much selected group. On the contrary, it was that much selected group that, probably by the grace of God, was saddled with the laborious necessity of spreading a rational creed that they, much better than others, were able to articulate — or so they (and almost everybody else) believed.

So, the struggle for worldwide implementation of what was at the beginning a very radical, almost lunatic, fringe of neoliberalism in economics in the early 1970s, went hand in hand with the fight to overturn at the same time 'actually existing Socialist' regimes and welfare systems in the West — seen as a sort of 'Socialism in disguise'.[11] The diffusion of the neoliberal creed found a very helpful and apt summary in the spreading of what Wacquant (1999) has called a new 'penal common sense' because the basic principles of such common sense seemed to be crucial to the neoliberal project — the central values of punishments, rewards, and individual responsibility. So, it is not a surprise if

---

[11] On this subject I recommend reading the essay by Bockman & Eyal (2002).

we find that some of the very same think tanks and right wing intellectuals are behind all of these ventures. All of which was seasoned, I should add, with a helpful dose of *machismo*, because the values of economic and military entrepreneurship are of course the privilege of valiant and self-reliant males — even when they are impersonated by females.

This neoconservative point of view seems to be well expressed in Robert Kagan's essay, *Of Paradise and Power* (2003). According to Kagan, there is a growing rift between Europe and the United States, a rift that he explores and explains in a very interesting fashion. On the one hand, the European no-end-in-sight 'enlargement', based for the first time in history on the democratic principle 'one person one vote',[12] would represent a true embodiment of the Kantian 'perpetual peace' Utopia, a haven of peace and law forever expanding. By contrast, such 'Kantian paradise' would be made possible by the United States spearheading order in a Hobbesian state of nature surrounding that Paradise, and being ready to use 'power' in order 'to man the walls of Europe's postmodern order' (Kagan, 2003: 76). Hence — and the reference to *manning* the walls could not be more telling! – Kagan coined what would become the catch phrase of his book, 'Americans are from Mars and Europeans are from Venus' (Kagan, 2003, see also Garton Ash, 2003; Judt, 2003).[13] If the Hobbesian metaphor is extended to the globe, however, one can well understand why, more and more in the last few years, the language of war and the language of punishment have tended to approximate one another. In the same way, according to the social contractualists from Hobbes to Beccaria, punishment constituted the signpost of the common repository of sovereignty in a social contract, ready to impart the lesson of *pacta sunt servanda* to transgressors, so in the new world order, the seed of a new global State is ready to punish those

[12] Actually, I am adding a bit of pro-EU enthusiasm of my own in this reconstruction that Kagan may not share.

[13] Unfortunately, we do not have the time and space here to probe into one of the most important cultural underpinnings of the general *Weltanschauung* that has emerged in this connection, what we have called, rather gently, *machismo*. The special connection between war, penality and an ideology of 'martiality' as a special attribute of masculinity, is quite evident in the language used by neoconservatives — an aspect of their more general aversion to what they call 'political correctness'. Mention should be made in this connection of the important work by Theweleit (1989), in his extensive analysis of letters from members of the proto-Fascist *Freikorps* in 1920s Germany — those who assassinated Rosa Luxembourg and Karl Liebknecht, among others — where he investigated the formation and nature of the Fascist psyche in 1920s Germany, exploring the male self-image, envisaged as 'armoured' against the threat and intrusion of 'the feminine'. Of course, other crucial investigations would come to mind, from Freud of course, to his wayward follower Wilhelm Reich, and more recently the writings of feminist theorist Pateman (1988) and an ample literature on the connection of gender and the Nation. On some of these issues, more recently, see Zarkov (2001) and Jefferson (1994) (I would like to thank Teresa Degenhardt for pointing the latter out to me).

'rogue states' that behave as the 'usurpers of the common good', in Beccaria's words (1764, p 9). The power of war and the power of punishment have therefore become less and less distinguishable, whether one thinks of 'punishing' the evil-doing of wayward states, or of bringing war to domestic enemies, terrorists, *narcotraficantes* and common criminals.[14] It may be objected that according to our contemporary sensibility the social contract has meanwhile progressed to becoming a 'democratic' social contract. In the same way, however, in which nation-states have been created by military powers which extended their reach over other previously independent states, to slowly evolve later toward domestic democratic rule so, on a global scale, the seed of the new order will have first to be established by might to be then developed toward a new democratic global order. Americans will plough the fields and sow the seeds, Europeans will then reap the fruits, democratic fruits that would however never grow without Americans' previous forceful actions. Forever enamoured with the epics of their West, American pioneers would circle the wagons around postmodern Europe — full with women and children! – and would then move on, exploring ever new territories, ready to 'circle the wagons' once more if necessary but this time around a much larger area!

PENALITY AND POLITICAL ECONOMY

Bockman & Eyal (2002) propose to speak about the 'travels' of the discourses that have accompanied such *Wahlverwandshaften* as an instance of 'diffusion through hybridisation'. By this I think they mean that the imperialist *élan* of ideological diffusion is in no way self-sustaining if it does not encounter local dispositions and orientations that welcome, facilitate, and creatively reproduce the 'message' that is being spread to the point of 'bouncing back', so to speak, toward the original point of diffusion — as it happened in their analysis with the contribution of 'Socialist' neoliberal economists to the neoliberal creed or, closer to our topic, with the reelaboration of the Italian Positive School doctrine in Argentina according to Sozzo (2006). However, in this process, the original message 'hybridises' with local themes and languages. This may be a useful way of thinking also in the sphere of penality, as Sozzo showed. If the 'quality' of such events tends to converge, their 'quantity', as suggested above, may better respond to cultural specificities that resist a 'structural' kind of explanation. We are back therefore to Weber's *Wahlverwandshaften*. It is indeed a consistent

[14] Ronald Dworkin writes: 'Conservatives have for many years wanted government to have the powers that administration officials now claim are legitimate: September 11 may have served them only as an excuse. John Ashcroft's Justice Department has been using its new powers under the Patriot Act, which were defended as emergency provisions against terrorists, to investigate and prosecute a wide variety of more ordinary crimes, including theft and swindling' (Dworkin, 2003, p 38; Lichtblau, 2003).

type of rationality, a *Weltanschauung* maybe, which is constructed by the converging action of such different actors in different domains. We do not have to think of such two- or three-pronged attacks through the obsolete language of 'superstructure'. Rather, we are faced by a complex and consistent project, a true moral vision of the world — of which crime and punishment are telling signs. Penality in this view rather than being the product or outcome of economic choices is on the contrary at the same time truly *constitutive* of such choices.[15]

We might be able to see the American 'great internment' of the last quarter of the twentieth century, in this perspective, not because of class conflict, rather as an integral *aspect* of class conflict and, indeed, at the same time, of international relationships, in so far as the increasing hegemony of a discursive punishment within the borders of the US would then fulfil a pedagogic function also in terms of international relationships. Americans' way of thinking about the world would tend to be structured more and more according to a basic narrative of crime and punishment.[16] This should not be seen however — softened European intellectuals, be aware! – as the outcome of simplistic minds. To the contrary, this would be simplification in action, a simplification that is the result of action, and of American supremacy, resulting in the tendential establishment of the seed of a new state, through the construction of a 'monopoly of violence', worldwide!

These connections between penality and class conflict, between imprisonment and social structure, have probably been the case from the very beginning. When, many years ago, I wrote of 'ancillary' institutions in describing the relationship of 'prisons' to 'factories' (Melossi & Pavarini, 1977), I was struggling with the stilted language of *The German Ideology* (Marx & Engels, 1845) or of the famous 'Preface' to *A Contribution to the Critique of Political Economy* (Marx, 1859). However, 'penality', in the English *Bridewells* as in Dutch seventeenth-century institutions, was at the very core of the constitution of a 'capitalist' mode of production. It was no detail, no occasional 'help'. Rather, it was at the centre of the 'making' of the working-class, because only a 'disciplined' 'working class' could become 'labour-power', ie a section of capital, ready to produce profit. At the same time, however, this overall project was at the service

---

[15] Cfr, in a similar vein, Miller & Rose (1990).

[16] And, unfortunately, a basic narrative of crime and punishment structured around a specific way of conceiving 'crime' which spans through both dominant criminological discourse and dominant international relation discourse, where the roots of 'crime', as well as of 'terrorism', are seen in the 'evil choice' of given individuals rather than in the overall situation within which those choices are made. This kind of view that started to become hegemonic in American culture starting in the 1970s, explains both the frightening increase in punishment and the kind of action taken in 'the fight against terrorism'. While I am writing these notes, in November 2003, the tragic consequences of this way of conceiving 'crime' and the reactions to it, are under the eyes of the whole world. In this sense, one could really say that the consequences on the American public and American elites, of understanding crime as 'evil', could not have been more disastrous.

of a certain vision of man, woman and society, of a certain kind of rationality that was to reform and transform all aspects of social life, morality as well as work. In this sense, a certain way of thinking imprisonment is an indicator of the historical change that was taking place in those centuries as coherent and as telling as the introduction of the factory, the market and all the other accoutrements of capitalism.[17]

In similar manner, the 'great internment' in the United States between the early 1970s and the early 1990s was as preparatory of the economic boom of the 1990s as the massive introduction of computers and the obsolescence of a 'Fordist' style of production. For vast sectors of the American working-class, or would-be working-class, imprisonment was the other face of 'mcdonaldization' (Ritzer, 1993). Only a defeated, humiliated, demoralised and beaten working-class, after the insurgent times of the 1960s–1970s, could succumb to working in the kitchens of Mr McDonald. This was a specific course of action that American capitalism took. American 'neo-liberal' elites reacted to that period of insurgency by following two different, but not alternative, paths. On the one hand, they pursued the high course of robotisation, automation and the information economy, giving a strong boost to productivity by pursuing the available brains around the centres of intellectual life, such as Boston or Silicon Valley. By contrast, the penal *revanche* that took off between the Nixon and Reagan Presidencies, obliged millions of young men and women from African American ghettoes or from poor white working-class suburbs to feed an economic recovery largely built on cheap labour (and therefore scarcely productive).[18] In this very specific sense, it is wrong to read penality, through nineteenth-century lenses, as a 'superstructure' of the economy. Rather, penality — as a form of 'government' of human conduct — is part and parcel of the overall project of a 'political economy'. Indeed, such fundamental function of the whole sectors of penality and welfare is reaffirmed repeatedly, when necessary, not only in seventeenth-century theorists and merchants' words, but also in late twentieth-century political scientists' writings, when Lawrence Mead for instance, in an admirably outspoken way, wrote of a 'new paternalism':

---

[17] In such connection, I should recall a *boutade* by my main dissertation adviser in Santa Barbara, Don Cressey, the style of which his many former students will not have any difficulty in recognising. Once, in his office, we were struggling with trying to identify an 'indicator' for the situation of class relationships, to relate to changing punishment levels (the 'obvious' indicator for which was the imprisonment rate). Suddenly Don snapped, 'the imprisonment rate!' Don was not a Ruschean, but he had an uncanny ability for reading through his students' minds!

[18] Alfred Blumstein and Richard Rosenfeld connected the economic recovery of the 1990s and the sudden availability of 'McDonald jobs' for the marginal sectors of the 'ethnic' working class, with the steep decline in crime rates in those years (Blumstein & Rosenfeld, 1998; Rosenfeld, 2002).

> Political discussions of freedom in America tend to define it as the absence of restraint. But people who live without limits soon sacrifice their own interests to immediate gratifications. To live effectively, people need personal restraint to achieve their own long-run goals. In this sense, obligation is the precondition of freedom. Those who would be free must first be bound. And if people have not been effectively bound by functioning families and neighbourhoods in their formative years, government must attempt to provide limits later, imperfect though they must be (Mead, 1997:23).

One does not really need to be a 'Marxist' to see the connection between the kind of 'work discipline' that makes profit, hence capitalism, possible, and the more general 'social discipline' which is so strictly articulated with workplace discipline. If, therefore, the realm of penality is particularly effective in marking the rules of social discipline (which has been particularly the case in the last quarter of century in the United States, less in other, European, countries (Melossi, 2001)), penality could very well be seen as *driving* (a certain kind of) social and economic development, rather than *being driven* by it.

CONCLUDING REMARKS: GLOBAL ANXIETIES?

In conclusion, we can see how, in the case of Italy, the conjunction of a historically-based scepticism on the role of violence and stern punishment in the conduct of human affairs with a traditional Catholic vocabulary of indulgence, tended to de-emphasise the push of socio-structural forces in the direction of an increasing role of punishment (and amplify a tension in the opposite direction). On the contrary, in the 'American' case, the conjunction of a 'cultural cockiness' articulated to the increasing role of the US in the world, with the availability of a Protestant based vocabulary of intransigence and toughness, tended to amplify the pressures coming from socio-structural forces (and de-emphasise the opposite ones).

In this respect, it may be instructive to read the comments by two mid-twentieth-century authors who both tried to capture the making of the contemporary American mind. In a crucial passage of Richard Wright's autobiography, *Black Boy* (1945), Wright tries to come to terms with the difficulty he had in relating with his white co-workers. Such reflections bring him to comment on 'white-American' culture from the perspective of a young black man in 1940s Chicago:

> If the nation ever finds itself examining its real relation to the Negro, it will find itself doing infinitely more than that; for the anti-Negro attitude of whites represents but a tiny part — though a symbolically significant one — of the moral attitude of the nation. Our too-young and too-new America, lusty because it is lonely, aggressive because it is afraid, insists upon seeing the world in terms of good and bad, the holy and the evil, the high and the low, the white and the black; our America is frightened of fact, of history, of processes, of necessity. It hugs the easy way of damning those whom it cannot understand, of excluding those who look different, and it salves its conscience with a self-draped cloak of righteousness. Am I damning my native land?

No; for I, too, share these faults of character! And I really do not think that America, adolescent and cocksure, a stranger to suffering and travail, an enemy of passion and sacrifice, is ready to probe into its most fundamental beliefs[19] (Wright, 1945:272–73).

Richard Wright's implicit and explicit sociology was very close to the Chicago School's (Cappetti, 1993:182–210). The words written by Wright remind us of another author who moved his first steps from the Chicago School and who, a few years after him, concluded in a not very dissimilar way that 'life in a society of masses implants insecurity and furthers impotence; it makes men uneasy and vaguely anxious…' (Mills, 1956:323). Is it not this insecurity and anxiety that makes us long for the spectacle of a stern punishment by means of which we continuously try to restore reassurance in our lives? If this is a condition increasingly common to our contemporary experience, also in this respect American culture has won the dubious primacy of being the first to show the way.

REFERENCES

Archer, D & Gartner, R (1984) *Violence and Crime in Cross-National Perspective* (New Haven (CT), Yale University Press).

Baker, R (2003) 'The Awful Truth' *New York Review of Books*, 6, November, 6–12.

Beccaria, C (1764) *On Crimes and Punishments and Other Writings* (Cambridge, Cambridge University Press, 1995).

Berk, RA, Rauma, D, Messinger, SL & Cooley, TF (1981) 'A Test of the Stability of Punishment Hypothesis: The Case of California, 1851–1970' *American Sociological Review*, 46, 805–829 [DOI: 10.2307/2095080].

Blumstein, A & Cohen, J (1973) 'A Theory of the Stability of Punishment' *Journal of Criminal Law and Criminology*, 64, 198 [DOI: 10.2307/1142990].

Blumstein, A & Rosenfeld, R (1998) 'Explaining Recent Trends in U.S. Homicide Rates' *Journal of Criminal Law and Criminology*, 88, 1175–1216 [DOI: 10.2307/1144254].

Bockman, J & Eyal, G (2002) 'Eastern Europe as a Laboratory for Economic Knowledge: The Transnational Roots of Neoliberalism' *American Journal of Sociology*, 108, 310–352 [DOI: 10.1086/344411].

Cahalan, M (1979) 'Trends in Incarceration in the United States Since 1880' *Crime and Delinquency*, 25, 9–41.

---

[19] Wright's text goes on: 'I know that not race alone, not color alone, but the daily values that give meaning to life stood between me and those white girls with whom I worked. Their constant outward-looking, their mania for radios, cars, and a thousand other trinkets made them dream and fix their eyes upon the trash of life, made it impossible for them to learn a language which could have taught them to speak of what was in their or others' hearts. The words of their souls were the syllables of popular songs'.

Cappetti, C (1993) *Writing Chicago* (New York, Columbia University Press).

Carrabine, E (2000) 'Discourse, Governmentality and Translation: Towards a Social Theory of Imprisonment' *Theoretical Criminology*, 4, 309–331 [DOI: 10.1177/1362480600004003004].

Cayley, D (1998) *The Expanding Prison: The Crisis in Crime and Punishment and the Search for Alternatives* (Cleveland (OH), Pilgrim Publishing Group).

De Giorgi, A (2002) *Il governo dell'eccedenza* (Verona: Ombrecorte).

Drew, E (2003) 'The Enforcer' *New York Review of Books*, 1, May, 14–17.

Durkheim, E (1969 [1900]) 'Two Laws of Penal Evolution' *Cincinnati Law Review* 38.

Dworkin, R (2002) 'The Threat to Patriotism' *New York Review of Books*, 28, February, 44–49.

—— (2003) 'Terror and the Attack on Civil Liberties' *New York Review of Books*, 6, November, 37–41.

Garland, D (1990) *Punishment and Modern Society* (Chicago, University of Chicago Press).

—— (2001) *The Culture of Control. Crime and Social Order in Contemporary Society* (Oxford, Oxford University Press).

Garton Ash, T (2003) 'Anti-Europeanism in America' *New York Review of Books*, 13, February, 32–34.

Graham, J (1990) 'Decarceration in the Federal Republic of Germany' *British Journal of Criminology*, 30, 150–70.

Michael, H & Negri, A (2000) *Empire* (Cambridge (MA), Harvard University Press).

Hobsbawm, E (1994) *The Short Twentieth Century 1914–1991* (London, Abacus).

Howe, RH (1978) 'Max Weber's Elective Affinities: Sociology Within the Bounds of Pure Reason' *American Journal of Sociology*, 84, 366–385 [DOI: 10.1086/226788].

Jamieson, R (ed) (2003) *Special Issue on War, Crime and Human Rights*, *Theoretical Criminology* 7, 259–414.

Jankovic, I (1977) 'Labor Market and Imprisonment' *Crime and Social Justice*, 8, 17–31.

Jefferson, T (1994) 'Theorising Masculine Subjectivity' in Newburn, T & Stanko, EA (eds) *Just Boys Doing Business?* (London, Routledge).

Judt, T (2003) 'America and the World' *New York Review of Books*, 10, April, 28–31.

Kagan, R (2003) *Of Paradise and Power: America and Europe in the New World Order* (New York, Alfred A Knopf).

Kovandzic, TV, Vieraitis, LM & Yeisley, MR (1998) 'The Structural Covariates of Urban Homicide: Reassessing the Impact of Income Inequality and Poverty in the Post-Reagan Era' *Criminology*, 36, 569–600 [DOI: 10.1111/j.1745-9125.1998.tb01259.x].

Krugman, P (2003) *The Great Unraveling: Losing Our Way in The New Century* (New York, Norton).

Lichtblau, E (2003) 'US Uses Terror Law to Pursue Crimes from Drugs to Swindling' *The New York Times*, 28 September [PubMed: 12842228].

Marx, K (1859) 'Preface to A Contribution to the Critique of Political Economy' in Tucker, RC (ed) *The Marx-Engels Reader* (New York, Norton).

Marx, K & Engels, F (1970 [1845]) *in The German Ideology* (New York, International Publishing Group).

Mead, LM (1997) *The New Paternalism: Supervisory Approaches to Poverty* (Washington, DC, Brookings Institution Press).

Melossi, D & Pavarini, M (1981) *The Prison and the Factory: Origins of the Penitentiary System* (London, Macmillan and Totowa; NJ, Barnes and Noble)

—— (1985) 'Punishment and Social Action: Changing Vocabularies of Punitive Motive Within A Political Business Cycle' *Current Perspectives in Social Theory*, 6, 169–197.

—— (1993) Gazette of Morality and Social Whip: Punishment, Hegemony, and the Case of the USA (1970–92). *Social and Legal Studies* 2, 259–79.

—— (2000a) 'Changing Representations of the Criminal' *British Journal of Criminology*, 40, 296–320 [DOI: 10.1093/bjc/40.2.296].

—— (2000b) 'Translating Social Control: Reflections on the Comparison of Italian and North-American Cultures Concerning Social Control, with a Few Consequences for a "Critical' Criminology"' in S Karstedt & KD Bussmann (eds) *Social Dynamics of Crime and Control* (Oxford, Hart).

—— (2001) 'The Cultural Embeddedness of Social Control: Reflections on the Comparison of Italian and North-American Cultures Concerning Punishment' *Theoretical Criminology*, 5, 403–424 [DOI: 10.1177/1362480601005004001].

—— (2003) 'Introduction to the Transaction Edition: The Simple 'Heuristic Maxim' of an 'Unusual Human Being' in Rusche G & Kirchheimer O *Punishment and Social Structure* (New Brunswick, Transaction Publishing).

Miller, P & Rose, N (1990) 'Governing Economic Life' *Economy and Society*, 19, 1–31 [DOI: 10.1080/03085149000000001].

Mills, C Wright (1956) *The Power Elite* (New York, Oxford University Press).

Pateman, C (1988) *The Sexual Contract* (Cambridge, Polity Press).

Pavarini, M (1994) 'The New Penology and Politics in Crisis: The Italian Case' *British Journal of Criminology*, 34, 49–61.

Peterson, WG (1994) *Silent Depression: The Fate of the American Dream* (New York, Norton).

Putnam, RD (2000) *Bowling Alone* (New York, Simon and Schuster).

Rennstich, JK (2002) 'The New Economy, the Leadership Long Cycle and the Nineteenth K-Wave' *Review of International Political Economy*, 9, 150–182 [DOI: 10.1080/09692290110101135].

Ritzer, G (1993) *The McDonaldization of Society* (Thousand Oaks (CA), Pine Forge).

Rosenfeld, R (2002) 'Crime Decline in Context' *Contexts*, 1, 25–34 [DOI: 10.1525/ctx.2002.1.1.25].

Rusche, G & Kirchheimer, O (2003) [1939] *Punishment and Social Structure*. (New Brunswick, Transaction Publishing).

Savelsberg, JJ (2000) 'Kulturen staatlichen Strafens: USA und Deutschland' in Gerhards, J (ed) *Die Vermessung kultureller Unterschiede: USA und Deutschland im Vergleich* (Wiesbaden, Westdeutscher Verlag).

Schor, JB (1991) *The Overworked American* (New York, Basic Books).

Sozzo, M (2006) '"Traduttore traditore" Traducción, importación cultural e historia del presente de la criminología en América Latina' in M Sozzo (ed) *Reconstruyendo las criminologías críticas* (Buenos Aires, Ad-Hoc).

Steinert, H (2003) 'The Indispensable Metaphor of War: on Populist Politics and the Contradictions of the State's Monopoly of Force' *Theoretical Criminology*, 7, 265–291 [DOI: 10.1177/13624806030073002].

Sutherland, EH (1956) [1934] 'The Decreasing Prison Population of England' in A Cohen, A Lindesmith & K Schuessler (eds) *The Sutherland Papers* (Bloomington, Indiana University Press).

Theweleit, K (1989) *Male Fantasies. II Male Bodies: Psychoanalyzing the White Terror* (Minneapolis, University of Minnesota Publishing Group).

Vanneste, C (2001) *Les Chiffres des Prisons* (Paris, L'Harmattan).

Van Swaaningen, R (1997) *Critical Criminology: Visions from Europe* (London, Sage).

Wacquant, L (1999) 'How Penal Common Sense Comes to Europeans: Notes on the Transatlantic Diffusion of Neoliberal Doxa' *European Societies*, 1, 319–352.

Wright, R (1945) *Black Boy (American Hunger): A Record of Childhood and Youth* (New York, HarperCollins).

Zarkov, D (2001) 'The Body of the Other Man' in CN Moser & F Clark (eds) *Victims, Perpetrators or Actors?* (London, Zed Books).

4

Theorising the Embeddedness of Punishment[1]

DAVID NELKEN

In isolation a piece means nothing — just an impossible question, an opaque challenge. But as soon as you have succeeded in fitting it into one of its neighbours, the piece disappears, ceases to exist as a piece

Georges Perec Life: a User's Manual (1987)

Mexico City, 13 February 2004. During a conference visit I am taken by Massimo Pavarini, who is a visiting professor at the UAM, to dinner at the home of his host and colleague, Fernando Tagle, who is the Professor of Criminology there. Conversation turns to the subject of Dario Melossi's thoughts about the 'embeddedness' of punishment. Isn't it curious, says Fernando, that in Spanish when we speak about embeddedness we mean its rootedness in the truth. When I leave, he gives me copies of some of his books. When I look through these later I find that his work has been strongly influenced by the Critical Criminological school of Sandro Baratta and the work of Massimo Pavarini, Melossi and others. But then I recall that Melossi has himself commented critically on the danger that too ready export of critical criminological ideas to Latin America could sometimes have unintended consequences in such a different context (Melossi, 2000)! So where does that

[1] This chapter was written in 2003 as a specific response to earlier thought-provoking papers on the theme of embeddedness authored by Dario Melossi. Although it has not appeared in English, a substantially similar version was published in Italian in 2006 (Nelken, 2006). I have not attempted to update it despite the long gestation of this collection, and have not read Melossi's finalised contribution here. More recent general discussions that have benefited from reading Melossi's work, can be found in Nelken 2009, 2010. I would like to thank Dario for his helpful comments on the original paper which I took into account as far as possible.

leave the truth of embeddedness? To what extent can we say that ideas and practices of punishment are embedded in their social and cultural context while also recognising that, for better or worse, they also travel?

In this paper I shall be exploring the question of what Dario Melossi calls the embeddedness of punishment, taking as my starting point a series of writings in which he contrasts punishment practices in USA and Italy. I shall be relying in particular on Melossi (1994, 1996, 2000, 2001), and as background also Melossi (1990, 1993, 2002). Melossi's views about the embeddedness of punishment have changed over time (and represent an exciting model of intellectual curiosity and honesty from which there is much to learn). It may be that some of the questions I raise are now otiose. His earlier arguments are worth examining, however, in their own right given that he is by no means the only social scientist who has sought to link practices of law and criminal justice to the specific contexts in which they are found. Among sociologists, before talk of globalisation, this was the rule rather than the exception. Among comparative lawyers, by contrast, the field tended be divided between those who traced the way institutions were borrowed from elsewhere and those who insisted on a necessary cultural affinity between a given society and its law (Nelken, 2003b).

In what follows I shall first briefly summarise Melossi's comparative project and then go on to provide an extended critical examination of the way he theorises what he calls the embeddedness of punishment. I shall end by discussing another and parallel comparison between Italy and the USA, this time one drawn by Edwin Lemert, which has to do with the system of juvenile justice in each country. Although I shall start and finish with efforts to explain specific contrasts between the USA and Italy, hopefully this chapter will also succeed in showing that the question of embeddedness has relevance to general theoretical debates about the current and future direction of criminal justice worldwide. It is interesting for example that David Garland changed his approach from an earlier emphasis on how punishment needs to be seen as a profoundly cultural phenomenon to more recent work in which he predicted the spread of what he called — in the singular — '*the* culture of control' (Garland, 1990, 2001). Are modern systems of punishment necessarily converging? If so, why? If we are to develop conceptual tools for analysing this problem we will almost certainly need to make some reference to issues of embedding and disembedding, even if we do not necessarily use these words.

COMPARING PUNISHMENT IN THE USA AND ITALY

Melossi's enquiries into embeddedness turn on the question why it is that in the United States so many more people are sent to prison compared with Italy, even though, he claims, they have roughly similar crime levels. He notes that those who fill the prisons in both countries are young men drawn from the groups of the poor, the marginal and racial minorities. The 'function' of the prison in these and other capitalist societies may be understood in terms of Rusche and Kirchheimer's Neo-Marxist theory which links the use of prison to long cycles of the economy (Rusche & Kirchheimer, 1939). He argues, however, that this type of theory is ill-equipped to explain why there should be such large differences in prison numbers in these two capitalist countries. Hence the need to look for 'cultural' explanations that can reveal how different conceptions and policies regarding punishment are 'embedded' in idiosyncratic, historically shaped political systems, religious traditions and the sense of a countries' role in the world.

With a richness of insight and wealth of detail to which I cannot do justice here Melossi draws on historical evidence and the views of foreign observers to point out some of the telling contrasts in the American and Italian conceptions of punishment and use of imprisonment. In his earliest work on the problem he placed major stress on the differences between Protestant and Catholic religious heritages, as well as forms of state formation and contrasting approaches to equality, inclusion and citizenship (Melossi, 2000). In particular, he showed how the American project of creating self-governing individuals involved the use of imprisonment as a means to *include* and educate those who could be considered potential citizens.

But Melossi did not remain satisfied with this first attempt to account for the difference in imprisonment rates in terms of religious traditions. He raises two objections. If religion is the key to all this, he asks, how can we explain the case of Holland which combines a strong Calvinist background with a tradition of tolerance which (until recently) produced the lowest prison rate in Europe? Perhaps more damaging still, why should American prison numbers have grown steadily and quite disproportionately only recently, whereas not so long ago Italy had relatively more people in prison.[2] Surely, he submits, the influence of religion should have become less rather than more important in a period of increasing modernisation and secularisation? To deal with these objections Melossi suggests that we must treat religion and other aspects of culture not as determining causes but as something that provides a 'repertoire of motives' that may or may not be taken up in given circumstances. And both Protestant and Catholic heritages, he suggests plausibly, can be inflected towards more or less punitiveness.

The problem with this solution, of course, is that it does not tell us when and why we should expect high or low rates of imprisonment. In his more recent work therefore, Melossi offers a new attempt to account for the changing rates of imprisonment in US and Italy. This places less emphasis on the consequences of differences in their religious traditions, and treats each historical period, especially the current one, as a separate problem to be explained. Melossi

[2] Melossi does not deal with the point that the observers whose ideas about high punitiveness in the United States he endorses are actually writing about that earlier period in which his statistics do not suggest that incarceration rates were high.

now sees the recent expansion of imprisonment in the USA as an aspect of the 'Macdonaldisation' of the workforce that prepared the economic boom of the 1990s by forcing the working-class into poor paying and insecure jobs. This was a process that was less pronounced in Europe. In addition he suggests that high levels of punishment in the US have a pedagogic function in terms of the role the US plays internationally. There is a connection between a certain way of building the discourse about criminals and crime (as the product of 'evil individuals') and the way in which the discourse of international relations is built: similarly terrorists are 'evil individuals' — this is connected both to a certain established mode of thinking the problem of crime, especially in the US, and also to a tendency to extend the reach of the US legal order worldwide in such measures as 'the Patriot Act'. Again, this is a factor that is less applicable to countries with low incarceration rates, such as Italy or Holland. In addition, policy makers in these European countries, he suggests, may also have been reacting against their experience of suffering and imprisonment during wartime.

Melossi has not yet attempted to correlate this new variable with the international role played by other countries with particularly high or especially low incarceration rates. A postulated correlation between high prison rates and strategic involvements could find some confirmation by examining the international role of other societies with high rates, such as the Russian Federation, China, Turkey, etc. This would not, however, help us explain Finland's post-war high rate of imprisonment. This thesis would also not explain why the prison rate in the USA was low during the Cold War period of intervention against communism (including the Korean and Vietnamese wars). Nor would it account for the many examples of regimes that are repressive only to their own populations. It also has little to tell us about sudden shifts in attitudes towards prison building, such as that which took place in Holland in the 1980s. In any case, even if the factors that Melossi discusses have somewhat changed, what remains constant in his various essays is the view that in some sense punishment can only be properly understood by showing its 'embeddedness' in its local and wider cultural context.

THE MEANING OF EMBEDDEDNESS AND
THE EMBEDDEDNESS OF MEANING

But what does embeddedness mean? In his earlier papers Melossi uses the idea of embeddedness mainly to signal the claim that criminal justice policy and practice cannot be taken as merely a response to levels of criminality and that we need instead to investigate how ideas about punishment are linked to wider historically shaped aspects of society. However, as his arguments have developed, Melossi's discussions of embeddedness have come to depend on and raise a variety of more fundamental theoretical issues. To get at these we need to ask: in what way is punishment embedded? How far is it embedded? When and why is it embedded? How can we grasp the way it is embedded? Nor are these matters only theoretical. There are obvious practical implications in learning about the roots of punitiveness in a given society. Melossi offers some interesting suggestions about the significance of the spread of certain styles of punishment beyond their home cultures, criticising both the too ready export of procedural formalisms from Italy to Latin America, and also the dangers of importing the current obsessive concern with crime reduction from the United States.

For Melossi the concept of 'embeddedness' of specific historical institutions means that such institutions cannot be conceived separately from the historical evolution and development of the larger setting of social action within which they have emerged — a setting constituted also through given cultural traditions (Melossi, 2001). In terms of its role in constructing explanations of levels of imprisonment, however, it can be argued that using the language of embeddedness provides us with a spatial *metaphor* of the relationship between punishment and the wider context(s) to which it is and must be related. But if we cannot manage without using metaphors in making arguments we do have to be careful not to take metaphors literally or to allow them to stand in for properly thought out theory (Nelken, 2002c). Thus, though a spatial metaphor is heuristically useful for some purposes, the claim that institutions are necessarily embedded 'inside' something else can sometimes obscure as much as it illuminates.

Take for example, the part played by Catholicism in influencing the form taken by state punishment. Melossi is absolutely right to suggest that this is an important factor in Italy. Catholicism, however, shapes punishment in a multiplicity of ways that are hard to pin down. As a religious tradition it shapes the ideas of those who work 'inside' the system as well as the expectations of the public (for example in the demand that the victim be forgiving). But, as a large and powerful social institution, the Church is also 'outside' the legal system and on many occasions even saps legitimacy from it, contributing in this way to reducing the state's 'power to punish'. This ambiguous and protean relationship in which Catholicism is both inside and outside is not easily presented in terms of the spatial metaphor of embeddedness.

By contrast, even for Melossi, the spatial dimension of embeddedness sometimes completely disappears. He argues that 'punishment is deeply embedded in the national/cultural specificity of the environment which *produces* it' (Melossi, 2001: 407). But it is not clear how we are to reconcile the idea of punishment as being embedded *within* a larger unit with the suggestion that the same phenomena is something that is produced *by* the whole.[3] The logic becomes still harder to follow when we are told that punishment is actually 'constitutive' of the wider context in which it finds itself, as in the claim that 'prison is constitutive of liberal democracy'. On this view there would be nothing

---

[3] As with Perec's analogy of the jigsaw, Melossi seems to want the elements of culture to be both separable and yet constitutive of a whole. But jigsaws, unlike cultures, are deliberately created in just this way.

'outside' for the prison or punishment to be embedded in.[4] As he has developed his arguments over time, the problems in using the term embeddedness have increasingly begun to make themselves felt. In attempting to integrate the claim that America's prison rate is the result both of long-standing religious ideas and also an aspect of deliberate national and international strategic choices by power holders, Melossi now uses the concept of there being 'an affinity' between each of these factors and levels of punishment. It is not clear, however, how this (Weberian) idea relates to the spatial metaphor of embeddedness.

In constructing his argument Melossi places considerable weight on a central distinction he draws between what he calls 'structural' and 'cultural' aspects of punishment. Structural explanations apply across societies (at least for societies of a certain type and at a certain stage of their development), are deterministic, can be expressed in mathematical indices and studied with positivistic methods. As already noted, in comparing the role of the prison system in USA and Italy Melossi takes as a common 'structural' pressure, 'capitalism's' need to impose 'less eligibility' by means of imprisoning those surplus to the labour force. Such explanations, he argues, have their limits. 'Structural variables can be used to explain in part variation internal to each society concerned as a cultural unit but they will be largely powerless to explain cross-cultural variation because the latter are characterised by the unique features of a certain society' (Melossi, 2000: 147). To understand variation in the level of punishment, in what Melossi calls the 'qualitative' level of punishment, it is necessary to grasp how punishment forms part of a given cultural whole. Cultural interpretations are non deterministic, historical and singular.

How, and how far, can these aspects to be synthesised? Melossi is concerned both to draw a line between structure and culture, but also to put them together. The 'cultural dimension' has both to be articulated with Rusche and Kirchheimer's type of explanation but also kept autonomous from it. Melossi's view is that there is a background structure that is more or less dominated by a world system/globalised development — otherwise one would be hard put to explain why in all societies the emergence of detentive punishment followed development and 'modernisation' at the same time we have to take into account the historically given individuality of each country that 'fine-tunes' so to speak that background structure (Melossi, this volume).

On the other hand it is far from easy to distinguish structure and culture.[5] Are the role of politics and the media — important factors shaping punishment

---

[4] The journalists who reported on the Iraq war were described as 'embedded' because they were obliged to make their observations on the war subject to constraints imposed by their presence within the American and British invasion forces.

[5] Melossi draws a distinction between the tasks of explaining who is sent to prison and accounting for how many end up there, citing Durkheim's distinction between quantitative and qualitative differences in his 'Two laws of penal evolution' (Durkheim, 1973). But Durkheim's distinction had nothing to do with historically-shaped specificities and our attempts to grasp this.

responses — to be considered structure or culture? In other words, how far do justifications for punishment rest on their argumentative force and how far does their success depend on structural conditions? (Melossi, 1993; Melossi, 2002). A well-known issue that all those who use the term 'culture' face is whether culture can really be treated as a *distinct* explanatory variable. Certainly, it makes little sense to talk of embeddedness if we believe that culture, like language, produces meaning though the co-presence of a series of 'differences'. It is hardly surprising then that Melossi often prefers to argue that cultural trends, political ideology or penality itself are actually 'constitutive' of the whole.

Culture is not just an aspect of that which has to be explained: it is also that which makes possible and plausible our effort at explanation. A second set of issues to which Melossi rightly gives attention (Melossi, unpublished; Melossi, 2001), has to do with the way the theorist herself/himself is embedded in one culture even as she/he tries to understand another. In writing about the possibility of understanding another culture Melossi seeks to navigate between the alternatives of an implausibly scientific (but really ethnocentric) universalism and a solipsistic cultural relativism[6] (see especially but not only Melossi, 2000). He does this not so much by finding an epistemological middle way as by trying to keep the two enterprises apart, each in its proper place. On the one hand, he endorses in principle the *cross-cultural* applicability of a Neo-Marxist thesis, such as that put forward by Rusche and Kirchheimer. By contrast, he acknowledges the potential untranslateability and incommensurability of cultural worlds. Any term, he argues, is embodied within a cultural context or milieu that gives it its meaning. Hence we need direct experience of the other culture to appreciate that meaning. What we are engaged in, therefore, is more a process of translation than an effort at explanation. Any translation will necessarily be imperfect; all that we can ask is that members of different cultures engage in conversation.[7] But sometimes (inevitably?) this conversation can turn back into a scientifically legitimated monologue.

The ambitious synthesis to which Melossi aspires can make some of the argument hard to follow. In stressing the need for giving attention to cultural specificity, Melossi tells us more than once that 'a genealogy of punishment cannot therefore be a genealogy of punishment in general' (Melossi, 2001: 407). Yet, unless we can in some sense indeed have access to the idea of 'punishment in general', how else could we show that it varies from one context to another? If, as he sometimes suggests, embeddedness really was what he calls 'deep' or 'radical', we would not even be able to tell whether we were comparing like with

---

[6] On which see Beirne (1983); Leavitt (1990); Nelken (1994) (all reproduced in Beirne & Nelken, 1997).

[7] In a recent textbook Melossi (2002) makes ample use of anomie and labelling theory in explaining crime and social control in modern day Italy while at the same time insisting on the relativity of all theories to their time and place. He seems confident that, even if the theories he draws on are not good for all times and places, they are apparently, still good for our time and place.

like. By contrast, Melossi takes some ideas about how punishment relates to its wider social context to be general or universal when they may in fact be only culturally specific. Thus, he recommends Sutherland's assertion that we should expect consistency between the prevailing cultural values of a given society and its punitive system' (Melossi, 2000: 147; 2001: 406). When engaged in a cross-cultural comparative exercise, however, it is misleading to assume such consistency. We would do better to treat the degree of 'consistency' between official practices of punishment on the one hand, and wider values and mores, on the other, as a cultural *variable* rather than a constant.

The point is particularly relevant to the comparison between the United States and Italy. Sutherland's claim could itself be seen as reflecting his local Anglo-American culture. We should certainly *not* expect the same level of consistency as between a common law jurisdiction like that of the US, where public involvement in the making of criminal justice is considered an important part of living in a democracy, and a continental jurisdiction like Italy where it is considered inappropriate to allow the response to crime be shaped by public opinion and much of the value of law lies in its capacity to resist and remould public sentiment. Instead of ruling out the existence of differences in the weight given to public opinion and public participation in influencing ideas about punishment in the two societies he compares, Melossi could rather have examined this variable empirically as a clue to the solution of his puzzle about why these two societies produce such different rates of punishment.

To be fair, there is no easy way to resolve the fundamental theoretical and methodological dilemmas that Melossi raises. His comparisons of United States and Italy have the great merit of helping us identify many of the issues that need to be addressed in seeking to understand social and cultural differences in punishment and the way they relate to other factors. As we have seen, there is also need to clarify and take further many of the points he discusses and some he does not. In what follows I shall try to do this with respect to the embeddedness of the object called punishment, the processes that shape its embedding and disembedding, and the embeddedness of the observer who seeks to explain its level and meaning.

THE EMBEDDEDNESS OF THE OBJECT

To develop an analytical framework for talking about the embeddedness of punishment we first need to decide *what* is being embedded, and what it is embedded *in*. Our definitions of punishment may refer to rates of imprisonment, other practices of official social control not involving prison, or even patterns of so-called 'informal' social control. Alternatively, we may want to tap into ideas, official policies and ideologies about punishment, or popular attitudes to punishment. In all these cases we need to be clear how and how far these objects can be measured. If we do use techniques of measurement we shall need to be sure that we are measuring the same object in different places, and over time.

Melossi is not always consistent in describing the object that is embedded. Prison rates are certainly a central focus, but he also talks of the embeddedness of 'penal institutions'. He entitles one paper the 'embeddedness of social control' and also offers to explain differences in 'official policies towards punishment', which he describes as 'conceptualisations about how to organise the world'. At his most reflexive he also makes reference to academic writing itself and includes 'the embeddedness of discourses on penality'. But it is not always clear how these different aspects of punishment are related and how far, if at all, one can be taken (in a Durkheimian sense) as the 'index' of another. Should prison rates and the other aspects of punishment he discusses be seen as all part of the same embedded object, as in the way, for example, state punishment could be seen as one delimited aspect of formal and informal control? Or is each itself embedded in the other like a Russian doll? It makes a difference what we choose as the object of analysis. As we move from considering incarceration rates to discussing official policies towards crime and even criminology itself are we increasingly moving from structural factors to cultural phenomena? At what point have we gone from discussing what punishment is to what it is embedded in?

Most of the evidence Melossi uses to show that Italy is a less punitive society than the USA revolves around a consideration of its level of incarceration rates. Whatever the limits of these rates, of which Melossi is well aware, there can be little doubt that the USA is the more punitive society and that Italy belongs with other European countries. Yet there are aspects of punitiveness in Italy which need highlighting if we are to avoid reading these rates as some sign of deliberately lenient policies. The Italian situation cannot be understood without taking into account the many stages of trial,[8] and the many complex procedures and delays which mean that trials often fail to be completed because of overrunning set time limits. The large variety of technical measures of mercy or conditional forgiveness which undo the effects of a sentence or punishment are also important and in some ways unique.

Nor can we simply treat all these features of penal procedure and organisational practice as themselves aspects of Italy's low level of punitiveness. For similar or even more extreme delays and complexities in trials are found in the handling of civil cases, where the reluctance to punish cannot be the explanation (Nelken, 2004c, 2004, 2008). Compared with common law countries, in Italy there is also

---

[8] Kommer has recently argued that for the purposes of international comparison 'the imprisonment rate is only a very weak indicator of punitiveness' (Kommer, 2004.) There are the obvious problems of comparability here having to do with how crimes are defined, the details of criminal procedure, and the types of sentences imposed on offenders at the different stages of the criminal process (as well as difficult questions concerning the reliability of the statistics in different societies). Changing how we define imprisonment makes a big difference to where Italy stands in relation to other countries in Europe. It is true that it has one of the lowest rates of convicted prisoners in Europe. by contrast, Italy comes out high in terms of gross sentences of imprisonment and has one of the highest average detention periods.

a relatively high risk of being exposed to the criminal process even for relatively powerful groups, such as politicians, administrators and businesspeople(as well of course for the poor and marginal groups who are the normal fodder of the criminal courts). The powerful quite often have a taste of pre-trial detention even if they usually get off in the end. For Malcolm Feeley, a leading scholar of the American criminal process, 'the process is the punishment' (Feeley, 1976). In these terms even when comparing Italy with the USA the pains of the pre-trial process might well loom larger in Italy.

The picture becomes even more complicated (though interestingly so) if we move beyond incarceration rates to wider aspects of official and unofficial social control. The level of state punishment may depend on how much it needs to replace or can rather rely on other forms of control. Considered as a crucial cross-cultural variable, the choice how far to look beyond the criminal justice system to include other forms of 'punishment' can make all the difference to any comparison. As Melossi himself explains, at the time that slavery still existed in the USA there were fifteen times less black people in prison than after its abolition! In Italy the number of people leaving the country as emigrants, especially from the south, had considerable consequences for reducing the number of people in prison (Melossi, 2002).

If we assume as a reasonable hypothesis that social control in Italy compared with the USA is more exercised by family and family-like groups. No comparison of the embeddedness of 'social control' (the title of one of Melossi's papers) could safely leave this out of the picture (though Melossi does). It would be the opposite error to assume a sort of equilibrium whereby each society must have the *same* amount of punishment, as one reading of Donald Black's famous argument about the relationship between formal and informal social control might suggest (Black, 1976). It is much more plausible to imagine that the USA and Italy have different levels of both formal and informal social control. So if we are studying the cultural embeddedness of 'punitiveness' we certainly do need to do more than merely compare prison rates and then link this to general dispositions of elites or populations towards punishment.[9]

Let us turn now to the question *where* punishment is embedded. As we have seen already there is more than a little uncertainty about where to draw the line between *what is being embedded* and *what it is embedded in*. Punitiveness is usually seen as anchored in the nation state, whether it be the USA, Italy, or sometimes Holland. But what is being referred to when we speak of the 'USA' or 'Italy'? The range of elements signified by these terms is almost without limit. And the idea of embeddedness likewise suggests that everything in the wider context is connected to that which is embedded in it. Yet, inevitably, the need for explanation pushes us to single out only some elements. If Melossi leaves out some factors, such as the role of the media or the family that would seem to be

---

[9] Of course, even when all these matters are taken into account we may still plausibly conclude that the United States is a more punitive society compared with Italy.

at least as relevant as those he discusses, he does draws our attention to many important factors, including aspects of economics, religion and international affairs, and he cannot be expected to cover everything.

We also need to give more thought to the meaning of the elements that Melossi has chosen to emphasise. In his initial efforts to solve the riddle of the large differences between the USA and Italy he plausibly took Catholicism to be an explanation of Italian tolerance as opposed to American Puritanism. Is this a feature of Catholicism, or of Catholicism in Italy? What of the considerable differences between Irish, Polish and Italian Catholicism (as well as those between Protestantism and Puritanism)? Melossi uses the example of the toleration associated with Dutch (Protestant) Calvinism to show us that cultures are toolkits, which can be drawn on in different ways. He could have made the same point just as well even from within the world of Catholic societies. Even as far as Italy is concerned, as Melossi reminds us, Italian Catholic society also provided a setting both for the inquisition and Mussolini's fascism.

The difficulties of deciding which aspects of culture are related to punitiveness can be better appreciated by considering the somewhat different explanation of international differences in the harshness of punishment that is proposed in an important recent socio-historical study (Whitman, 2003). Rather than focusing only on imprisonment rates as such, Whitman is concerned also with the quality and style of the use of imprisonment. He seeks to measure greater severity characteristic of the USA, which he calls 'harsh justice', along with ten dimensions of criminal law and penal practice that include matters, such as the length of prison sentences, the existence of the death penalty and what is done to and for prisoners in prison and afterward. For Whitman, the relative severity of punishment in America is connected to 'equal opportunity degradation', as well as to the distrust of the state. In continental Europe, by contrast, the more gradual abolition of a hierarchical class system kept alive the tradition of less degrading 'high status' punishments that eventually came to be applied across the board.

Like Melossi, Whitman is concerned to understand why America has such a tendency towards punitiveness. He thinks that the roots of this go back a long way (at least 300 years) rather than being limited to the explosion of prison rates in the last 30 years. As Melossi does, Whitman refers to Toqueville's ideas about the extensive use of prison in America as originally linked to a project of inclusion. But Whitman's other key variables are not the same as those pointed to by Melossi. For example, he makes little of the differences between Catholicism and Protestantism, nor does he refer to America's current military global role.

For present purposes, however, the most important difference between Whitman and Melossi's argumentative framework is the way that Whitman sees the crucial contrast as that between the USA and Europe – in particular France and Germany – rather than between USA and Italy. This is not just a question of his engaging in a different inquiry from that which interests Melossi. Given that America is the outlier in prison rates (as well as other aspects of harsh justice) compared with Europe it is the American–European difference that needs explaining.[10] If European rates are all so similar what sense would there be in seeking to explain Italy's relatively low rates compared with the USA as an aspect of the historical specificity of Italy's culture? Indeed, if the correct point of comparison is Europe we should probably not be giving weight to those factors which are unique to Italy, such as its type of Catholicism, or its particular recent habit of ruling through leniency (Melossi, 1994). We should rather be looking for what it has *in common* with the rest of Europe.

Whatever we may think of the rival explanations provided by Melossi and Whitman, however, it is worth noting that both may be mistaken in linking rates of punishment so directly to general aspects of the wider culture. It would rather seem essential to concentrate in the first place on the practices and decisions of the police, prosecutors, judges, lawyers and others who are the most proximate sources of these rates of imprisonment. For, whatever else they are influenced by, in the first instance imprisonment rates are measures of these official and bureaucratic responses to crime.

This has been well documented in explaining societies with low prison rates. The leading English-language account of the very low rate of imprisonment, which characterised Holland until the 1990s, attributes it to the role of prosecutors influenced by the Utrecht school who sought to limit the use of custody as far as possible (Downes, 1988). Likewise, the low conviction rate in Japan has been linked to the professional ideology of the prosecutors there who do not want to risk mistaken convictions (Johnson, 2001). The relationship between such ideologies and public sentiment is by no means straightforward. For example, Johnson found little evidence that prosecutors in Japan saw themselves engaged in what Braithwaite dubbed 'reintegrative shaming' in the community. Even in common law systems, the rise in prison rates can be related to attempts to restrict the autonomy of legal officials. In the USA a good part of the explanation for the recent increase in the imprisonment of those committing non violent crimes is attributed to determinate sentencing and such strict legal provisions as 'three strikes and you are out', etc.

Melossi (and Whitman) might reply of course that the behaviour and ideas of criminal justice officials ultimately reflect wider cultural expectations and trends. It is certainly true that they are not immune from political and policy control and rethinking and wider social changes. The increase in prison building in Holland in the 1980s for example coincided with the breaking down of the older system of political cooptation known as 'pillarism'. But we should not forget legal officials can and do create policies or pursue practices that do not correspond to the wishes of the population at large or even to that of

[10] Kagan (2001) sees the USA as distinctive in terms of its obsession with 'adversarial legalism', but see also Nelken (2003c). This would suggest that there is a correlation between high rates of punishment and a realm of formal social control which is particularly inflated.

the politicians and that the 'law in action' may also often have an unexpected relationship to legal provisions and policy intentions. In an apparently rigid continental prosecution system, such as Italy, where prosecutors work under cover of the constitutional requirement of 'obligatory prosecution', empirical research reveals a situation where they are forced in practice to make crucial choices about which cases to prosecute among the masses of cases that come before them (Nelken, 2002a; Nelken, 2007). It is alleged furthermore that the police may currently be avoiding processing 90 per cent of the cases that come to their attention, (Grande, 2000), though it is difficult to find hard evidence about this.

EMBEDDING AND DISEMBEDDING

Punishment is not only tied to its national context. Ideas and practices also travel widely. So embeddedness must be treated not only as a fact but also *as a process*. Any given aspect of apparently embedded practices and ideas of punishment must be considered the result of a dynamic relationship between the past and future and the 'here' and 'there'. In examining any given context in which punishment is embedded we also need to appreciate the processes by which it has been or is being embedded or disembedded. Law has always moved from place to place. It is enough to think of the way Roman law, Common law or Islamic law have spread. Such processes of 'embedding' and 'disembedding' are now speeding up at a time of globalisation. Disembedding, in particular, which 'involves the lifting out of social, relations from local contexts of interaction and their restructuring across indefinite spans of time-space' (Giddens, 1990, p 21), has been said to be a central feature of late modernity. Law, and more specifically systems of punishment, are good examples of the expert systems which participate in these developments and make them possible.

Melossi does draw our attention to the fact that ideas about punishment travel; he sees these as embedded in potentially transferable cultural trends, what he terms 'universal blueprints'. He gives less attention, however, than it deserves to the implications of this for talking about embeddedness. He also does not provide any explicit discussion of the processes of embedding and disembedding themselves. Nonetheless, in the course of his argument he can be found to put forward at least three distinct thesis that are relevant to such an inquiry. For Melossi, the use of prison or any other aspect of punishment is:

  a. A product of the general requirements of the capitalist economy and, per-
     haps also, a result of recent neo-liberal trends that transcend culture. Both
     of these could be said to be more disembedding than embedding forces.
  b. At the same time punishment is also an aspect of specific cultures. Thus,
     he repeats several times that punishment is produced by, and constitutive
     of 'national cultures'. Indeed his comparison of Italy, USA (and Holland)
     would not make sense otherwise.

c. Lastly, he also believes that practices of punishment are the result of the spread of what he calls blueprints.[11] As he puts it, '[c]ultural artifacts of more powerful social formations are imported into less powerful social worlds-whether these social worlds coincide or not with nation states' (Melossi, 2001: 406).

These three claims may not be incompatible. Indeed, most of Melossi's arguments, as we have shown, have to do with showing how the first two are both true. Adding in the third claim though does lead to some further complications that also need to be addressed. If, punishment can belong to social worlds that may or may not coincide with nation states why should we ever assume (thesis b) that the influences on punishment come from single nation states or are limited to what goes on within their boundaries? The term 'culture' gained its modern sense of national interconnectedness through the part it played in the writings of the German romantics. Identifying law with the nation state may have been no more than a post-Westphalian phase of recent centuries. Many cultural units or traditions relevant to the study of punishment, such as the differences between common law and continental civil law, transcend particular countries. By contrast, national 'legal cultures' (Nelken, 1997a, 2002b, 2004c) are themselves internally differentiated. Lawyers in some specialisms may share more with colleagues in foreign jurisdictions than they do with lawyers specialising in different areas of law in their own nation state. Criminologists, too, are likely to have more to say to criminologists in other places than to property lawyers working in their own legal systems.

Talk of the decline of the nation state can be taken too far. It would be a mistake to forget that in many places the state still provides the major boundaries of jurisdiction, politics, and language. Even if common influences, cultural interchange and increasing economic interdependence (or in many cases just dependence) can all produce similarities, local differences remain vital and 'increasing homogenisation of social and cultural forms seems to be accompanied by a proliferation of claims to specific authenticities and identities' (Strathearn, 1995: 3). Increasingly, as a result of globalisation, we will inhabit, it is claimed, a deterritorialised world where we can participate via the media in other communities of others with whom we have no geographical proximity or common history (Coombe, 2000). Because national cultures are influenced by global flows and trends, their purported uniformity, coherence, or stability will often be no more than an ideological projection or rhetorical device.

Much that is described as historical culture will be no more (but also no less) than 'imagined communities' or 'invented traditions'. What counts as culture will be manipulated by elements within the culture concerned or even by outside observers. Any given national system will be at least in part a reworking of ideas coming from elsewhere. The current working of Italian criminal justice, for

---

[11] These blueprints are not only American. For some discussion and criticism of 'globalising criminology' see Nelken (1997b, 2003a).

example, is moulded by doctrinal scholarship which reflects, on the one hand, the long standing hegemony of German penal law, which is still unchallenged among law professors of substantive criminal law, and, by contrast, the more recent influence of Anglo-American ideas which have come in because of the introduction of a large number of accusatorial elements in the penal process. This certainly complicates any effort to characterise Italian criminal justice merely in terms of other aspects of the same culture.

Can we consistently embrace both the claim that punishment is embedded and recognise the evidence of processes of embedding and disembedding? As already mentioned, much of the comparative law literature treats these processes as dichotomous. On the one hand, there are those who assert that there is an intimate and inviolable connection between law as culture and the legal traditions and national contexts in which it is embedded. Hence no genuine transfer from one tradition or context to another is possible (Legrand, 2001). By contrast, there is the diametrically opposed claim that all legal systems are nothing than other than borrowings from elsewhere, and that this process regularly includes flawed and imperfect understanding and application of foreign ideas. The evidence of such constant borrowing is taken to disprove the idea that law can ever be considered embedded in a given society (Watson, 1974).

This debate has significant implications for any study of embeddedness, and should prompt us to try to reconcile what is best in these competing approaches (Nelken, 2003b). The crucial point is that blueprints can modify contexts not only fit them. The ideas about crime and punishment put forward by Beccaria, or Bentham's plans for a model prison, for example, have exercised enormous influence. When they were first developed they were not already embedded in the contexts in which they emerged or in which they became important; on the contrary they were framed in angry reaction to them and became embedded in cultures rather different from those where they had originated (Whitman, 2003). Any living culture is certainly complex enough to include conflict as well as shared values. It is not clear what happens to any theses about embeddedness once we acknowledge that there is no a priori fit between social conditions and cultural ideas. As Melossi insists, ideas about punishment migrate not only to places where underlying conditions are similar but also elsewhere, and may thus be a means of changing rather than merely reflecting or consolidating such contexts. 'Penality', he now argues, 'seems to encapsulate a way in which dominant cultural trends "drive" change in the social structure from a specific cultural context to another, being creatively adapted (and translated) under very different social and historical conditions' (Melossi, in this volume).

But talking only of 'dominant cultural trends' may provide a misleading, and at best partial, account of how ideas travel. There is something tautologous (as well as dystopian) about arguing that it is always dominant cultural trends that are able to travel. It may also be over optimistic to assume that what travels is always creatively transformed. Comparative law scholars are able to cite numerous examples of legal transplants that have had more to do with the accidents of where politicians or legal scholars have studied than with global trends, as in the case of the Turkish code being modelled on that of Switzerland. The results of taking on practices from abroad are not always predictable or univocal. The odious Nazi occupation of Holland left behind legal institutions which are still functioning well there even after the collapse of that regime and after they have been abandoned in their native Germany (Jettinghoff, 2001). The legal institutions introduced in Japan after the second world war work well enough there but the original need to accept ideas from abroad continues to serve as a source of unease (Tanase, 2001).

As opposed to any assumption of cultural hegemony, it is well to consider the variety of internal and external factors that can influence ideas and practices of punishment through processes of imitation, diffusion, immigration and conquest. To account for differences in punishment we need to understand the relevant mix of both local and wider factors. Only careful empirical investigation can reveal the actual weight of these influences in a given society. For example, the global boundaries of crime control are changing because of the threat from terrorism and organised crime. Melossi (in this volume) suggests that the export of American punitive ways goes together with the 'tendential establishment of the seed of a new state'. American neo-conservatives have a certain project about the new world order which involves the extension of American supremacy — and therefore a supra-ordinated legal order — over larger and larger areas of the globe. An aspect of this is the tendency to see American citizenship as the only 'full' citizenship and therefore the individual guarantees of all other citizenships are somewhat reduced. At the same time, however, much collaboration in transnational law enforcement is still most often geared to local low-level crime (Nelken, 1997b; Sheptycki, 2002; Nelken, 2003a). American ideas, such as those having to do with situational prevention, the risk society, and private policing, are slowly spreading to Italy. But the rhetoric of crime prevention in towns across the country would hardly have found a hearing if it had not been for the arrival of immigration as a political issue and the move to having local mayors elected directly rather than being proposed by political parties.

As with the metaphor of embeddedness, we also need to ask whether the embedding adds anything to already existing ones, such as transplanting, exporting, borrowing and so on (each of these of course have their own problems. When did anyone give back a borrowed idea?). But no single metaphor is likely to allow us to grasp the empirical complexities of the spread of ideas and practices (Nelken, 2001c, 2002d) and Melossi himself makes use of some of these other terms, most recently talking of 'diffusion through hybridization' (Melossi, in this volume).[12] Arguably, the term embedding could

[12] Trying to reduce these empirical complexities by using a metaphor whose sense is defined by its place within a theoretical framework, as with Tuebner's use of the term 'irritant' which is taken from Luhmann's systems theory, is even more counterproductive (see Nelken, 2001a).

be particularly useful for describing the way cultural imports can find a place in otherwise dissimilar environments. Examples of this would be the way English common law 'successfully' became embedded in the apparently quite different circumstances of colonial India, where it is has continued to evolve, or the relatively 'successful' importation of foreign legal models in Turkey and Japan. These examples would show yet again that specific legal institutions do not necessarily have to conform to wider aspects of national culture, a situation which is chronic in the many societies characterised by legal pluralism because of successive conquests and migrations (Harding, 2001). On the other hand this was not at all the point that Melossi was trying to make when he started out talking about the embeddedness of punishment in the USA and Italy.

Melossi's illustrations of the way penality travels include the application of British criminal justice policies in the colonies, the spread of Italian critical criminology to Latin America, or the importation of American sociology of deviance into the UK in the 1970s. He also links currently popular approaches to crime control to the American inspired neo-liberal doctrines of deregulation and downsizing of the state of the 1990s. In terms of his discussion of the USA as the land of high punitiveness it is interesting that these examples include at least one where American ideas (through the arguments of the 'labeling school') were intended to, and did, serve to reduce penality. For Melossi the influence of labelling theory offers us an example of what happened in the sixties, in a cycle phase of decarceration and depenalisation. What happened afterward is the sum of the 1970s 'revanche' plus the worldwide role of the USA. This is not the only such example we could find of less punitive ideas travelling in different directions. Even today innovations involving diversion, probation or mediation typically travel from common law jurisdictions, despite their more populist or 'community' oriented criminal justice systems, to continental Europe jurisdictions (see, eg Crawford, 2000). The history of such influences goes back well beyond the sixties as with the modern notion of a separate system of juvenile justice (of which more later).

The speeding up in processes of embedding and disembedding means that the assumed significance of embeddedness can easily become itself part of the debate about whether a particular cultural import respects existing tradition or whether it puts at risk long standing values and practices.[13] The arrival of foreign ways can offer an ideal opportunity to reaffirm existing values and to define what constitutes a local tradition. By contrast, given that traditions are complex, there is usually also room for some argument that the new is not after all foreign. Alternatively, new ideas may be invited precisely for their perceived capacity to bring about change in existing traditions. Sometimes legal institutions are borrowed with the hope that they may have an almost magical capacity to bring into being the wider conditions in which they are embedded in their places of origin.

---

[13] There may also, or above all, be economical or political interests at stake, but this is usually less emphasised.

Questionable assumptions about embeddedness are usually presupposed when scholars and policy makers discuss whether a proposed solution fits the problem — or will create new problems (Nelken, 2001b). Melossi too suggests that the spread of ideas can be deleterious, as in the case of Latin America borrowing the Italian ideas of extreme protections for the accused (then misused by the powerful), or the importation of American practices. But it would be misleading to imply that the problem was simply that these ideas were embedded in other places, rather than offer objections to the ideas and practices in themselves or to their likely effects. We would surely not want to criticise the spread of human rights or the campaign for the abolition of the death penalty on the grounds that they were not yet embedded in the places where they were to be taken on.

Local ideas of what punishment practices are appropriate may be shaped as much by resistance as through processes of borrowing or imitation. For example, the Italian criminal justice system can define its values through its opposition to the use of the death penalty in the USA as well as to the use of curfews and other harsh measures to handle juvenile crime in the UK. Interestingly, a system may resist foreign ideas even when these might be considered consistent with its own values. The famous reform of criminal procedure in 1989 in Italy was based on the American adversarial model and was intended to introduce American-style greater protections for the accused. But those working in the Italian criminal justice system were then blamed for resisting a reform which would have strengthened the position of the accused. Prosecutors and judges, it was said, found it hard to give up control over the criminal process, and the Constitutional Court intervened to avoid the reform offering too many possibilities to organised criminals to exploit it for their own advantage (Grande, 2000).

With the growth of international communication and exchange, members of national legal cultures are likely to become ever more conscious of where they stand in 'relation' to others. More than fact, beyond being a process, embeddedness is thus becoming a relationship. Elites in nation states often feel under international pressure to show that their laws and practices fall within the overall norm. When it comes to prison rates, it is relevant to note that when comparative European prison rates first began to be published in the 1980s, Finland, which came out high in the list, decided to cut back on prison building to move nearer to the 'Scandanivian norm', whereas the then Dutch justice Minister called for a prison building programme emphasising that they were well below the European Norm. An important part of the explanation for the high rate of punishment in the USA is hence likely to be the fact that its elite does not seem to feel the same need to be 'normal', just as it also fails to sign up to some international agreements, such as the international criminal court.

THE EMBEDDEDNESS OF THE OBSERVER

Given that cultures exist ever more in relation to their perceptions of other cultures, it is increasingly important to examine the role in these exchanges which is played by those individuals and groups, including academics, who provide interpretations of their own and other peoples' cultures. Whether they are right or wrong, policy makers' summaries, or legal actors interpretations, for certain purposes help constitute the facts they claim to be describing. Likewise, scholars' visions of a society can come to be taken as versions of the reality, especially by other academics. All such observers, however, are always themselves 'embedded'. This means that what is said about other cultures will always come from a given 'starting point' (Nelken, 2000b). Outsiders' accounts of other places, including what they find to be 'significant absences' in other approaches to criminal justice (Lacey & Zedner, 1998), often tell us at least as much about the cultural expectations of the observers than about that which they set out to describe and explain.[14]

By contrast, as Melossi rightly points out, grasping the way punishment is thought about and administered in another society requires some experience of the society and the ability to translate its meanings from the original language in which they are embedded. It means seeing things as an insider does. How else are we to decide whether Italy is characterised by a healthy refusal of harsh punishment or is rather prey to an elite which cynically rules 'through leniency' (Melossi, 1994)? One promising route to making sense of the apparent reluctance to punish in Italy would involve a hermeneutic exegesis of terms, such as 'garanzie pelose', 'perdonismo', 'buonismo', that offer critical judgements about the excessive leniency of existing punishment practices (see now Nelken, 2009). It would also require an analysis of the occasions in which such appraisals are offered. Melossi hints at the need for this approach when he points out that 'tolerance' and 'indulgence' are not the same, though he does not follow it through. By contrast, his comparison of punishment in the USA and Italy prefers to rely mainly on the sociological interpretations of non–native commentators, such as Toqueville or Paz.

Of course, both native and non-native accounts of other cultures have their strengths and weaknesses (Nelken, 2000a, 2004d). The insider is privy to the meaning of his or her own culture in a way that no outsider can be. The outsider, however, can see more, precisely because he or she has some external point of comparison. Where possible it may be particularly valuable to have the views of those who are 'insiders-outsiders', such as Melossi himself, with extended periods of living and working in more than one culture.[15] But is it safe to rely

---

[14] A valuable and wide-ranging discussion of recent developments in criminal justice in Italy (Clarke, 2003) is weakened by the assumption that trends in punishment can be attributed to the pressures of public opinion as they would be in the United States.

[15] See the discussions in Nelken (2000a, 2004b), and Roberts (2002).

so much on Toqueville when he made only a limited research visit to the USA (to report on their prisons which he did favourably!), and 200 years have passed since he made his observations?

Whitman, by contrast, argues that Toqueville's predictions have actually turned out to be wrong (Whitman, 2003). Toqueville, he claims, distinguished two competing themes in what Melossi would call the American cultural toolkit. On the one hand there was the 'manly and legitimate passion for equality', on the other, 'the depraved taste for equality'. Toqueville believed that the former would prevail and that a democracy able to mobilise popular consensus could dispense with the harsh use of punishment characteristic of absolute centralised states (cf Durkheim, 1973). Whitman, for his part, tries to explain why the second of these trends in fact prevailed. Whether or not we go all the way with him, his comments certainly warn us to be cautious about allowing observers to constitute the phenomenon they describe. We need if possible to be able to observe the observer. To complete and conclude this analysis of the embeddedness of punishment I therefore want to consider another relevant example of the way the views of an outside observer has been taken to constitute the phenomenon in question. I shall again underline the need to see how and why such observers are themselves embedded.

JUVENILE JUSTICE IN ITALY: A SPURIOUS INSTITUTION?

If the notion of embeddedness is to be useful it must also be possible to point to cases where an institution is not well embedded. In a paper called 'Juvenile justice: Italian style' published in the 1980s, a distinguished criminologist, Edwin Lemert sought to show that Italy's juvenile justice system was not really embedded in Italian society (Lemert, 1986). Lemert's argument deserves our attention even if at first sight it seems bizarre. Lemert was one of the most original criminologists of his generation, a pioneer of the 'labelling' approach to crime, as well as being an expert in national and comparative aspects of juvenile justice. More to the point, his account is still used as the standard English-language authoritative guide to the history and current workings of the Italian system (Reichel, 1999). So it is worth trying to discover what he meant by such a strange sounding claim.

In simple terms, Lemert set out to explain how and why welfare-oriented juvenile justice institutions had not succeeded in taking root in Italy. In the course of doing so he also provided figures to show that courts in California were arresting something like 30 times as many young people as in Italy and sending considerably higher proportions of young people to prison. Melossi would quickly tell us that these differences in levels of punishment are in line with those he has been seeking to explain. Indeed, the differential level of arrests for young people itself goes part of the way to explaining the overall difference in prison rates. It might be expected that Lemert, concerned as he was elsewhere with avoiding the 'secondary deviation' that often follows from official intervention in the control of crime, would also have seen this as a reason to praise the Italian approach to juvenile justice as a more lenient alternative to the heavy emphasis on punishment in the USA. Surprisingly, however, rather than compliment Italy's system for its restraint, Lemert instead described its approach as 'spurious'. The abstract of his article runs as follows. 'I propose that the juvenile court in Italy has been a spurious development, reflecting contradictions between the culture of legal certainty and familism, and the adoption of a pattern of discretionary justice based on the positivism of Ferri. Operations of the juvenile court resemble rituals aimed to satisfy conflicting values. Signs are that its legitimacy has been weakened and that other forms of social control have emerged or re-emerged'.

It should be said immediately that we are dealing with an article published more than 20 years ago. Some of the data about the workings of the system on which Lemert relied go back as far as the 1960s! The 1970s and 1980s, the period on which he mainly concentrates, were, in retrospect, very much the nadir of the system. A major procedural reform in 1989 gave a much greater role to the courts and increased their legitimacy as well as introducing a more substantial role for social work in relation to the (still relatively few) cases that were now dealt with by means of pre-trial probation ('messa alla prova'). Two lay experts (a man and a woman), usually with social work training, sit with the judges in trail hearings. A recent proposed bill from the Ministry of Justice designed to reduce this to one lay expert (as well as more generally to move the system in a more repressive direction) was defeated in parliament, with some members of the majority parties voting with the opposition.

On the other hand, many of Lemert's substantive insights into the Italian system are still relevant today, even after the changes and reforms that have taken place since his visit (Nelken, 2005). The system still makes less use of social work and community interventions than the USA or Britain. The 1989 reform introduced a type of pretrial probation but it is employed in only around 5 per cent of cases. Prison, rather than any form of community based alternative, remains the only post-sentence punishment available. But the number of young Italians who are sent to prison has actually gone down since the period of Lemert's research, even if, worryingly, prison is an increasingly common way of dealing with property offences if they are committed by unaccompanied young immigrants, or by gypsies.

The point that concerns us here, however, is not the degree to which Lemert's account has (inevitably) dated. Rather, the problem is what he meant when he described the system as 'spurious' and not embedded in its culture. His brief history of the system explained that juvenile justice came relatively late to Italy, and that most of its goals and structures were explicitly borrowed from the USA, and to a lesser extent, from England. But it was not the fact by itself that the institution originated elsewhere which proved that it was not embedded. The welfare oriented form of individualised response that Lemert viewed as juvenile justice has been 'successfully' transplanted to many other places. It is, rather that the growth of such a system in Italy was impeded by the factors that Lemert discussed in terms of 'formalism' and 'familism'.

The first of these factors Lemert called 'the myth of certainty'. He described it as follows: 'legal reasoning usually avoids any concern with concrete phenomena or their social and political consequences, focusing instead on legislation by the state, with a view to ordering and explaining principles and relationships of law' (Lemert, 1986: 511). 'Given this commitment', he argued, 'it is a tenable proposition for study that Italian legal culture was not a fertile ground on which to generate forms of administrative justice granting wide discretionary power to a single judge, American style, with dispositions freely made, in the interests of the child' (ibid). Hence, what we find, in place of individualised justice, is 'rather a mix of older formalistic classical jurisprudence with an overlay of positivism, threaded with the values of a familistic legal culture and more remotely affected by certain aspects of Italian culture in general' (*id*: 523). By contrast, if courts and social workers do much less than in America to sort out the problems of youth, 'residual resources within the family or extended family can be used to solve the problems of minors' (ibid: 540). In explaining public support for this reliance on the family Lemert discussed what he calls the Italian ethos of avoiding reliance on the state and preferring self-help. He also emphasised the power of the Catholic church as an agency competing with the state and heavily involved in work with youth and offenders.

Lemert's views about Italian juvenile justice were likely affected by his 'starting point', his familiarity with the American juvenile justice system, and his socialisation into American criminal justice in general. Like so many scholars who come from the world of the common law, Lemert was surprised by the depth of the contrast in continental legal systems between what is considered 'law' and what is treated as mere 'administration' (Goldstein & Marcus, 1977).[16] Likewise, his emphasis on the crucial role of the family as an alternative to the state may be seen as an example of the typical reaction of Anglo-American scholars to Italian social life, seen most notoriously in Banfield's ideas about 'amoral familism' (Banfield, 1958). Italian born authors, including Melossi, by contrast, tend to find this misleading or stale (see the Italian commentators whose views are included in Banfield, 1976) and are much less likely to use this factor in their explanations.

As an outsider there is much that Lemert saw about the Italian system that insiders might not have been in a position to register. But his interpretation may have also suffered from his not being embedded in the country he was describing. His picture may have been coloured by the fact that his brief visit focused mainly on Rome, which has always had a remarkably low number of social workers. Not speaking Italian he was bound to rely on scholarly contacts and interpreters who perhaps had their own agenda (which possibly included their bemoaning the lack of real commitment of welfare resources). Legal formalism may also be

---

[16] As they put it, 'the idea of the administration of law belongs to a lower and more flexible order of things' (Goldstein & Marcus, 1977: 281).

more a cover than a reality. There is much use of discretion in Italy that goes on behind the scenes in ways that may often aim at and produce sensible practical outcomes (Nelken, 2002a).

Above all, however, one senses the lack of a wider context of reference. A lot of what Lemert described with reference to juvenile justice — its formalism, proceduralism and lack of attention to results, its delays and so on-also characterise, to an even greater extent, the adult system of criminal justice. From an Anglo-American 'pragmatic-instrumentalist' approach to law we might then want to describe the *whole* criminal justice system as spurious. But the ethnocentrism of such a conclusion hardly needs underlining. From an Italian, and more broadly civilian, perspective, for example, it was and is the failure of the common law system of criminal justice to give sufficient importance to coherent doctrine and legal certainty that is inexplicable and scandalous. This view was even shared by some American scholars, such as Pound and Cardozo who were well versed in continental jurisprudence, for whom American penal law was therefore 'a field for charlatans' (Grande, 2000). It would hardly advance the debate to say that Anglo-American criminal law was therefore spurious.

Since Lemert wrote his piece, the juvenile court in the USA has itself increasingly shifted away from its welfare orientation towards a more legalistic approach. Does this mean that juvenile justice in the USA has also now become spurious, or would it not be more correct merely to say that its orientation has changed? What was Lemert really trying to get at by using a term that so easily conflates the descriptive and evaluative registers?[17] The working definitions he provides in the course of his argument are intriguing but in the end contradictory. On the one hand, we have the following definition that refers to the place of juvenile justice in relation to the rest of Italian culture — "here I use the word in the sense of 'anomalous' to suggest that the Italian juvenile court was an alien development with the appearance — but not the genuine characteristics — of Italian culture" (ibid: 511 n 1). By contrast, spuriousness is a quality which is said to depend on the differences between Italian developments and those elsewhere. Juvenile justice in the American or British mode, with its emphasis on the individualised treatment of delinquent youth, he argues, was ill suited to Italian legal doctrine. It could not create a differentiated special role for judges, and could not bring in a major role for positivistic science. When the attempt failed 'the courts acquired a spurious quality, more culturally synergistic than genuine' (*id* 527). Hence juvenile justice in Italy was 'a precariously institutionalised form of justice likely to disappear or be replaced by other types of social control' (*id*).

---

[17] The bibliographical references Lemert provided to earlier uses of the word by Sapir and Tumin are of little help because these authors tend to apply the description to whole cultures that are thus categorised as somehow inauthentic. Paradoxically, in terms of Lemert's criticisms of the formalism of Italian juvenile justice, they even suggest that the term is more applicable to American culture precisely because of what they criticise as its 'obsession with 'instrumental outcomes'!

Lemert cannot have it both ways. The system cannot be spurious in relation to an American blueprint because it is being true to its local context, and, at the same time, be spurious because it does not fit in with the rest of Italian culture. To put the same point somewhat differently, we need to decide how far it is the American model itself that is spurious for Italy, and how far it is Italy's juvenile court that can be judged to be spurious in its own terms. We should be very wary of Lemert's assumption that the failure to embed the American model as such rendered what happened in Italy spurious in terms of its own cultural context. This becomes still clearer when with hindsight we can now see that the Italian system has since gained in welfare orientation while the American system has retreated.

Ideas and practices of punishment do not exist only in the eye of the beholder. The object we call punishment is lived and reproduced in the everyday experience of those who undergo it, those who apply it, and those who make policies about it. But for that very reason it becomes important to see how academic discourse does play a part in constituting the object it describes — and seek for ways of showing it to be partial or in other ways misleading. The truth about embeddedness is that to some extent it cannot be otherwise: there can be no view from everywhere. This very embeddedness of the observer is also that which makes the 'conversation' about other cultures, of which Melossi speaks, both possible and valuable.

REFERENCES

Banfield, E (1958) *The Moral Basis of a Backward Society* (Glencoe, Free Press).
—— (1976) *Le Basi Morali di una Società Arretrata* (Bologna, Il Mulino).
Beirne, P (1983) 'Cultural Relativism and Comparative Criminology' *Contemporary Crises*, 7, 371–391 [DOI: 10.1007/BF00728670].
Beirne, P & Nelken, D (1997) (eds) *Issues in Comparative Criminology* (Aldershot, Dartmouth).
Black, D (1976) *The Behaviour of Law* (New York, Academic Press).
Clarke, DS (2003) 'Estilos italianos: La justicia penal y el ascenso de una judicatura activista' in HF Fierro, LM Friedman & RP Pérez Perdomo (eds) *Culturas jurídicas latinas de Europa y América en tiempos de globalización* (México, Universidad Nacional Autónoma de México).
Coombe, RJ (2000) 'Contingent Articulations: A Critical Cultural Studies of Law' in A Sarat & T Kearns (eds) *Law in the Domains of Culture* (Ann Arbor, University of Michigan Publishing Group).
Crawford, A (2000) 'Contrasts in Victim/Offender Mediation and Appeals to Community in Comparative Cultural Contexts: France and England and Wales' in D Nelken (ed) *Contrasting Criminal Justice* (Aldershot, Dartmouth).
Downes, D (1988) *Contrasts in Tolerance* (Oxford, Oxford University Press).
Durkheim, E (1973) 'Two Laws of Penal Evolution' *Economy and Society* 2, 285–308 [DOI: 10.1080/03085147300000014].

Feeley, M (1976) *The Process Is the Punishment* (New York, Russell Sage)

Garland, D (1990) *Punishment and Modern Society* (Oxford, Oxford University Press).

—— (2001) *The Culture of Control* (Oxford, Oxford University Press).

Giddens, A (1990) *Consequences of Modernity* (Cambridge, Polity Press).

Goldstein, A & Marcus, M (1977) 'The Myth of Judicial Supervision in Three Inquisitorial Systems: France, Italy and Germany' *Yale Law Journal*, 87, 240 [DOI: 10.2307/795651].

Grande, E (2000) 'Italian Criminal Justice: Borrowing and Resistance' *American Journal of Comparative Law XLVLLL*, spring 2: 227–260.

Harding, A (2001) Comparative Law and Legal Transplantation in South-East Asia' in D Nelken & J Feest (eds) *Adapting Legal Cultures* (Oxford, Hart Publishing).

Jettinghoff, A (2001) 'State Formation and Legal Change: On the Impact of International Politics' in D Nelken & J Feest (eds) *Adapting Legal Cultures* (Oxford, Hart Publishing).

Johnson, D (2000) 'Prosecutor Culture in Japan and USA' in D Nelken (ed) *Contrasting Criminal Justice* (Aldershot, Dartmouth).

Kagan, RA (2001) *Adversarial Legalism: The American Way of Law* (Cambridge, MA, Harvard University Press.

Kommer, M (2004) 'Punitiveness in Europe Revisited' in *Newsletter of the European Society of Criminology*, 3(1), 1, 8–12.

Lacey, N & Zedner, L (1998) 'Community in German Criminal Justice: A Significant Absence?' *Social and Legal Studies*, 7, 7–25 [DOI: 10.1177/096466399800700102].

Leavitt, G (1990) 'Relativism and Cross-Cultural Criminology' *Journal of Crime and Delinquency*, 27, 5–29 [DOI: 10.1177/0022427890027001002].

Legrand, P (2001) 'What Transplants' in D Nelken & J Feest (eds) *Adapting Legal Cultures* (Oxford, Hart Publishing).

Lemert, E (1986) 'Juvenile Justice; Italian Style' *Law and Society Review*, 20, 509–544 [DOI: 10.2307/3053465].

Melossi, D (1990) *The State of Social Control* (Cambridge, Polity Press).

—— (1993) 'Gazette of Morality and Social Whip: Punishment, Hegemony and the case of the USA'. 1970–92 *Social and Legal Studies*, 2, 259–279 [DOI: 10.1177/096466399300200301].

—— (1994) 'The Economy of Illegalities: Normal Crimes, Elites and Social Control in Comparative Analysis' in D Nelken (ed) *The Futures of Criminology* (London, Sage).

—— (unpublished) 'The Radical Embeddedness of Social Control (or the Impossibility of Translation): Reflections Based on a Comparison of Social Control in Italian and North American Culture'. Unpublished Paper presented at the Onati International Institute for Sociology of law, Spain.

—— (2000) 'Translating Social Control: Reflections on the Comparison of Italian and North American Cultures Concerning Social Control, with a Few

Consequences for a "Critical Criminology"' in S Karstedt & K Bussmann (eds) *Social Dynamics of Crime and Control: New Theories for a World in Transition* (Oxford, Hart Publishing).

—— (2001) 'The Cultural Embeddedness of Social Control: Reflections on the Comparison of Italian and North American Cultures Concerning Punishment' *Theoretical Criminology*, 5, 403–424 [DOI: 10.1177/1362480601005004001].

—— (2002) *Stato, Controllo Sociale, Devianza* (Milano, Bruno Mondadori).

—— in this volume 'Neoliberalism's "Elective Affinities": Penality, Political Economy and International Relations'.

Nelken, D (1994) The Future of Comparative Criminology' in D Nelken (ed) *The Futures of Criminology* (London, Sage)

—— (ed) (1997a) *Comparing Legal Cultures* (Aldershot, Dartmouth).

—— (1997b) 'The Globalization of Crime and Criminal Justice: Prospects and Problems' in M Freeman (ed) *Law at the Turn of the Century* (Oxford, Oxford University Press).

—— (editor) (2000a) *Contrasting Criminal Justice* (Aldershot, Dartmouth)

—— (2000b) 'Telling Difference: of Crime and Criminal Justice in Italy' in D Nelken (ed) *Contrasting Criminal Justice* (Aldershot, Dartmouth).

—— (2001a) 'Beyond the Metaphor of Legal Transplants?' 'Consequences of Autopoietic Theory for the Study of Cross-Cultural Legal Adaptation' in J Priban & D Nelken (eds) *Law's New Boundaries: The Consequences of Legal Autopoiesis* (Aldershot, Dartmouth).

—— (2001b) 'The Meaning of Success in Transnational Legal Transfers' *The Windsor Yearbook of Access to Justice*, 19, 349–366.

—— (2001c) 'Towards a Sociology of Legal Adaptation' in D Nelken & J Feest (eds) *Adapting Legal Cultures* (Oxford, Hart Publishing).

—— (2002b) 'Comparative Sociology of Law' in M Travers & R Banakar (eds) *Introduction to Law and Social Theory* (Oxford, Hart Publishing).

—— (2002c) 'Legal Transplants and Beyond: of Disciplines and Metaphors' in A Harding & E Orucu (eds) *Comparative Law for the 21st Century* (The Hague, Kluwer).

—— (2002d) 'Changing Legal Cultures' in MB Likosky (ed) *Transnational Legal Processes* (Cambridge, Cambridge University Press).

—— (2003a) 'Criminology: Crime's Changing Boundaries' in P Cane & M Tushnet (eds) *The Oxford Handbook of Legal Studies* (Oxford, Oxford University Press).

—— (2003b) 'Comparativists and Transferability' in P Legrand & R Munday (eds) *Comparative Legal Studies: Traditions and Transitions* (Cambridge, Cambridge University Press).

—— (2003c) 'Beyond Compare? Criticising the American Way of Law' *Law and Social Inquiry*, 28, 181–213 [DOI: 10.1111/j.1747-4469.2003.tb00216.x].

—— (2004a) 'Comparing Legal Cultures' in A Sarat (ed) *Blackwell Handbook to Law and Social Science* (Oxford, Blackwell).

—— (2004b) 'Being There' in L Chao and J Winterdyk (eds) *Lessons from Comparative Criminology* (Ontario, De Sitter Publications).

—— (2004c) 'Using the Concept of Legal Culture' *Australian Journal of Legal Philosophy*, 29, 1–28.

—— (2004d) 'Doing Research into Comparative Criminal Justice' in R Benakar & M Travers (eds) *Doing Socio-Legal Research Differently* (Oxford, Hart Publishing).

—— (2005) 'When Is a Society Non-Punitive?' in J Pratt et al (eds) *A Case Study of Italy in the New Punitiveness: Current Trends, Theories, Perspectives* (Cullompton, Willan Publishing).

—— (2006) 'Il radicamento della penalità' in A Febbrajo, A La Spina, and M Raiten (eds) *Cultura Giuridica e Politiche Pubbliche in Italia Milano*, ed Giuffré.

—— (2007) 'Comparing Criminal Justice' in M Maguire, R Morgan and R Reiner (eds) *Oxford Handbook of Criminology* 4th edn (Oxford, OUP)139–57.

—— (2008) 'Normalising Time: European integration and Court delays in Italy' in H Petersen, H Krunke, A-L Kjær and M Rask Madsen (eds) *Paradoxes of European Integration* (Aldershot, Ashgate) 299–323.

—— 'Comparative Criminal Justice: Beyond Ethnocentricism and Relativism' (2009) 6(4) *European Journal of Criminology* 291–311.

—— *Comparative Criminal Justice: Making Sense of Difference* (London, Sage Publications, 2010).

Reichel, PL (1999) *Comparative Criminal Justice Systems: A Topical Approach* (New Jersey, Prentice Hall).

Roberts, P (2002) 'On Method: The Ascent of Comparative Criminal Justice' *Oxford Journal of Legal Studies*, 22, 529–561 [DOI: 10.1093/ojls/22.3.539].

Rusche, G & Kirchheimer, O (1939) *Punishment and Social Structure* (New York, Russell and Russell).

Sheptycki, J & WE (2002) *In Search of Transnational Policing* (Aldershot, Dartmouth).

Strathern, M (1995) *Shifting Contexts: Transformations in Anthropological Knowledge* (London, Routledge).

Tanase, T (2001) 'The Empty Space of the Modern in Japanese Law Discourse' in D Nelken & J Feest (eds) *Adapting Legal Cultures* (Oxford, Hart Publishing).

Watson, A (1974) *Legal Transplants* (Edinburgh, Scottish Academic Press).

Whitman, J & Q (2003) *Harsh Justice: Criminal Punishment and the Widening Divide Between America and Europe* (Oxford, Oxford University Press).

Part II

Diffusion of Post-Fordist Penality

5

State Form, Labour Market and Penal System: The New Punitive Rationality in Context

IÑAKI RIVERA BEIRAS[1]

Around the turn of the nineteenth century, Vincent van Gogh painted — to subsequent international renown — his famous picture 'The Round of the Prisoners'. It presents a well-known image: a circle of prisoners that completely embraces the perimeter space of a prison courtyard. This circular vision is composed by people who truly seem to be moving around, painted by a magic hand.

One century later, we can think about another circular view, rather less artistic. The new millennium presents a terrifying figure: according to the most rigorous and official data (from the UN), there are at present about 8,700,000 prisoners all over the world. Nowadays, this human contingent can form another 'round', another circular view: such a number could go twice around the world. A gloomy and hard vision for a sensitive artist: what has happened? What is going on?

(Pavarini (2002))

POLITICAL SCIENCE, CRIMINAL POLICY AND CHANGES IN PARADIGMS

In addressing the problem of the right to punish, Ferrajoli (2001) reminds us that criminal law and punishment were among the grounds on which, in the 17th and 18th centuries, the rationalist philosophy of the Enlightenment

[1] I want to thank Prof Pat Carlen for all her help in reading and discussing this work with me. This paper is a revised, updated and extended version of an essay published in *Punishment & Society* (2005) vol 7: 167–82.

fought its battles against the repressive and intrusive despotism of the *Ancien Regime*. Here the values of modern juridical civilisation and the guidelines of the Rule of Law began to be defined: respect for human beings, the value of life and personal freedom, the link between legality and liberty, tolerance and freedom of thought and expression, and the function of the state as a protector of rights. Later on, diverse influences have contributed to attempts at tearing down that building of modernity. Among the most relevant topics, Ferrajoli mentions the reactionary retreat of late nineteenth century liberal thought; a coarse and non-critical positivist epistemology supportive of the status quo; a kind of paradoxical 'naturalisation' of criminal law as an external and independent phenomenon that jurists saw as susceptible of being known and perhaps explained, but never justified or, conversely, de-legitimated. For this reason, we witness the reduction of its external or political legitimisation to an internal or juridical one, or the confusion of its justice with its mere existence.

In the political-criminal field, the second half of the nineteenth century was a period of widespread change. From the Italian Scuola Positiva, to the German School of Marburg, or from the Spanish *Correccionalismo* to the *New Penology* in the United States (following the experiments of the Elmira reformatory), a new punitive rationality began to be imposed as a penal counterpart of the etiological paradigm of criminality. The early Penitentiary Congresses in both Europe and the Americas provided the most emblematic stage for the representation of the new 'scientific, criminological and penological' knowledge. Those discussions not only revealed a new faith in correcting individual pathologies through the penal system but also insisted that those debates had succeeded in founding a whole new body of scientific knowledge. Their discussions about penal architecture, regimes and methods of treating criminality, or the problems arising from alcoholism, pornography, and prostitution (as 'new' causes of deviant behaviour), the treatment of insane people and the organisation of asylums, problems relating to youth and the creation of the first reformatories, or the discussion of justifications for punishment and the creation of security measures, provided a defence of (more or less) indeterminate sentences, albeit in some geographical areas more than in others.

The martial disasters of the Second World War, the Jewish Holocaust and the task of reconstructing Europe after 1945, would mark — at least for continental Europe — the beginning of a new State-form with a constitutional model inherited from the '*Resistenza*' (in the particular Italian case) of those people who had themselves suffered the effects of authoritarian penal regimes. The Italian Constitution initiated the so-called 'social constitutionalism' which would prove — through a form of adaptive reinterpretation of continental European culture — receptive to the establishment of a welfarist tradition. All these facts had a decisive impact on the ways in which juridical-political intervention came to be legitimated. This requires an explanation.

In speaking about the origins of welfare, one should go back to the second half of nineteenth century and the importance of the so-called 'social question' (the birth of the worker's 'movement', the first collective struggles, the beginning of syndicalism, and so on). In England in 1900 we see the enactment of important social/manufacturing legislation. In Germany, the first programmes of compulsory provision for insurance against sickness and invalidity similarly appear. In this brief outline, it can be also said that this trend towards intervening on the 'social question' would be followed by similar Danish and Swiss legislation in the first years of twentieth century. Thus, a new form of welfare came into being. To fund the new measures of 'assistance' that they had undertaken states had to resort to one main resource: tax collection. In this sense, it can be said that modern social assistance and modern taxation come into being in a contemporary relationship. The idea that the state had to assume responsibility for maintaining some essential minima for the whole population through a gathering and distribution of resources and a dispersion of risks was born.

The first theories about the fiscal support of the welfare model would come along with the concept of 'Fiscal State', thanks to a couple of decisive authors. As Gough (1979) has shown, Goldscheid, in 1919, and Schumpeter, in 1918, noted the importance of studies on fiscal sociology when recognising that the fiscal history of a nation is an essential part of its general history (the idea of 'Budget as the State's skeleton'). As a consequence of these approaches, the expression 'Fiscal State' arose. Following these contributions, the early forms of welfare would present certain characteristics: the state begins to involve itself more in regulating the labour market; strikes, syndicates and the first social legislation begin to be understood as a part of the 'social question' that the state must regulate and 'protect'. Labour regulation, schedules, rest, holidays, emergent social rights, and so on, characterised the early forms of state-provided welfare 'assistance'.

The influences of welfare on the political and economic culture of the United States and Britain at the end of nineteenth century and the first decades of twentieth century were orientated in these directions. On the other hand, the development of continental European 'assistance' (born with Bismarck in Germany at the end of nineteenth century) underwent, as we have seen, an abrupt rupture with the emergence of the European totalitarianisms and the era of dictatorships. Following the devastation of Europe by World War II the task of social reconstruction had to begin. The reconstruction was based upon two central assumptions: international cooperation (which had to serve to rebuild the continent and improve people's living standards) and the emergence of international legislation on human rights (as the necessary concomitant of reconstruction and the means of avoiding the repetition of these atrocities for ever). The 'modernised' recovery of the welfare would be understood as 'the group of social services provided by the State, in cash or in kind, as well as the regulation of the activity of individuals and enterprises' (Gough, 1979: 22).

In the political-criminal field, and closely related to the social constitutionalism of the post-war period (which asserts the formula of the social and democratic state allied to the Rule of Law), Ferrajoli argues that, in the second half of twentieth century, a real change of paradigm in the positive law of the advanced democracies took place. This leads to an epistemological revolution in penal sciences and, in the framework of law as a whole.

As Ferrajoli indicates, in the cultural and political environment that saw the birth of post-war constitutionalism — the foundation of the UN, the Universal Declaration of Human Rights (UHDR) from 1948, the Italian Constitution from 1948 and the German one from 1949 — there was an understanding that popular consent alone (to which the fascist dictatorships had also laid claim) was not sufficient to guarantee the quality of a political system. A new emphasis was thus placed upon the value of the Constitution as the limit and link of any kind of power, even a majority one. Consequently, a structure of juridical order, a lot more complex and doubly artificial, was being built up: (1) not only because of the positive character of the produced norms (that is the specific feature of Juridical Positivism); (2) but also because of its subordination to Law. In this latter case, the very juridical production is disciplined by norms of positive law not only in relation to its generation but also to its contents. Ferrajoli calls this legal framework the guarantee model or system (op cit: 25).

In such a framework, the penal system — Law's guarantee — and punishment will persist in being justified with the purpose of fulfilling both old and new aims. Indeed, when facing the old resocialising and reforming aspiration, Ferrajoli accords punishment the function of being useful to prevent the penal transgressor from being subjected to an informal (spontaneous, wild) punishment, something potentially much worse than the pains imposed by lawful punishment. As is well-known, however, all of this would require support, investment and expenses from the social state. As will be seen next, this foundation is exactly the one that has latterly grown weak.

STATE (FISCAL) CRISIS AND THE EMERGENCE OF
THE PENITENTIARY BUSINESS IN THE USA

James O'Connor pointed out — in the USA at the beginning of the 1970s — that 'every class and economic and social group wants the Government to spend larger amounts of money on an increasing number of things. But no one wants to pay new taxes or greater indexes on the old taxes. As a matter of fact, almost everybody wants lower taxes, and many groups have successfully carried out campaigns to get them reduced' (1981: 20). O'Connor defined the situation in very exact terms: 'We have defined 'State fiscal crisis' as the trend of government expenditure to increase faster than its income. It is not the case that there is a rigid rule through which spending always has to rise faster than revenue, but there is no doubt that the increasing necessities to which only the state can respond produce greater claims on the state budget' (op cit: 26). However, he recognised that diverse factors, individually or in combination, may counteract the crisis. For instance: the state may leave unfulfilled the needs of people depending on public services; it may happen that the big companies applying for government loans and subventions do not obtain them; the government may freeze salaries and wages in an attempt to alleviate the fiscal crisis; or it may also compel citizens to pay higher taxes. As can be seen, the pressure under which the welfare state begins to crack and split is an economic-budgetary one. What kind of consequences would this bring to the American penal system?

The Fall of the Rehabilitation Myth

The fiscal crisis provoked the need to reconfigure the 'penal complex' that had been developed under the influence of the welfare model. The rehabilitative ideal could only work through the support of diverse professional groups (classification officers, parole boards, psychologists, psychiatrists, teachers, criminologists, social workers), to which one should add the great cost of the prison system itself. As has been already seen, the period of post-war economic expansion was reaching its end; this was the time for budget reductions and the American economy could not go on allocating so many resources to the management of certain social problems. The agencies and operators of this very wide reforming penal system had to begin to be reduced.

Meanwhile, the discrediting of the indeterminate sentence had already taken hold. The report *Doing Justice* remarked in 1976 that when the sentence is indeterminate, the harm is produced precisely by the agony of uncertainty. It is scarcely surprising that many prisoners came to regard the indeterminacy of their date of release as the worst feature of their life in prison. The distrust of medical, psychological or psychiatric predictions, or therapy in general, crystallised under the slogan 'nothing works'. As Zysman (2001) indicates, criticism started to come from two different fronts: the *conservative* one and another front of *liberal-radical* character. The former connected rising crime rates with the preventive failure of individual reformation and its unjustifiable benevolence, pointing out that the focus of attention is put on the criminals rather than the victims. The second front of criticism revealed the regrettable effect of prison on inmates, underlined its selective-racist character, criticised the ideology of treatment as a method for concealing manipulation, discrimination, violence, and the transgression of elementary rights, and asserted that it served as a control instrument for the penitentiary authorities to keep the population docile, disciplined and industrious. In sum, it was argued that rehabilitation had not achieved the declared functions of reformation but served instead as an instrument of disciplinary control. This critical movement in penology thus existed in an important relationship with the wider counter-culture and oppositional social movements of the period. It also called upon an increasing body of research in prisons (Clemmer, 1958) and other 'total institutions' (Goffman, 1970) that cast grave doubt upon the optimistic pretensions of the prevailing scientism. Furthermore, the bloody events at Attica on 9 September 1971, when an unprecedented number of people died during the authorities' assault on the prison, with the television cameras rolling, contributed to the tearing-down of the reformative edifice.

The Construction of the Penitentiary Business

The demise of the indeterminate sentence and the myth of rehabilitation in the USA during the 1970s gave way to very different sentencing models that, apart from some attempts to institute the reductionist objectives of the justice model (cf Von Hirsch, 1986), would come to be dominated by rationalities of the economic/technocratic type. The notions of *cost-benefit, calculation, statistical analysis*, along with the attempt at *anchoring penal scales* in a fixed and determinate way, explain the emergence of forms of sentencing that would eventually prioritise two tools from the new penal culture: mandatory penalties (culminating in the invention of 'three strikes and you're out') and guideline sentences. The theorisation of the individual as a rationally choosing risk-taker, prepares the way for the renewed 'enlightened-postmodern' rationality (De Giorgi, 2000: 30).

As Christie indicated some years ago, the new sentencing led American legislatures, for example through the establishment of Sentencing Commissions, to elaborate 'manuals to decide on pain' (2000: 137), expressly forbidding the courts from considering transgressors' personal qualities — age, education, professional instruction, psychiatric or emotional conditions, bodily conditions (including drug addiction, alcohol abuse, etc.), labour background, family links or responsibilities, cease to count. Thus, Christie argued, 'the legislators make it illegal for justice to consider precisely those factors which most of the prison population have as their common background: poverty and deprivation, the absence of a share in the good life, all those key attributes of the non-productive "dangerous class"' (Christie, 2000: 158). The scene has been set for the emergence of a new penitentiary industry.

Christie influentially claims that by comparison with other activities, the crime control industry finds itself in a very favourable situation. There is no lack of raw material: rather there is an 'unlimited reservoir of acts which can be defined as crimes'. Thus, 'the ground has been prepared. The crime control market is waiting for its entrepreneurs' (op cit: 23). Drawing on Bauman (1989), Christie documents the emergence of the punitive management of poverty in the USA as a major business opportunity. However, the confidence required for major investment decisions depended on the demonstration of a *sustained* expansion, a new 'great confinement' sufficient to permit the emergence of a new enterprise sector.

Wacquant (2000) has recently documented the burgeoning prosperity of the correctional industries and the transformation of the American penal system. As he points out, the expansion of the penal sector is not an exclusive patrimony of the Republicans but instead became a bi-partisan consensus. For example, during the later years of the Clinton administration the Federal State Reform Commission worked away steadily at chopping programmes and public employment. Meanwhile, some 213 new prisons were built. At the same time, Wacquant records, the number of employees in state and federal prisons (that is, excluding those in the now flourishing private sector) went from 264 000 to 347 000, including 221 000 guards. In total, the penitentiary world comprised more than 600 000 employees by 1993, just a little fewer than the industrial giant *General Motors* or the international supermarket company, *Wal-Mart*. Wacquant notes that the training and contracting of prison guards is, among all government activities, the one that presented the highest growth over the course of the 1990s (op cit: 86–87).

This presumably helps to explain why the major private sector companies (such as *Corrections Corporation of America, Correctional Services Corporation, Securicor* and *Wackenhut*) have enjoyed such strong investor support on Wall Street since they began to be quoted on the stock market. Wacquant notes that at one annual exhibition sponsored by the *American Correctional Association* in Orlando, the following products were exhibited: handcuffs with wrist protection, assault weapons, unbreakable locks and bars, cell furniture with fireproof beds, one-piece water closets, cosmetics and foodstuffs, immobilisation chairs, restraining uniforms (to be used to take the most problematic prisoners out of the cells), electrified belts, detoxification programmes for drug addicts, the latest lines in electronic surveillance and telephonic systems, identification technologies, computer programmes to process administrative data, antituberculosis air-purification systems, dismountable cells (that can be installed in a car park to absorb a massive influx of arrestees), key-in-hand jails and even an operating van to practise emergency surgery in the prison yard (Wacquant, op cit: 91). The industry, it seems, has indeed flourished. To better understand this success we need to return to the question of the new rationalities that allowed these punitive developments.

The Consolidation of 'In-tolerance Criminology'

As we have been seeing, the United States has for some time now been determinedly expanding the state's penal capacity while simultaneously drastically retrenching welfare assistance. Christie seriously called our attention to this as early as 1993; Young denounced it in 1996; and Wacquant has latterly lucidly developed the theme.

These tendencies have also had their analogues in the field of policing. When, in 1993, Rudolph Giuliani assumed the role of Mayor of New York he raised the banner of 'Zero Tolerance', understood as in-tolerance when facing drunkenness, graffiti, minor thefts, prostitution, vandalism, begging and other 'lifestyle' offences. The war 'against poverty' had begun. Urban insecurity, especially the anxieties of the privileged (energetically canvassed and prefigured through mass media) became an intense political issue. The expansion of the penal, begun more than a decade before, experienced a further remarkable rise.

The social state cut, the gradual demise of welfare culture, the establishment of highly repressive criminal policies, the constant reiteration of an *intolerance criminology* (Young, 1996); the propagation of all of this in the American *think tanks* (whose outlook was exported to Great Britain, and thence to continental Europe as we will see next); these all constitute examples of a 'manufactured' and transportable penality. The new poverty management is not assistance any more. Rather, this management now acquires police, penal and prison features.

THE WELFARE CRISIS AND THE EXPORT OF THE PENAL INDUSTRY TO EUROPE

Does the emergent 'crime control industry' exclusively belong to the American punitive-cultural sphere or has it spread to other regions of the world? As Wacquant further indicates the 'zero-tolerance' motif moved around the world with great rapidity (op cit: 26). Mayor Giuliani's innovation created emulators on both sides of the Atlantic Ocean. In regard to Europe, Wacquant notes the dissemination of the doctrine thanks initially to the role performed by British and American think tanks, and subsequently its infiltration of continental Europe. Conceived as 'thought power plants' or 'idea factories', the most notable right-leaning think tanks in this political-penal background include the *Manhattan Institute* and the *Heritage Foundation*, frequent stops in the itinerary of the 'forgers of the new penal reason', such as Giuliani or William Bratton. On the British side, the *Adam Smith Institute*, the *Centre for Policy Studies* and the *Institute of Economic Affairs*, are among the sources that have contributed to spreading neoliberal concepts in the social and economic fields and latterly the field of crime control also. This way, England becomes the European vanguard of the new American penal rationality. Very soon, the continental penetration would fructify, at least in three of the main European countries (France, Italy and Germany): Jospin in France, with the French version of zero-tolerance; the German Christian-Democratic Union (CDU) with the opening of the *null toleranz* in Frankfurt; Naples as the vanguard in Italy when applying its *tolleranza zero* to slight and common crimes. The foundations of that 'social constitutionalism', described by Ferrajoli, begin to break down.

However, in mainland Europe, the shipment of American penal strategies would meet another especially worrying political-criminal line of development. Since the 1970s, Europe had begun to experience its own social state crisis. In the penal field this took the form of the so-called 'culture of emergency and penal exceptionality'. These terms require further explanation.

As we have seen, following the Second World War, Western Europe moved towards what we have called *social constitutionalism*. The German and Italian Constitutions were emblematic in that sense. Shortly after, most European countries carried out penal reform processes in line with similar constitutional principles. Resocialisation — positive special prevention — became established as the principal objective of the 'new' freedom-depriving penalties. At the same time, however, the phenomenon of political violence and terrorism erupted across Europe. In responding to this states appealed to a range of antiterrorist laws and practices. These would later come to be known under the name of 'penal emergency' *and/or* 'culture of exceptionality'. There is no room here to discuss such criminal policy in-depth (but see works by, for example, Bergalli (1988); Piedecasas & Ramón (1988); Olarieta (1996); Rivera Beiras (1998) and Silveira Gorski (1998)). It is necessary at least to remark that it is very well attested that this policy contributed to a subversion of the very foundations of a framework of penal law anchored and founded on another liberal basis. From the penological point of view, the adoption of emergency powers opened the way for the era of maximum security regimes and prisons, prison isolation practices, the breaking-up of inmates' collectives, the rapid development of high-tech control systems and computerised surveillance, and so on. In brief, the bases of that penitentiary reform were also subverted. This segregative penality has provoked no small number of scandals, owing to the (more and more) 'corporal' character it has been assuming, not least as AIDS began to spread inside European prisons, with a consequent steep increase in deaths in custody.

The intersection of these two political-criminal trends (*Zero-tolerance*, on the one hand, and *Penal Emergency/Exceptionality* by contrast) have begun to a worrying extent to dismantle the 'guarantee' character of penal systems formerly committed to the social and democratic Rule of Law. The idea of 'emergency penal legislation' as a 'repealing hypothesis' of the elementary principles of the penal system has long been acknowledged (see Troncone, 2001). Lately, something of this kind is again becoming evident in the ways in which our cities are 'defended' (in architecture and via the application of military and paramilitary force) and, for example, the repression of anti-globalisation demonstrations in some European cities.

THE 'NEW' PUNITIVE RATIONALITIES
(GLOBALISATION AND POST-FORDISM)

If we wish to grasp current events in the context of deeper changes, we now need to resume the analysis of the socioeconomic transformations that underlie contemporary penal trends.

As Silveira Gorski (1998) remarks, there are several readings that can be made of the crisis of the social state. Let us pursue a *reading that connects the crisis to the failure of the 'Fordist' model of society*. Fordism presupposed the durability of certain basic characteristics: stock work, enhanced productivity leading to a commensurate rise in salaries and living standards and, alongside this, a degree of economic redistribution, effected in large part through a generalised system of social security. Ultimately, all of these would lead to the extension of welfare to the great majority of the population. This is to say, the 'stable life', jobs until retirement, the expectation that one's children and relatives would also find work in the factories — all of this accompanied the development of a distinctive value-system and lifestyle and went hand in hand with the emergence of new forms of class consciousness.

The very axis of the Fordist system of production was the social state. The so-called 'Keynesian equation' was based upon this form of state: the idea that it was possible to combine indefinite growth with a better wealth distribution and a greater degree of social fairness. The crisis of the social state and the international economic-political transformations of the 1970s and 1980s, however, bankrupted the Fordist model. Thus, we arrive at the gates of the so-called economic globalisation process and the Post-Fordist social model.

This has provoked important transformations in our understandings of time and space. As Silveira Gorski outlines (1998: 140), Fordist production implied a certain way of organising time and labour space. This in turn allowed workers to establish personal communications and common links and to structure a certain form of collective awareness. There was a concrete *praxis* among workers, entrepreneurs and unions. Post-Fordism has transformed these links and this praxis, separating the places where social needs are generated from the social reproduction of the agents of the labour process. For many, work has again become fragmentary, precarious, flexible and unstable. In the past workers had lost their own identity as a group; now they are isolated and without any form of links. They have passed from being citizens to being consumers — if they have means to consume. Those who lack the means are reduced to inhabiting the spaces of social exclusion. Little by little, we find ourselves entering what some have defined as the 'risk society'.

Beck (1986) defines risk society as one in which the production of new risks is to be seen as directly related to socio-technical advances and developments. Nuclear and other environmental dangers are the classical examples. Nowadays, as Beck remarks (2000a and 2000b), the list may be extended: labour risks, food and health risks, the risk of a high accident rate, the problems coming from psycho-social disorders, the harm caused by 'consumer pathologies' (anorexia, bulimia...). Bauman (1999) and Giddens (2000) have similarly enumerated the chronic uncertainties and anxieties that press in upon the inhabitants of late- or post-modern societies.

In the sphere of Anglo-Saxon penal culture, among the methods pursued to govern this critical situation has been the development of the new *administrative criminologies*, whose organising feature is the imposition of new modalities of risk management. The focus of these pragmatic-administrative interventions falls mainly on the regulation of behaviour in the interests of minimising risks (rather than on changing ways of thinking, as in the past). Such measures demand an inventory of the risks to be avoided. Indicative examples include the installation of surveillance video cameras in the streets; prohibitions against young people being around during the night; more stringent bye-laws on selling and consuming alcohol (especially in public). The common features in such measures include that authorities seek to act prior to the commission of an offence and that the measure may be applied to groups or categories of persons or behaviours rather than to specific individuals. These tasks of prospective risk-avoidance are not primarily the work of judges (indeed they are not infrequently resisted by them) but rather cede the initiative to administrators and local politicians.

Matthews & Francis (1996, 1999) suggests that in the British case the increasing emphasis on surveillance and monitoring became evident with the creation of 'intensive' intermediate treatments. In the 1970s these measures had emphasised the face-to-face provision of counselling and advice, whether individually or in group work. In the following decade they became more and more directed to the tracking of young people 'at risk'. The increasing interest in monitoring, supervision and tracking has been characterised by Stanley Cohen (1988) as a new 'behaviourism'. Cohen argues that this strategy is premised on the belief that it is unproductive to focus primarily on transforming individuals and that, therefore, before engaging on treatment programmes or providing advice we have to intervene by modifying circumstances and reducing opportunities (and in the field of women and penal policy, see also Carlen & Tchaikovsky, 1996).

Feeley & Simon (1995) have helped to reveal the new 'positive rationality' hidden behind this veil. The new administrative penology, they suggest, is not very normatively engaged or morally curious; neither is it much interested in causes, especially not at the level of individual lives. It has instead the limited objective of regulating dangerous human groups to optimise risk management. Statistical profiles generate knowledge of risk factors and their distribution, rather than an understanding of causes or pathologies. They provide a sketch of probabilities to be reduced or distributed and hence promote greater systemic efficiency. Actuarial justice, thus conceived, is not an ideology in the strict sense of a set or body of beliefs and ideas that direct action. Rather it is an array of methods or practices: 'in fact, it is powerful and significant, especially because it lacks a well-articled ideology and identification with a specific technology. Its amorphism contributes to its power' (ibid).

It is also crucial to note that penological 'actuarialism' has a strong elective affinity with a new functional justification for imprisonment, construed as the physical impediment that restricts criminality when other, extra-custodial preventive measures prove insufficient. Thus, it becomes clear that the objectives of the prison are reduced to the simple act of taking people out of society. The only certain thing that remains is that the spatial restriction greatly reduces opportunities for committing crimes; and this simple common-sense reflection promotes itself as the new scientific foundation of the freedom-depriving penalty.

SPAIN AFTER 9/11: A EUROPEAN EXAMPLE OF POLITICAL-CRIMINAL
RECEPTION IN PENAL INTOLERANCE

With all the foregoing background, there seems little doubt about the consequences that the crisis of welfare culture (in the British and American spheres) and the social state (in continental Europe) had produced for the penal system. Because of this, the paths taken in the days just following the attacks on the United States on 11 September 2001 cannot occasion too much surprise: the foundations were already laid.

Here we attempt briefly to analyse whether the measures related to the political-criminal order that Spain began to adopt during that period are really 'Spanish' or whether, on the contrary, they express the reception of 'guidelines' that are inherent in the *British criminology of in-tolerance* and in the *Continental European culture of emergency and exceptionality*.

Some time ago, Manuel Revuelta published, in *Le Monde Diplomatique*, an extensive article entitled: 'Spain: an Unstoppable Drift Towards the Right' (in Spanish: 'España: deriva hacia una derechización imparable') (25 July 2001: 8–10). In this article, the author mentioned, with regard to the last years of the then Spanish government that contrary to appearances, 'the Chief of the Government has a solid project about conquering power. This plan is based upon a national liberalism that has been set, since the late 1980s, around a staff of ambitious young people who populate the Foundation for Analysis and Social Studies (FASS) [in Spanish: Fundación para el Análisis y los Estudios Sociales {FAES}]. This is the most important of the six foundations of the PP (Popular Party), along with the Cánovas del Castillo's one, which was organised in connection with Fraga Iribarne during the last Franco years' (op cit: 8).

A little later Revuelta adds that 'the FASS men have copied the British and American think tanks, which were essential for Margaret Thatcher's triumph in 1979 and Ronald Reagan's one in 1980, with a modernised ideology. This last fact may explain the apparently excellent relations that prevailed between Aznar and Tony Blair' (ibid). Revuelta also commented that this mixture of liberal ideologies — Christian morality and Hayekian minimal statism, has been set up as the base of a 'deregulating and privatising way of thinking'.

Revuelta adds that all of this has created a 'security obsession' that Spanish society has been gradually internalising with detriment to freedoms and guarantees: 'the official statistics seem to confirm some features of that security trend assumed by the citizenship where there is a mix-up of scarce information and social disintegration. To take one striking illustration: most people think that the country is on the right track. According to official surveys, 81 per cent of the Spanish people believe that terrorism is the most serious problem in Spain, 49 per cent of those interviewed think that we are racist' (ibid).

Of course, all of this has been fertilised by the strategy of a terrorism which seems to adhere to the idea of 'the worse, the better'. With regard to this, Revuelta remarks that 'it is obvious that the strategic aim of achieving Basque independence remains a remote possibility, and perhaps indeed unattainable, even though the Spanish Government allowed the performance of a referendum that could apply the right of self-determination'. All of this, dealing with the media reductionism that is used by Madrid, ignoring and making silent the complex structure of a Basque left that is opposed to violence, 'reinforces the political roughness of the current terrorist offensive' and provokes easy identifications of contestable trends which are suspected of being in league with those ones who are practicing political violence. The stigmatising conflation between oppositional social movements, terrorism and criminality gives shape to a framework that stands out, according to Revuelta's words, as an 'uncontainable rightist process'.

After 11 September 2001, some of the measures being adopted by the Spanish Government of José María Aznar added momentum to the authoritarian drift begun some years before. For example, reforms were already proposed to the Penal Code of 1996 (the 'Democracy Code'), whose aim was to 'physically remove serious transgressors from the streets' (as was announced by the former Minister of the Interior, Mariano Rajoy, cfr *La Vanguardia*, 7 July 2001), through a serious intensification in penalties in cases of relapse or recidivism. This imitates the American debate on 'three strikes', no matter the claims about its unconstitutionality.

After 11 September 2001, several measures were announced by the Spanish Government. The following ones may be synthesised:

a. One week after the attacks against the United States, Spain announced that it would promote anti-terrorism Acts during its presidency of the EU (cfr, *El País*, 18 September 2001). This met with the full agreement of the main opposition party (the Spanish Socialist Labour Party [in Spanish: Partido Socialista Obrero Español (PSOE)]), reaching a great consensus on that matter.

b. Just one day later, the former Minister of Foreign Affairs of the Spanish Government, Josep Piqué, after expressing the possible connections of the 'Islamic extremist fundamentalism' in Spain, indicated that it was essential to fortify border security to fight terrorism. Strictly related to this, the president of the Catalonian Government, Jordi Pujol wrote that 'reinforcing the struggle against illegal immigration means reinforcing anti-terrorist struggle' (cfr, *El País*, 19 September 2001).

c. The following week, the Spanish Government announced that "the National Intelligence Center (NIC) [in Spanish: Centro Nacional de Inteligencia (CNI)] will be able to intercept communications and break into private homes without any previous judicial authorisation, provided that they are urgent cases or investigations on terrorism. This would be an exceptional procedure that was sketched in the draft bill that the former Prime Minister José María Aznar had approved. (*El País*, 4 October 2001).

d.   A little later, the Government of José María Aznar published its anticrime plan. Among the large number of measures announced in the days that followed it is important at least to mention the following headline-grabbing examples:

d.1. the Ministry of the Interior asks for 'zero-tolerance' for recidivist offenders. The Chief of Police lays the blame for the crime increase on irregular immigration (*El País*, 11 February 2002).

d.2. Aznar announces that the maximum prison sentence for terrorist offences will be raised from 30 to 40 years. The President promises that sentences for serious crimes will be served in full. (*El País*, 30 December 2002).

d.3. The Government decides to raise the maximum sentence for terrorists to 40 years. The release and reintegration of ETA prisoners will be only possible if they collaborate in the struggle against terrorism (*El País*, 4 January 2003).

d.4. A reform of the law on criminal prosecution is announced. The aim is to facilitate the implementation of preventive imprisonment. (*El Periódico*, 7 January 2003).

d.5. The Minister of the Interior announces the building of seven prisons with the purpose of handling the possible rush of inmates on remand. (*El País*, 10 January 2003).

d.6. The Socialist Party justifies its support for more severe penalties, favouring responsibility and not weakness. (*El País*, 11 January 2003)

d.7. The Ministry of Justice tries to extend preventive imprisonment to crimes committed before the legal reform was sanctioned. (*El País*, 13 January 2003).

d.8. Aznar will expel "undocumented" criminals. This is an offensive from the Government against citizen insecurity. The new measures will permit the deportation of immigrants who have committed minor transgressions. (*El Periódico*, 13 January 2003).

d.9. Four misdemeanours will be punished as a crime. Aznar announces a Penal Code reform with the purpose of hardening sentences. (*El País*, 14 January 2003).

d.10. Aznar adds more police and new prisons to his law and order offensive. The PP will deploy municipal police to security tasks and other officers will control traffic. (*El País*, 18 January 2003).

Aznar's offensive was largely agreed by the Socialist Party (then in opposition but elected into government on 14 March 2004, and reelected in March 2008). Several voices were raised in opposition to the erosion of elementary freedoms and the dismantling of the normative framework that, in criminal, legal, penitentiary, and juridical matters constituted the product of the consensus of the 'political transition to democracy' after 1976. For example, these measures came in for criticism from professional associations representing judges and magistrates. One spokesperson said:

[T]he fight against any kind of crime must be carried out within in the constitutional framework and the system of liberties, and it will not be coherent to disregard the basic principles of our legal system in order to defend democracy (*El País*, 5 October 2001).

To sum up, the immediate aftermath of 9/11 saw the wholesale dismantling of the penal guarantees typical of a social and democratic rule of law.

Muñoz Conde pointed out that these reforms took us closer to a 'new Criminal Law of the enemy' (*El País*, 15 January 2003) characteristic of political hard times (cf Krasmann, 2007), yet never seen even in 'the hardest and darkest time of Franco dictatorship'. In Catalonia, diverse collective groups of progressive jurists argued that the changes amounted to a covert way of introducing life imprisonment and they warned about the substitution of social state by penal state. Some months later, and in a similar way, more than a hundred scholars, judges and attorneys protested that, behind the reintroduction of 'political crimes' into the Penal Code, there was a real totalitarian drift on the part of Aznar's Government (*El País*, 29 November 2003).

The period in question saw an astonishing increase in the Spanish prison population, which rose for a time at a rate of 'a thousand new prisoners every month' (cfr *El País*, 3/3/02). Spain came to vie with England and Wales for first place in prison population league tables of European Union countries (71.000 inmates, or 157 inmates per 100 000 inhabitants).

With regard to Catalonia, where this study has been prepared, the increase in the prison population has been also astonishing. It is important to mention the revelations made by the Observatory for the Penal System and Human Rights in Barcelona University (in Spanish: *Observatorio del Sistema Penal y Los Derechos Humanos de la Universitat de Barcelona*) as to the main problems affecting the penitentiary situation from the point of view of respect for human rights. This institution denounced torture and mistreat meant on 20 inmates after incidents on 30 April 2004 in Quatre Camins prison, when its governor was seriously hurt (cfr *El País*, 17 and 18 June 2004). Deaths in custody throughout Spain have been persistently high (269 in 2006, at a mortality rate of 42 per 10 000 prisoners according to the Council of Europe's Annual Penal Statistics, with deaths in custody in Catalonia alone amounting to some 100 per year throughout the 1990s[2] the 'problem of insecurity' has been built up in a very populist way. The resort to the 'terrorist threat', to 'immigration dangers', to the so-called 'citizen insecurity' and other similar clichés, represent the sharpest version of punitive populism, which is employed

---

[2] It is important to remark the disregard from penitentiary authorities towards those organisations, associations, social movements, etc. trying to inspect and monitor prison conditions. The former Director General of Penitentiary Services of Catalonia (Ramón Parés) denied permission for Professors from the *Observatory of the Penal System and Human Rights* (University of Barcelona) of this region to see prisoners' living conditions when performing a European research project.

– not only by the political parties from the ideological right-with strictly electoral purposes and to consolidate consensus in the interests of maintaining power. What is going on? Is this an inheritance from *zero-tolerance* or a renewed version of the *culture of emergency*? Is this perhaps the exact result of both lines getting together? We will see how long the diffusion of this 'new' criminal policy lasts in being verified in European countries. The trend is clear: punitive management of poverty, completely flexible economic market, more and more criminalisation of political dissidence, and reduction in the 'social' goals of the state.

REFLECTIONS (TO KEEP ON THINKING...)

By way of conclusion we might just refer to some words from a great writer, one of the most brilliant minds still engaged with this disordered time. Not so long ago, when commenting on one of his last works, José Saramago remarked:

> We will be back to the 'cavern' –or the 'big mall'–. Before now, mankind searched for the outer place, the 'outside', the light from Enlightenment. Today, people do not look for 'the inside' but the 'inner security', and inside it there is only a grey, cold, dry and, specially, artificial light. We all will finally be in the Mall –as a paradigm of the new City–: there we will have air, light and temperature and artificial climate...We will also have private security and we will be finally doing 'inside' what we used to do 'outside': so, what to get out for? It will be better a grey life than an insecure life. Those who can pay for security will have their village, their neighbourhood, their town, their private, artificial and secure-Centre and what about those ones will not have the money or the means to support it (these people will be more and more desperate and will act in a desperate way)? Therefore, the Penal System (the 'outside' one) will always remain for them...

Final Excursus

Let us not finish on a note of hopelessness. In 2003, millions took to the streets of Barcelona (where this paper was written) and of other cities to cry 'No to War'. The attacks on Madrid in March 2004 left more than 200 people dead and 1500 hurt. Sorrow was immediately accompanied by people's indignation when faced with the lies and the manipulation of the conservative Aznar Government that tried to distract attention from the authors of the attacks towards ETA political violence, with the aim of holding power and winning the elections planned for 14 March. Fortunately, the electoral overturning that gave victory to the Socialist Party established a new framework. Perhaps history will record that this turned out to be a milestone in Europe taking some distance from the hegemony of the United States. If all that has been mentioned before is inscribed into the frame of political irrationality, with its particular consequences on the penal system, there may also be scope for citizen movements that allow us to recover a rationality that helps us to survive as a civilisation and to avoid the triumph of barbarism.

REFERENCES

Bauman, Z (1989) *Modernità e Olocausto* (Bologna, Il Mulino).
—— (1999) *La società Della incertezza* (Bologna, Il Mulino).
Beck, U (1986) *La sociedad del riesgo. Hacia una nueva modernidad* (Barcelona, Ediciones Paidós Ibérica).
—— (2000a) *La democracia y sus enemigos* (Barcelona, Ediciones Paidós Ibérica).
—— (2000b) *Un nuevo mundo feliz, La precariedad del trabajo en la era de la globalización* (Barcelona, Ediciones Paidós Ibérica).
Bergalli, R (1988) 'Presentación. La emergencia: Una cultura específica' in JR Serrano Piedecasas (ed) *Emergencia y crisis del estado social. Análisis de la excepcionalidad penal y motivos de su perpetuación* (Barcelona, Ed Península) I–XVII.
Carlen, P & Tchaikovsky, C (1996) 'Women's Imprisonment in England at the End of the Twentieth Century: Legitimacy, Realities and Utopias' in Matthews & Francis (eds) *Prisons 2000. An International Perspective on the Current State and Future of Emprisonment* (London-New York, Macmillan Press, St Martin's Press).
Christie, N (1993) *Il Business penitenziario. La via Occidentale Al Gulag* (Milano, Editrice Elèuthera).
Clemmer, D (1958) *The Prison Community* (New York, Rinehart and Winston).
Cohen, S (1988) *Visiones de control social. Delitos, castigos y clasificaciones* (Barcelona, Promociones y Publicaciones Universitarias).
De Giorgi, A (2000) *Zero Tolleranza. Strategise e pratiche Della società di controllo* (Deriveapprodi, Roma).
Feeley, M & Simon, J (1995) 'La nueva penología: Notas acerca de las estrategias emergentes en el sistema penal y sus implicaciones' *Delito y Sociedad Revista de Ciencias Sociales*, 4, 33–58.
Ferrajoli, L (2001) 'Sobre el papel cívico y político de la ciencia penal en el estado constitucional de derecho' in RE Zaffaroni (ed) *Crimen y castigo. Cuaderno del Departamento de Derecho Penal y Criminología de la Facultad de Derecho* (Buenos Aires, University of Buenos Aires).
Giddens, A (2000) *Il Mondo Che Cambia. Come la globalizzazione ridisegna la Nostra Vita* (Bologna, Il Mulino).
Goffman, E (1970) *Internados. Ensayos sobre la situación social de los enfermos mentales* (Madrid, Editorial Amorrortu-Murguía).
Gough, I (1979) *The Political Economy of the Welfare State* (London, Macmillan).

Krasmann, S (2007) 'The Enemy on the Border: Critique of a Programme in Favour of a Preventive State' *Punishment and Society*, 9, 301–318 [DOI: 10.1177/1462474507077496].

Matthews, R & Francis, P (eds) (1996) *Prisons 2000. An International Perspective on the Current State and Future of Imprisonment* (London-New York, Macmillan Publishing Group)-St. Martin Press.

Matthews, R (1999) *Doing Time. An Introduction to the Sociology of Imprisonment* (London, Macmillan Publishing Group).

O'Connor, J (1981) *La Crisis fiscal del estado* (Barcelona: Ediciones Península).

Olarieta, JM (1996) 'Los delitos políticos en el Proyecto de Código Penal' *Panóptico*, 1, 63–85.

Pavarini, M (2002*) Il business penitenziario*' ('Conference, Pisa, Italy, April 20').

Rivera Beiras, I (1998) 'La irrupción de la "emergencia" en Europa y sus consecuencias en las políticas penitenciarias' *Cathedra, espíritu del Derecho*, 100–132.

Piedecasas, S & Ramón, J (1988) *Emergencia y crisis del estado social. Análisis de la excepcionalidad penal y motivos de su perpetuación* (Barcelona, Península)

Silveira Gorski, H (1998) *El modelo político italiano. Un laboratorio: de la tercera vía a la globalización* (Barcelona, Edicions Universitat de Barcelona)

Troncone, P (2001) *La legislazione penale dell' emergenza in Italia. Tecniche normative di incriminazione e politica giudiziaria dallo Stato liberale allo Stato democratico di diritto* (Napoli, Jovene Editore).

Von Hirsch, A (1986) *Doing Justice: The Choice of Punishments* (Boston, North-Eastern University Press)

—— (1998) *Censurar y castigar* (Madrid, Editorial Trotta).

Wacquant, L (2000) *Las cárceles de la miseria* (Madrid, Editorial Alianza).

Young, J (1996) *The Criminology of Intolerance: Zero-Tolerance Policing and the American Prison Experiment* (London, Middlesex University).

Zysman, D (2001) *El papel de la determinación de la pena (sentencing) en la justificación del castigo penal de los Estados Unidos, en el último tercio del siglo XX* (Barcelona, University of Barcelona).

6

Post-Fordism and Penal Change: The New Penology as a Post-Disciplinary Social Control Strategy*

ALESSANDRO DE GIORGI

INTRODUCTION: POLITICAL ECONOMIES OF PUNISHMENT

We live in a globalised world. The term 'globalisation', widely adopted in academic as well as everyday discourses, seems to make sense only if one refers it to another word — generally used in its 'negative' meaning: this word is *border*. Hegemonic descriptions of contemporary society suggest that a global world is, basically, a borderless world: a world in which national frontiers fall, cultural divisions tend to disappear, free movement and circulation is granted to everything and everybody. In this new 'global world', nation-states and their peoples are interlinked through real time communication systems which neutralise geographical distances and replace 'time' with 'simultaneity': *universal connectedness* seems thus to become the main feature of the post-modern condition.

However, the experience of modernity taught us to be diffident toward the concept of universality itself: whenever modern values, rationalities and ideas made some claims to universality, they later revealed all their partiality and the oppressed — be they women or colonised subjects, industrial workers or deviants — had to discover at their own expenses how selective the universality of universalism could be.

Once again, the hegemonic discourse represents the attributes of globalisation — particularly freedom, communication and movement — as universals, but

* I would like to thank Dario Melossi, Richard Sparks, Maximo Sozzo and Stefania De Petris for their enlightening comments on earlier drafts of this essay.

behind this apparent universality it is not difficult to discover how selectively these operate. Freedom of movement is not granted equally to everything and everybody: some people can circulate freely, other die in the attempt to cross militarised borders; capital and finance can circulate freely, whereas 'third world' workers cannot. In the field of ideas and discourses too the abolition of frontiers is selective: neo-liberal orthodoxies have crossed each and every border (especially after the end of the Soviet Union), whereas oppositional discourses (especially in the aftermath of 11 September) run the risk of being constantly assimilated to 'terrorist' or anti-Western ideologies. In the same vein, punitive practices and discourses inspired by populist slogans like 'war on crime', 'war on drugs' and 'zero tolerance' reach every corner of this global world, whereas counter-discourses or critical analyses of contemporary social control strategies find it difficult to circulate and even more difficult to capture the attention of political leaders.

In this process of 'selective globalisation', new punitive and stigmatising discourses on crime, immigration, the 'underclass' and more generally the new 'public enemies' of Western societies (to which Islamic fundamentalists have been recently enlisted) impose themselves, thus contributing to the construction of what Loïc Wacquant defines a 'new penal commonsense': on both sides of the Atlantic what we observe is a trend toward harsher penalties, increasing prison populations, overtly discriminatory policing practices against migrants and ethnic minorities — all this in conjunction with dramatic reductions in welfare provisions, labour protections and social security measures. The dark side of the neo-liberal 'invisible hand' dispensing freedom, enterprise, individual empowerment and upward social mobility is the 'iron fist' of mass incarceration, urban surveillance, administrative detention and structural marginality.

Following Wacquant (1999) and other critical theorists, I would argue that these two aspects of the contemporary condition are deeply connected. Therefore, a radical critique of the punitive discourses and practices emerging in the Western world to neutralise the 'social surplus' produced by the neo-liberal economy — and by the *exclusive society* built around it — should start from an analysis of the *structural determinants* of the new social control strategies.

The objective of the 'political economy of punishment' is precisely to investigate the relationships between economic systems and forms of punishment, its main hypothesis being that the institutions and policies of social control play an important role in the reproduction of capitalist relations of production. In this vein, on the one hand the so-called 'revisionist' histories of punishment which appeared in the 1970s linked the birth of the penitentiary to the 'invention' of the factory, thus describing the peculiar role played by the prison in the formation of an industrial working class (Rusche & Kirchheimer, 1939; Foucault, 1977; Melossi & Pavarini, 1981). On the other hand, some scholars applied this analytical framework to contemporary societies, investigating the current developments of the relationship between economy and punishment. Here, criminologists like Greenberg (1977, 1980); Jankovic (1977); Box &

Hale (1982, 1985, 1986); Melossi (1983, 1985, 1998) discovered that economic transformations, particularly variations in the level of unemployment, affected penal policies — especially rates of imprisonment. Therefore, these authors concluded that crime control policies do not represent simple 'reactions' to the problem of crime: in fact, the 'politics of punishment' — both historically and in the present — are influenced by several social factors, among which the economy seems to be the crucial one.

The economic system which these criminologists investigated and connected to penal policies was based on the Fordist model of production: a system characterised by mass factories, extended welfare, reduced unemployment and low levels of labour flexibility. In this respect, the 30 years following the Second World War exhibited an intrinsic coherence between penal practices and socio-economic policies. The correctional prison and the Taylorist factory, the philosophy of rehabilitation and the development of welfare, low incarceration rates and low unemployment: all these features gained some degree of coherence within an inclusive model of social citizenship based on waged work.

However, from the early 1970s onward a significant transition took place in Western economies: these shifted gradually from a Fordist and Keynesian model to what some critical theorists define as a post-Fordist and neo-liberal order, characterised by high unemployment, increasing labour flexibility, work insecurity and widespread social vulnerability. All this, in a context of welfare 'reform' and rising income inequalities. Thus, concepts like 'the underclass', 'working poor' and 'social exclusion' reappear in economic, sociological and criminological discourses. The internal coherence mentioned earlier seems now to be leaving way to a contradictory socio-economic order in which the mechanisms of social regulation — and penality in particular — undergo significant processes of change. This paper argues that a renewed political economy of punishment should take these transformations into account, and suggests some possible directions of inquiry into the relationship between post-Fordism and social control.

POST-FORDISM AND SOCIAL SURPLUS

In the last 30 years, we witnessed a process of transformation of Western economies, characterised by the decline of the industrial (Fordist) model and by the emergence of new relations of production. The post-modern 'global cities' are no longer theatres of heavy industrial productions, but territories in which information, images, finance and symbols circulate through networked and decentred circuits (Sassen, 1991).

The mass-industries — those 'productive monuments' inspired by a panoptic utopia of total control over the labour force — lose their appeal in post-industrial economies. The new sites of production tend to be either 'immaterial' (small, automated and hyper-technological factories) or 'invisible' (deregulated sweatshops in which heavy labour is often performed by an immigrant, hyper-exploited and female labour force). The process of production is thus becoming increasingly dispersed, molecular and diffused. No longer does any rigid organisation of the labour process (such as Taylor's 'scientific management') seem to be eligible here: mobility, flexibility and decentralisation replace the fixity, rigidity and centralisation of the Fordist factory (Reich, 1991).

At the same time, the Fordist strategy of wage regulation seems to be collapsing because the new fragmented labour force, dispersed as it is in small and de-unionised factories, has lost much of its power over working conditions: 'flexibility' is in fact synonymous with the loss of contracting power. To this we must add the dismissal of those welfare policies that were developed in the second half of the twentieth century in order to keep the market imbalances and their disruptive social consequences under control (Piven & Cloward, 1972; O'Connor, 1973).

In the meantime, the geographies of the global economy are being rewritten. No longer is capital just transnational and mobile: it is becoming a truly global entity. Financial power is free to circulate, taking full advantage of the real time information technologies now available (Ohmae, 1990). The new territory of capital appears indeed as a 'smooth' global space in which fluxes of money, information and labour force circulate under a diversified regime of control — money and information are virtually free, whereas the labour force is constrained by restrictive immigration laws. In this sense, Hardt & Negri (2000) define the new territory of capitalist development as a borderless 'Empire'. According to these authors, in the contemporary 'world economic system' we see the emergence of a unified global labour force, scattered through the different corners of the world and positioned differentially within the global hierarchies of labour.

Some fractions of this global labour force are highly mobile, others are constrained by restrictive immigration laws; some experience a situation of social 'vulnerability', others live in conditions of plain 'exclusion' from the formal economy; some are defined as 'employed' according to official statistics, others figure as 'unemployed' even if they are involved in the over-exploitative circuits of informal production. Growing portions of the so called 'third world' can now be found in the global cities of the 'first', whereas 'first-world' economic and financial powers can easily 'migrate' to those global peripheries in which they will find cheap labour and unregulated markets. Less people work for longer and harder, and more people are either formally 'out of work' or prisoners of the 'informal economy'.

At the same time, we witness a steady increase in the number of (traditionally out-of-the-market) activities now being more and more marketised. I think here of those 'reproductive' activities (care, education, 'affective' labour in general) that were once confined within the boundaries of the family and are now industrially organised and exploited in the service economy. A crucial point is that these activities are seldom recognised as real 'employment'. It is here that precarisation and insecurity reach their peaks, and the 'working poor' (especially poor women) concentrate more. Let us consider, for example, the field of domestic labour: here work tends to be unguaranteed, insecure, hidden, unregulated and sometimes as invisible as the undocumented immigrant women who perform it. Thousands of domestic workers appear as 'unemployed' in official statistics, not to mention those who do not appear at all, because they are 'illegal' and thus virtually non-existent.

Work is fragmented and segmented by the massive introduction of new technologies into the production system and by the deregulation of the market (Fumagalli, 1997). As a consequence, a large fraction of the working class has been expelled from restructured productive sectors, thus joining the growing mass of the 'unemployed', underemployed, part-timers and flexi-workers. A large portion of these people work in the emerging 'third sector', in those economic niches complementary to industrial production, in which hyper-exploitative conditions of work often prevail (Gorz, 1999). Meanwhile, the neo-liberal assaults on welfare tend to abolish social guarantees, spreading those situations of insecurity, flexibility and new poverty that are now an existential and paradigmatic condition of the new labour force (Ehrenreich, 2001).

Reduced access to regular, full time and guaranteed employment, together with the political assault on social rights and the 'culture of dependency' they supposedly foster, produces a hypertrophy of the hidden economies and of those productive circuits where 'the new excluded' must look, in search of alternative sources of income. Whole productive sectors rely now on deregulated markets, often on the border between legal and illegal economies (Piore & Sabel, 1984).

The main consequence of all this is the transition from 'work' individually perceived (and socially constructed) as a biographical event capable of narration, toward 'work' experienced as a fragment (or a 'life in fragments' in Bauman's words). It is here that the contemporary process of 'corrosion of character' described by Sennet (1998) has its roots.

If it is true that what we witness is not the end of 'full employment', but rather its fragmentation, its uneven diffusion throughout the whole of society and its explosion into an archipelago of regular and irregular, guaranteed and unguaranteed, part-time and overtime jobs; if it is true that production and reproduction are merging, with the former recognised as proper 'work' and the latter exploited and yet deprived of any guarantees and social rights; if it is true that an increasing portion of the new poor are working poor and that a significant fraction of workers is exposed to poverty; if all these assumptions are plausible, the question becomes: is the distinction between 'employment' and 'unemployment' — on which the old political economy of punishment was grounded — still meaningful? In other words, do 'rates of unemployment' offer a meaningful indicator of contemporary economic conditions?

I would suggest that once the concept of unemployment is contextualised within the new post-Fordist model, it refers to something different from a simple condition of non-work (Beck, 1999). French economist André Gorz (1999, 2) argues that 'unemployment' is the abolition of

> (t)he specific 'work' peculiar to industrial capitalism: the work we are referring to when we say 'she doesn't work' of a woman who devotes her time to bringing up her own children, but 'she works' of one who gives even some small part of her time to bringing up other people's children in a playgroup or a nursery school.

In this respect, 'unemployment' is no longer associated with inactivity (as was the case in the Fordist economy) but becomes something like an official measure of the distance separating the many and diversified productive 'activities' in which people are involved, and the conditions under which these activities achieve their social recognition as 'work'. Thus, more than measuring exclusion from the field of production, official rates of unemployment illustrate the growing inadequacy of official statistics to capture the reality of contemporary economies. What we see here is a radical separation between 'work' as it is experienced by 'the new labour force', and a system of social rights and citizenship still linked to the Fordist concept of work as *job*, as a full-time, life-long employment.

The fragmentation of 'work' excludes from social citizenship a significant fraction of the population, whose productive activities are not socially recognised as a gateway to economic inclusion and full social integration (Gorz, 1989).[1] A dramatic contradiction emerges here: the right to income, social inclusion and full citizenship is based on a model of work that is gradually disappearing from the horizon of Western societies. According to Guy Standing (2000: 13) the Fordist system of social citizenship

> (…) while never powerfully redistributive, was mostly universalistic in principle, linked firmly and unequivocally to the performance of labour (…). Social security was based firmly on the image of an industrial society in which the working class was expected to remain or become the overwhelming majority of the population and the norm for social behaviour.

If until the second half of the XX century, following Thomas Marshall (1992), it was reasonable to conceptualise citizenship as a complex of rights 'of' work grounded on a generalised right (and duty) 'to' work, this seems no longer to be the case today. The crisis of the Fordist-Keynesian pact implies that the institutions for the (economic) government of society can no longer guarantee social inclusion through work. The dissociation between the 'material' constitution of society (its productive forces) and the 'formal' constitution of citizenship (its 'mode of regulation') becomes structural.

---

[1] It should be noted, however that the question of what is recognised as 'work' and what is not, with all the consequences this distinction has for the labour force, has always been a field of struggle between labour and capital. Think about the feminist struggles over the gendered division of labour and for the recognition of 'domestic' labour as 'real' work (Federici, 1975).

Under the Fordist paradigm it was possible to see unemployment and social exclusion as consequences of an individual deficit, as the inability of some social groups to find their place within a system that was able to guarantee 'universalised' inclusion and citizenship. I would suggest that this has changed, because those instruments of social regulation are disappearing, and there seems to be neither a social order to be re-established, nor any individual deficit to be recovered through discipline. Rather, we see only a growing *surplus* of labour force easily depicted as a 'dangerous class' to be controlled.

The welfare state belonged to a historical period in which the labour force had to be disciplined to the industrial organisation of work: a system characterised by full-employment, in which 'waged labour' was an effective gateway to social citizenship. In that context, the labour force appeared to be inadequate and unprepared, and needed some discipline to reach the degree of cooperation and economic efficiency required by capital: those who remained outside had to be reintegrated through the penal-welfare complex. Penal control functioned there as a *disciplinary* machine whose aim was to defeat the resistance of the labour force, to fill its deficits, to enforce its cooperation within the production system, and to promote individual self-control.

In *Discipline and Punish*, Michel Foucault deals explicitly with the problem of penality in its historical configurations, paying great attention to the processes of transformation of the capitalist economy and to their effects upon the universe of punishment. With the transition from a 'sovereign' toward a 'governmental' rationality (Foucault, 1991; Dean, 1999), the concept of 'power' came to define the capacity to regulate a population and to govern a 'social body'. Centred as it was around the emerging political economy, *governmentality* marked the appropriation of a capitalist economic rationality by the science of government. In the words of the French philosopher (Foucault, 1997: 69):

> the working-out of this population-wealth problem (in its different concrete aspects: taxation, scarcity, depopulation, idleness-beggary-vagabondage) constitutes one of the conditions of formation of political economy. The latter develops when it is realized that the resources-population relationship can no longer be fully managed through a coercive regulatory system (...).

Together with this new rationality, Foucault describes also the formation of those dispositives and practices of 'security' whose function was to guarantee the correct functioning of the governmental apparatus, and to preserve the principle of economic maximisation which sustained it. Foucault refers here to various practices for the control and surveillance of the population, but also to public education, social insurance and national health: all the technologies necessary to guarantee and sustain the productive management of a population.[2] Social

---

[2] The following is Foucault's definition of the 'apparatuses of security', formulated during a lecture at the *Collège de France* in 1978: 'The setting in place of mechanisms of security (...) mechanisms or modes of state intervention whose function is to assure the security of those natural phenomena, economic processes and the intrinsic processes of...

control and the field of penality belong to this set of apparatuses of security: it is here, according to Foucault that the 'analytics of governmentality' meshes with the 'microphysics of disciplinary power'. Governmentality has to do with the productive government of the population as a whole, whereas disciplines concentrate on the individual body as a particular component of the same population. In this context, penality became a process through which subjects could be *produced, not destroyed*: subjects whose utility — both as individuals and as parts of the productive population — would be realised in the process of work (Foucault, 1997).

The same body on which the destructive violence of the sovereign power was exercised, becomes now the peculiar object of the disciplinary practices. It catalyses new regulatory knowledge (biology, statistics, medicine, psychiatry, social psychology, criminology), institutions (schools, hospitals, asylums, prisons, barracks) and regulatory practices (inquiry, survey, exam, therapy and sentence):

> The factory, the school, the prison, or the hospitals have the object of binding the individual to a process of production, training, or correction of the producers. It's a matter of guaranteeing production, or the producers, in terms of a particular norm. This means that we can draw a contrast between the confinement of the eighteenth century, which excluded individuals from the social circle, and the confinement that appeared in the nineteenth century, which had the function of attaching individuals to the producer's apparatuses of production, training, reform or correction (Foucault, 2000:78).

This is a very important point for the argument presented here: the dispositives of disciplinary power and control had to be activated because there was a widespread lack of productivity, a latent dispersion of resources and a deficit of productive cooperation. Here, *capitalist relations of production needed to produce their own labour force*, disciplining it to a cooperation for which it appeared to be inadequate, unprepared, insufficiently socialised and often explicitly reluctant.[3]

The synchronisation of movements, the regulation of masses of individuals within the factory, the connection between the body and the machine: these were all aspects of a peculiar economic rationality shaped by the emergence of industrial production and consolidated by the development of Fordist capitalism: the disciplinary technologies of control were an expression of this

population: this is what becomes the basic objective of governmental rationality' (Quoted in Burchell, 1991: 19).

[3] I agree with Vaughan (2000:28) that 'The development of the prison, as an alternative to capital punishment, is the story of how the burgeoning middle class tried to impose their own standards of behaviour upon those who were thought to be worthy of inclusion within society but not yet able to take their place voluntarily'. Criminals were, in other words, 'incomplete citizens', who could be 'completed' through discipline and rehabilitation. This idea synthesises the 'inclusive' project of modern penal institutions.

rationality, once it could be translated into specific forms of punishment.[4] The lines of this evolution would develop both inside the factory, where Taylor's *Principles of Scientific Management* would regulate the productivity of labour, and outside it, where Keynesian policies would set the framework of the state's intervention in the social processes.

Economic management, state regulation and the social control of deviance: these were all disciplinary strategies whose objective was to prepare the labour-force for the capitalist organisation of production. The factory had to be governed 'scientifically' to limit the loss of productivity; the social body had to be governed 'scientifically' to reduce the loss of inclusion produced by the anarchy of the market; deviance had to be treated 'scientifically' to limit the loss of socialisation which derived from the failure of other practices of government:

> The proper treatment of offenders required individualized, corrective measures carefully adapted to the specific case or the particular problem — not a uniform penalty tariff mechanically dispensed. One needed expert knowledge, scientific research, and flexible instruments of intervention, as well as a willingness to regulate aspects of life which classical liberalism had deemed beyond the proper reach of government. The normative system of law had to give way to the normalizing system of science, punishment had to be replaced by treatment (Garland, 2001: 40).

What these different fields of state intervention had in common was an ideology that saw the social body as affected by scarcity and disadvantage: a structural deficit to which the power to punish (and more generally the governmental 'power to regulate') could oppose effective remedies. David Garland defines this as the 'modernist project', whose expected result was, borrowing Jock Young's definition (1999), an 'inclusive society'. These policies aimed to maximise the productive capacity of a labour force in need of socialisation and discipline, whose productive deficits emerged in the form of deviance, criminality, illness, unemployment and poverty. The transformative project of disciplinary control was inscribed within a broader project of universalised citizenship, and the role of the disciplinary prison was to produce 'full citizens', by producing efficient workers.[5]

---

[4] 'People's time had to be offered to the production apparatus; the production apparatus had to be able to use people's living time, their time of existence. The control was exerted for that reason and in that form' (Foucault, 2000: 80).

[5] 'Punishment is used against those who have fallen below the standards which are expected of all citizens but is also used to mould them into citizens — hence punishment is not only a deterrent but is also deployed as a device for character-transformation. It is used on those who are conditional citizens, people who may be moulded into full citizens but who are, at present, failing to display the requisite qualities expected of citizens' (Vaughan, 2000: 26). The term 'universalised citizenship' should be taken with some caution: modern Western citizenship has never been a truly 'universal' system, as many feminist and postcolonial thinkers have shown. Nonetheless, I would agree that its underlying 'logic' was inclusive, tough this inclusion was tailored around the hegemonic image of the male/white/working subject.

Our question is: what technologies of control and rationalities of power emerge from the crisis of Fordism and of its practices of social regulation? What technologies of control follow the end of the industrial phase of capitalist development? What new governmental rationalities are announced by the transition from a regime of *scarcity* toward a regime of *surplus*?

CONTROL AS 'NON-KNOWLEDGE'

The post-Fordist 'surplus' can be represented as a complex of subjectivities whose condition of poverty, vulnerability and exclusion marks a growing contradiction between a model of social citizenship firmly based on the Fordist paradigm of work, and a sphere of production that is abolishing precisely that kind of work — through flexibility, precarisation, deregulation, etc. In other words, access to income, citizenship and social integration is linked to a requisite that is disappearing from the landscape of the post-Fordist 'material constitution'.[6] Here I would identify a first side of a contradiction which the contemporary strategies of control try to contain, repress or inhibit because of its potentially dangerous consequences for the social order. The old dichotomy which saw the poor, the marginalised and the excluded at the same time as 'threats' and 'resources' for capitalist development, takes now a different tone: as social exclusion becomes an ontological condition for a growing fraction of the post-Fordist labour force, new strategies of control become necessary, because every 'resource' can easily turn itself into a 'threat' to the stability of the whole system (Adamson, 1984).

The emergence of a social 'surplus' — the underclass, the permanently unemployed, the working poor, informal workers, etc. — suggests that the old disciplinary technologies (based on the industrial work ethic and work organisation) lose their meaning, because the economic structure on which they were grounded is gradually disappearing. The model of power which informed the disciplinary technologies was grounded on an individualised knowledge about individuals and the forms of cooperation to which they had to be forced. The knowledge-power complex on which disciplinary control was based, shaped a process of individualisation and allowed a precise cartography of the productive dynamics of the population. This is a framework which Foucault discovered inside the prison, but also in factories, hospitals, schools, asylums, barracks and the wider society. Knowledge had to be scientifically extracted from the human body to be later re-applied to it reflexively (in the form of disciplinary practices of control), whenever a multiplicity of bodies had to be organised within the field of production:

[6] On the concept of 'material constitution' (the economic structure of a society) as opposed to the 'formal constitution' (the legal/political institutionalisation of this structure) see Negri (1989).

In an institution like the factory, for example, the worker's labour and the worker's knowledge about his own labour, the technical improvements — the little inventions and discoveries, the micro-adaptations he's able to implement in the course of his labour — are immediately recorded, thus extracted from his practice, accumulated by the power exercised over him through supervision. In this way, the worker's labour is gradually absorbed into a certain technical knowledge of production which will enable a strengthening of control. So we see how there forms a knowledge that's extracted from the individuals themselves and derived from their own behaviour (Foucault, 2000: 83–84).

However, what seems to be vanishing with the transition toward a regime of surplus is precisely the possibility to gather this knowledge from the productive body of the post-Fordist labour force. If the *regime of scarcity* could be defined as a universe in which a 'power-knowledge' operated, we would describe the regime of the post-Fordist surplus as the field of exercise of a power characterised by a condition of *non-knowledge*. The post-Fordist labour force — flexible, mobile and permanently on the border between inclusion and exclusion, work and non-work, formal and informal economies, legal and illegal activities — does not offer itself to the knowledge of power and control. This difficulty (on the side of power) to make clear distinctions between 'threats' and 'resources', 'dangerous' and 'labouring' classes, 'social junk' and 'social dynamite' (Box & Hale, 1986) compels the institutions of social control to categorise whole sectors of the post-Fordist labour force as 'risk-groups', and to deploy consequent strategies of mass confinement, incapacitation and surveillance.

In such a post-disciplinary order, individuals seem to disappear. Indeed, the emerging model of control incorporates risk based, insurance-inspired and probability-driven strategies, whose aim is to reduce a social complexity out of control. Unknowable individuals are thus replaced by artificially constructed categories.

BEYOND THE PANOPTICON: SIGNS OF A POSTDISCIPLINARY ORDER

The metaphor of Panopticon has been recently rediscovered by some authors in the attempt to analyse the transformations of social control in post-modern societies. Thomas Mathiesen (1997) has argued that contemporary strategies of control are converging toward the creation of a 'post-panoptical' regime called *Synopticon*. In what Guy Debord defined as the 'society of spectacle', it is no longer the 'few' who observe the 'many' to ensure that they conform to the rules, but the many — constantly transformed into a docile and uncritical 'public opinion' — who watch the (often televised) gestures of the few and thus interiorise the models, attitudes, behaviours and values through which they can become responsible individuals and trustable consumers.

Mathiesen grounds this analysis of social control in the transition from a 'producer society' toward a 'consumer society' (Bauman, 1998), and I agree that the importance of this transition cannot be overlooked. The 'aesthetic of consumption' pervading contemporary society is something very different from (and to some extent even in contradiction with) the 'ethic of work' which shaped industrial society. While the reproduction of a work ethic could be enforced by a complex of disciplinary strategies aiming to normalise individuals, the instillation of a consumerist aesthetic requires something different: perhaps a system of control that leaves the individual — at least in theory — as free (to choose what and how to consume) as possible. If the panoptical model struggled to generalise conformity, the *synoptical* strategy must allow different lifestyles to express themselves freely, channelling them into the theatre of consumption.

However interesting this argument might be, it does not seem to give a substantial contribution to our effort at reconfiguring the territories of the political economy of punishment. In fact, it is based on the category of *consumption*, whereas at the core of our analysis stands the category of *production*. It is at the transformations of work — more than at those changes affecting the styles of consumption — that we should look in order to understand the transition from Fordism to post-Fordism and its impact on the field of social control. Crucially, however, the image of the *Synopticon* points to a crisis of the disciplinary utopia: the assumption is in fact that this grand narrative of modernity leaves way to technologies of control which explicitly reject the disciplinary project.

If we try to follow the footsteps of this rejection, we discover the emergence of technologies of control based on three peculiar practices: *generalised surveillance, selectivity of access* and *mass confinement*. Not always do these practices imply the creation of new institutions of control: in fact, the post-panoptical order is often characterised by the persistence of old institutions (and especially the panoptical institution par excellence: the prison), whose rationality, however, seems to be undergoing a process of transformation. The peculiar settings in which I think these practices are becoming more visible are the *metropolis*, the *Internet*, the *prison* and the *immigration detention centre*.

At first sight, it would seem that each of these 'social control-scenarios' displays the prominence of one kind of practices in particular. Thus, the prison and the immigration detention centre would be clear examples of mass-confinement; the urban landscape would represent the field of new practices of generalised surveillance, and the Internet could be seen as a public sphere increasingly affected by strategies of privatisation and control of access. However, the point of view suggested here is different: these sites seem to be paradigmatic (for their strategic role in the neo-liberal order) of the current transformations of social control, but the three mentioned technologies of control characterise to some extent all of them at the same time. Just to offer a few examples: the task of confining the 'social waste' produced by the neo-liberal economy and by the downsizing of the welfare state, is performed by the prison and the immigration detention centre as well as by the urban ghettoes

— and this seems true in particular for the American cities where, following Loïc Wacquant, a 'deadly symbiosis' connects the prison to the ghetto, thus entrapping the African-American poor (Wacquant, 2001). In the same way, the aim of excluding systematically some categories of people (defined, as we will see, by their *actuarial profile*), characterises the post-modern cities (in which the poor, the homeless and the new 'strangers' are kept out of many public and privatised spaces) as well as the post-disciplinary prisons. Similarly, the selectivity of access finds its peculiar exemplification in the urban landscape, with the diffusion of 'no-go areas' and 'gated communities', but the same logic inspires some emerging policies for the control of information (and particularly electronic information), based on the imposition of limits to access. The same applies to the generalisation of surveillance.

In this paper I will concentrate on the strategy of 'mass confinement' as exemplified in particular by the American experiment of 'mass incarceration'. The apparent exceptionality of the United States should not prevent the new political economy of punishment from scrutinising the diffusion of comparable policies in other areas and different contexts. In fact, the renewed role of imprisonment and of other related practices of confinement, such as the detention of undocumented foreigners in immigration detention centres around the world, as an instrument for the control of the huge social contradictions produced by the transition to a neo-liberal order, can be observed also in many European countries, whose 'variously' detained populations are growing as well.

MASS IMPRISONMENT FROM THE 'WELFARE STATE' TO A 'PENAL STATE'?

In the aftermath of World War II, the US prison population followed a constant downward trend, which intensified particularly in the 1960s due to a variety of factors. The 'tolerant' moral climate characterising the era of the civil rights revolution, the extension of the *welfare state*, the increasing resort to alternatives to imprisonment: each of these elements played a peculiar role. According to David Garland, this was the period of 'penal welfarism', in which a set of ideas, practices and institutions oriented toward the rehabilitation, reintegration, socialisation and treatment of offenders became hegemonic:

> In the penal-welfare framework, the rehabilitative ideal was not just one element among others. Rather, it was the hegemonic, organising principle, the intellectual framework and value system that bound together the whole structure and made sense of it for its practitioners (Garland, 2001: 34).

This trend toward a reduction in the centrality of the prison was felt also in other Western countries (for example in European penal systems) whose prison populations declined steadily, until they reached in many cases a historical minimum. Deviance was seen as the result of a multiplicity of social, economic, and cultural factors which had to be addressed by the penal-welfare complex. Crime was just one among many possible effects of individual and social deficits, whose deep economic causes had to be identified and removed through inclusive social policies and rehabilitative penal treatments.

Towards the end of the seventies, however, the correctional model entered a sudden crisis which produced a reversal in the official languages, practices and strategies on crime and crime control:

> In the course of a few years, the orthodoxies of rehabilitative faith collapsed in virtually all of the developed countries, as reformers and academics, politicians and policy-makers, and finally practitioners and institutional managers came to dissociate themselves from its tenets. With surprising speed, a liberal progressive ideal came to appear reactionary to the very groups that had previously championed it. And nowhere was this about-turn more spectacular than in the USA which, until then, had been the nation most fully committed to correctionalist policies and practice (Garland, 2001:54).

This crisis was in fact part of a larger shift in the political climate of the United States. As many scholars have documented, it was not until the end of the 1970s (with the presidential election of Ronald Regan) that 'law and order' became a major issue of US politics. What seemed to emerge was an attitude of 'revenge' by the American establishment (Melossi, 2000). Such revenge had to be launched against an intrusive welfare whose taxation system had taken too much from the white middle classes at the advantage of the poor, now depicted as 'scroungers' and 'parasites'. Moreover, revenge was invoked also against the black community, whose cyclical 'urban riots' were perceived as unacceptable acts of ingratitude toward American society. It was only with Reagan's election that the 'race-welfare-crime' complex emerged as a new 'governmental rationality', and a new rhetoric of war ('war on crime' and 'war on drugs') became hegemonic in the public discourse. This was targeted mainly at the black community, scapegoated for the increasing rates of crime, the diffusion of lethal drugs and the fiscal crisis of the welfare state (Parenti, 1999).

The new political climate influenced also the practices and rationalities of punishment. If until that time the main indicator of the effectiveness of crime (and drug) control strategies had been rates of recidivism and re-offending, some studies conducted in those years revealed that the correctional ideology had failed. Statistics showed an increase in street crimes, thus proclaiming the failure of those policies of treatment and rehabilitation whose aim was to reintegrate offenders by eliminating the social causes of delinquency.[7] Actually,

---

[7] If it is undeniable that the 1960s witnessed an increase in crime, it should also be noted that already in 1973 this upward trend had ceased, leaving way to a steady decline in criminal activity. More precisely: 'From 1973 through 1994, the rates of violent crime victimisation had intervals of stability, increase and decrease, while the rates of property crime underwent a virtually uninterrupted decrease' (Bureau of Justice Statistics, 1998, p 1). This means that the 'get tough' policies started when crime rates were already

this increase was not so 'dramatic' as some governmental 'think tanks' argued. But the consequence was that a public attitude of strong enthusiasm for individual treatment and correction — a sort of 'criminological progressivism' — gave way to sentiments of delusion, whose immediate translation was a kind of 'criminological scepticism'.

'Understand less and punish more' became the new common sense (Matthews, 1999). Sociological theories of deviance, 'realist' criminologists argued, worked only to justify crime and to legitimate the supposed leniency of criminal courts: the image of the 'deprived' and deviant was thus replaced by that of a 'depraved' and rational delinquent. Rehabilitation had to give way to deterrence and incapacitation (Van Den Haag, 1975; Wilson, 1983).

The project was no longer to adopt measures adequate to the social conditions of the single deviant, but to apply those sanctions which, on average, would be harsh enough to deter people from committing crimes. Where this economic model could not work, the solution of last resort would be the neutralisation of offenders. In this sense, 'selective incapacitation' represented an important step toward a new exclusionary rationality of punishment, whose effects are stilll visible in our times (Greenwood, 1982). In fact, to speak of 'selective incapacitation' means, on the one hand, to theorise explicitly the dismissal of any rehabilitative ideal and, on the other hand, to see punishment only as an instrument for the physical separation of the deviant from the wider society. The plan is to isolate, within the mass of actual or potential deviants, a small number of 'born criminals', 'incorrigible deviants' or 'chronic recidivists' who cannot be reintegrated into the community. What is crucial here is the logic behind this perspective: the idea that it is possible to select some categories of people who, all the rest being equal, should be punished more than others because they display some indicators of a structural propensity to crime.

Initially, the 'selective incapacitation' approach was presented by its advocates as a 'deflationary' measure: its (declared) aim was in fact to reduce the prison population by limiting detention only to some groups of persistent offenders. What tends to go unnoticed is that the underlying logic of selective punishment could be extended discretionally, thus reaching larger social groups defined as dangerous — by practitioners, probation officers, judges, and to a greater extent by the mass-media, public opinion or politicians. This is exactly what seems to have happened in the United States (Sparks, 2000).

The short step between 'selective incapacitation' and 'mass-incapacitation' was covered rapidly. This comes as no surprise, if one considers that the criteria according to which criminals are judged as 'dangerous' depend on many factors, not always purely 'criminological' ones, but also political and cultural. In other words, when the 'degree of tolerance' toward deviant behaviour is high, only few

declining. This paradox reappeared in the second half of the 1990s, when a dramatic reduction in criminal offences was accompanied by 'tough' laws like the 'Three strikes and you're out' legislations.

people will be selected for incapacitation; but in times of 'law and order', 'war on crime' and 'zero tolerance policing' it is not difficult to understand to what extent those categories of people perceived as deserving long-term imprisonment will become larger. Even more so, if one considers that 'the factors identified by persistence studies are factors shared by many of the underprivileged: socio-economic deprivation; low family income and high family size; frequent unemployment; broken homes and early parental separation; criminal, anti-social and alcoholic parents' (Hudson, 2001, 155). In other words, the target of 'selective incapacitation' soon became the growing army of the American poor and the 'underclass'.

I would argue that mass incarceration started here: prison and jail populations started to grow steadily — from 400,000 in 1975 (a historical minimum) to 750,000 in 1985, to almost 2 million in 2000 (Bureau of Justice Statistics, 2000). Direct public expenditures for justice and corrections grew while welfare, education and health spending suffered dramatic cuts.[8] Incarceration rates have thus reached levels never touched before in the whole history of the United States, surpassing even those of South Africa at the time of *apartheid*: on average, the United States incarcerates today five times more than European countries. If to the incarcerated population one adds all those who live under some form of penal supervision, the total 'penal population' reaches 6,5 millions (Bureau of Justice Statistics, 2002).

It would be impossible to explain this trend by looking at criminal activity in the US. In fact, in the last 50 years rates of crime remained stable, if one excludes the rise in violent crimes that took place in the 1980s — due mainly to the diffusion of the crack market and culture in the inner cities, particularly among the African American and Latino youth (Bourgois, 1996). Since the early 1990s these rates are declining steadily for all the main categories of crime, while prison population continues to grow.[9] Another important element to be considered is that almost one million of US prisoners — that is, half the total — are behind bars for non-violent offences: crimes against property or public order, less serious drug offences and, in the case of immigrants, violations of immigration laws (Irwin, Schiraldi & Ziedenberg, 2000).[10] The overall picture shows quite clearly

[8] According to the Bureau of Justice (2002b), in the years 1982–99 expenditures for justice grew in the United States by 419% at Federal level, 369% at State-level and 310% at County-level.

[9] According to the Bureau of Justice Statistics (2001), serious violent crimes remained stable between 1973 and 1983; they increased during the period 1985–93, and finally declined sharply between 1993 and 2001. See also Tonry (2001). It should be noted that the trend toward mass incarceration in the US seems to have slowed down since 2000. In 2001 the annual rate of growth of prisoners was 1.1% (the smallest increase since 1979). However this was compensated by higher rates of growth in Federal prison population, and (after the events of 11 September) by a dramatic increase in the foreign population supervised by the INS (Immigration and Nationalisation Service).

[10] According to these authors, between 1978 and 1996, 77% of prison population growth was accounted for by non-violent offenders.

that the new 'great confinement' experienced by the United States is linked to a shift in crime control policies and more generally to a transformation in the politics of deviance, rather than to any significant change in criminal activity.

The commonsensical explanation for the upsurge in US rates of incarceration holds that politicians — from Reagan to GW Bush — only 'responded' to a growing public demand for punishment, by introducing new punitive measures, promoting tough legislations and waging periodic wars on crime and drugs. In other words, the public — made insecure by a real increase in crime and by the crisis of traditional American values caused by civil rights activists, feminist movements and anti-authoritarian ideologies — asked for harsher penalties, while the political system only satisfied this demand. The results would be plain to see: 'truth in sentencing', 'three strikes and you're out', 'Megan's laws', 'mandatory minimum sentences' and 'real offence sentencing schemes'.

Katherine Beckett has showed that this narrative is in fact very questionable. It is true, she argues, that the American public opinion has become more punitive — as have many other Western public opinions — but this increased punitiveness was not the leading force behind political choices and discourses about crime: on the contrary, it was produced by them. In other words, the mass media and the political system pushed the American public opinion toward a more punitive attitude, by turning crime into a big issue (Beckett, 1997; Beckett & Sassoon, 2000). It is true, however that such shift, synthesised by the transition from the 'war on poverty' to the 'war on crime', was easier and more successful in the United States than elsewhere.

To explain this apparent exceptionality of the American case, I would follow Jonathan Simon, who argues that the shift was facilitated by the 'single-issue' patterning of American politics. Drawing on Mary Douglas' theory of risk and blame, Simon suggests that crime became a suitable field for the emergence of a 'border' political discourse, in which 'sectarian' attitudes could impose themselves. The crime issue was suitable for a 'good against evil' rhetoric, through which the state could present itself as the defender of unspecified 'us' against suitable 'others'. In this way, Simon concludes, a new strategy of government has emerged in America, a strategy of 'governing through crime'. The mass-mediated discourse about crime as a major social problem affecting honest citizens, facilitates the social construction of some categories of people — the poor, the African-American youth, the 'underclass' — as a 'public enemy' against which a war must be waged. This war, the war on crime, works to re-legitimise in the eyes of the public a de-legitimated nation-state (Caplow & Simon, 1999; Simon, 2001).

In other words, the politicisation of crime succeeded in two peculiar ways. On the one hand it allowed the American establishment to reassert its 'sovereign' power, thus constructing a new legitimisation of the state through a series of 'wars' against internal enemies (who replaced the crumbling Soviet Union, no longer fit to the role). On the other hand, by representing the poor and the 'outsiders' as the main threat to collective welfare, public opinion's attention could be diverted from other sources of insecurity, fear and suffering — economic restructuring, increasing unemployment, work insecurity, etc. — thus confirming its attachment to the existing political system, given that 'scapegoating not only transposes the anxiety felt by many, but also offers to anchor the worth of objects according to the threat that is allegedly arrayed against them' (Vaughan, 2002, p 207).

If we look at the ethnic composition of American prisons, we realise that this strategy of selective neutralisation has been very successful. African Americans represent 12 per cent of the American population, but since the 1980s they are the absolute majority of the US prison population. In 1950, this population was composed by a 66 per cent of whites and a 32 per cent of blacks. Today, these proportions are inverted: whites represent only 30 per cent, while African Americans are about 60 per cent of the total. If one looks at incarceration rates, what emerges is that if whites are incarcerated at a rate of 919/100,000, blacks behind bars are almost 7000/100,000. This means that the chances for a black (male) to end up in prison during his lifetime are more than seven times higher than for whites (Wacquant, 1999; Bureau of Justice Statistics, 2001, 2002a): one in three African Americans aged 18–35 is in prison or under some form of penal supervision (Miller, 1996).

These data should always be taken in conjunction with those concerning the class-composition and the educational level of the prison population.[11] As I mentioned earlier, the expansion of the penal system has coincided — almost in a perfect timing — with a substantial downsizing of the welfare state. For instance, just in the years 1993–98 there has been a 44 per cent decrease in the number of American families receiving 'Aid For Families With Dependent Children' (AFDC), the main subsidy granted by the American welfare system. A recent study by Katherine Beckett and Bruce Western shows that the increase in penal severity (and in prison population) has been more pronounced in those American states in which welfare provisions have been reduced more — like Texas, California, Louisiana and Arizona (Western & Beckett, 2001).

The exclusionary logic of the American 'penal state' is also confirmed by the side-effects of the so-called 'invisible punishments', which join imprisonment as further instruments for banning whole categories of people from civil, social and political life. A good example is offered here by the 'Felony Disenfranchisement Laws': in the United States, 46 states deprive convicted offenders of the right to vote while they are in prison; 32 States extend this ban to those on parole; 14 states disenfranchise also ex-offenders, and 10 states disenfranchise ex-felons for

---

[11] According to the Bureau of Justice Statistics (2003), prisoners in Federal and State Prisons — as well as jailers and probationers — were much less educated than the general population. In particular, 27% of Federal prisoners, 40% of State inmates, 47% of jailers and 31% of probationers had no high school education at all, compared to 18% of the general population. The same *Report* shows that ethnic minorities were less educated than whites and in 1997 17% of inmates were unemployed at the time of admission.

life, thus excluding them permanently from political participation. Because of these provisions, '(...) an estimated 3,9 million US citizens are disenfranchised, including over one million who have fully completed their sentence' (Human Rights Watch/The Sentencing Project, 1998: 1). But the impact of these measures is not equally distributed within the American population: once again, blacks are disproportionally represented. In fact 13 per cent of African-American men – 1,4 million – are disenfranchised, representing just over one third of the total disenfranchised population (Human Rights Watch, 1998:1). And the logic of exclusion is not limited to political rights: it involves also the denial of housing and welfare benefits to drug offenders,[12] as well as the termination of parental rights and occupational bars (Travis, 2002).

If one takes these developments into account, it becomes difficult to argue that the rehabilitation, reintegration and inclusion of deviants in the social pact are still among the aims of contemporary punishment.[13] What these punitive strategies seem to pursue is the pure and simple 'exclusion' of whole fractions of the population from society, by reproducing a cycle of deprivation and marginality which in turn justifies their representation as threats and public enemies. The fact that the absolute majority of the prison population is composed by poor people, the unemployed, precarious and unskilled workers is not new: indeed, it is a *leitmotiv* in the history of the institution itself. The prison was invented for the confinement of these categories of people, and continues to perform its task.

What is new, however, is the relation between penal and social policies in the management of poverty and the control of the labour force. The new 'problem

[12] According to the 'Personal Responsibility and Work Opportunity Reconciliation Act' signed by President Clinton in 1996, which ' (...) imposes a lifetime ban on eligibility for TANF (Temporary Assistance to Needy Families) on individuals with drug felony convictions' (Rubinstein & Mukamal, 2002:41).

[13] As suggested, for example, by Dario Melossi when — following Thomas Dumm he argues that "(...) the penitentiary and the other 'ancillary institutions' (...) can be conceived as machines to process those who were not 'naturally' within the scope of the social contract, ie those who have been perceived historically as incarnations of 'otherness' (criminals of course, but also proletarians and those socially constructed as too distant from the anthropological model in power — a model usually male and 'white', whatever 'white' means" (Melossi, 1998, xix). More precisely, I agree entirely with this author when he refers his analysis to the 'birth' of the prison — and to its development until the crisis of the industrial society: as Melossi himself suggests, this is in fact an important aspect of the disciplinary project described by Michel Foucault. I would disagree with this perspective, however, if it is applied to contemporary punishment: my point of view is that mass incarceration and its related 'invisible punishments' are exclusionary both in instrumental and symbolic terms. Instrumentally, it reproduces a dynamic of exclusion of growing fractions of the post-Fordist labour force; symbolically, it reasserts hierarchies and divisions within the labour-force, thus preventing it from forming political coalitions which could question the legitimacy of the neoliberal order.

population' — the 'surplus' labour force produced by the post-Fordist economy — is managed less through the instruments of 'social' regulation of poverty, and more through penal technologies. The consequence is the transition from the 'social state' to the 'penal state', which Loïc Wacquant refers to when he defines the 'irresistible growth of the American penal state' as a strategy for the 'criminalisation of poverty' that is functional to the 'imposition of precarious and under-paid waged labour' (Wacquant, 1999).

It would be difficult to suggest that the American experiment with mass imprisonment and social exclusion is being replicated in the same way in other areas of the world, and particularly in Europe. We know that the European scenario is different, and that in particular the persistence of a 'welfare-model' of social regulation has prevented to some extent the diffusion of a model of 'governing through crime'. If it is true, as Western and Beckett argue (and Wacquant agrees) that in the United States the emergence of a neo-liberal model has given a substantial contribution to the expansion of the penal realm as an instrument for the control of social contradictions, then we might argue that the limited diffusion of this model in Europe has prevented a full development of the new penal strategies described so far.

However, Wacquant himself warns that this trend toward the penalisation of poverty is not peculiar to the United States, given that a 'neo-liberal penal commonsense' is also spreading across Europe. Indeed, we can identify some commonalities between the American and the European context. In the last decade, incarceration rates grew by 43 per cent in England; 39 per cent in France; 49 per cent in Greece; 140 per cent in Portugal (now the country with the highest rates in Europe); 192 per cent in Spain and 240 per cent in the Netherlands. The only countries witnessing a slight reduction in prison populations are Germany, Finland and Austria (Tournier, 1999; Kuhn, 2001). But more than these quantitative aspects — showing at least that the trend toward mass incarceration is not unique to the United States — what deserves our attention is the class and ethnic composition of the European prison population.

If the American prison is affected by a process of 'blackening' and 'impoverishment', the same pattern is observable also in European prisons: immigrants are dramatically overrepresented in all European penal systems. In Italy, between 1990 and 2000, the percentage of foreigners on the total prison population has shifted from 15 to 30 per cent: a shocking percentage if one considers that immigrants represent just 2.5 per cent of the general population (Palidda, 2001). In Greece 39 per cent of prisoners are immigrants; 34 per cent in Germany; 38 per cent in Belgium and 32 per cent in the Netherlands. More crucially, however, the 'detention' of immigrants is not limited to prisons. In fact, prompted by the diffusion of anti-immigration policies, new institutions for the confinement of 'illegal aliens' are being built across the European territory. The external borders of the European Union are now disseminated with 'Immigration Detention Centres' whose function is to 'detain' immigrants (in some cases indefinitely and without trial) on the ground of their administrative position of 'irregularity'. Finally, in Italy as in the rest of Europe, the hyper-incarceration of foreigners goes systematically hand in hand with the overrepresentation of drug addicts and poor people.[14]

INCARCERATING RISK

I would agree here with those scholars who in the early 1990s hypothesised that contemporary crime policies — and in particular the American experiment of mass incarceration — follow a new rationality which is configuring the realm of a 'new penology' (O'Malley, 1991, 1992; Feeley & Simon, 1992, 1994).

The leitmotiv of this new rationality is represented by the concept of risk. Increasingly, recent social control technologies, and the post-Fordist prison in particular, seem to be performing the task of managing risks and incapacitating those social groups which are considered (by the mass media, politicians, public opinion, and the criminal justice system itself) as 'risk-producers'. No longer focusing on the neutralisation of individual risk-factors through the incapacitation of individual dangerous offenders (as was indeed the case with 'selective incapacitation') the system would concentrate thus on the 'categorial management' of a burden of risk which cannot be reduced.

In this respect, the rationality of control we refer to is no longer disciplinary but *actuarial*. I am not suggesting here that the European and American criminal justice systems adopt statistical technologies to manage their deviant populations. In fact, the term 'actuarialism' is used here as a metaphor for two recent trends in crime policies: first, the fact that crime tends to be considered (in the technical language of practitioners and experts) as a 'normal fact', as a social phenomena which cannot be eliminated (as was believed at the time of 'criminological progressivism'); second, the fact that whole categories of people, defined by peculiar factors like poverty, social exclusion, welfare 'dependency', ethnic origins or nationality, become the privileged targets of contemporary punitive policies — because they are socially perceived as 'dangerous' and 'threatening'. The hypothesis is that these policies do not treat the members of these 'undeserving' categories as individuals — by deploying 'inclusionary' strategies of social control targeted at removing the 'social causes' of deviance — but as members of wider 'dangerous classes' to be neutralised, incapacitated and warehoused. In this respect, the recurrence of concepts like 'underclass' in political (and criminological) discourses is crucial. In fact, according to Feeley & Simon (1994: 192):

> The underclass is a permanently dysfunctional population, without literacy, without skills and without hope; a self-perpetuating and pathological segment of society that is not integrable into the larger whole, and whose culture fosters violence. Actuarial

---

[14] According to Tournier (1999) drug-related prison convictions represent 21% of total convictions in France, 32% in Spain, 36% in Portugal and 33% in Italy.

justice invites it to be treated as a high-risk group that must be managed for the protection of the larger society.

It is not difficult to find evidence of the shift toward a risk-based model of social control: one should consider how discriminatorily some federal or state 'sentencing guidelines' are applied in the United States,[15] or how routinely some categories of people — stereotyped as dangerous in public discourse — receive harsher penalties for the same crimes.[16] Another significant example is also offered by the evolution of drug-testing policies in the United States. If until recently taking drugs would expose an individual to rehabilitative treatment, and therefore the priority of drug-control agencies was to identify drug-takers to plan for the most suitable programme, today the situation looks quite different. Individual drug-treatments have been gradually replaced by random drug-testing, whose aim is no longer to deliver suitable programmes to rehabilitate individuals, but to identify and isolate whole categories of drug-users within the wider population. Random drug tests help to isolate a whole class of subjects and to prevent the risks they are deemed to pose to the community — by excluding them from the workplace, the neighbourhood, the gym, and other public places (Simon, 1987; O'Malley & Mugford, 1991).

Some recent developments in the field of alternatives to imprisonment, in particular parole in the United States, seem also to be leading toward an actuarial model. No longer do rehabilitation, support, counselling and the reduction of recidivism represent the main objectives of the parole service: perhaps these ideals survive as rhetorical tools in the minds of some well-intentioned practitioners, but their operational model has shifted toward a different framework. The main task of the parole officer is now to identify those categories of people who — given their actuarial 'status' — are most suitable for parole revocation, so that 'parole and probation as sources of prison admissions have become almost as important as the court system itself' (Caplow & Simon, 1999: 102; Petersilia, 1999). The indicators of success and failure of parole schemes have been thus

---

[15] I refer here in particular to the '1986 Anti-Drug Abuse Act', clearly an 'actuarial' legislation. This law punishes the possession of five or more grams of crack cocaine with 5–20 years of imprisonment. To get the same sentence for possession of powder cocaine, one has to be found with 500 g. How can such a disproportion be justified? Only if one considers who is the average possessor of each variant of the same drug: crack is the poor, 'black' version of cocaine, whereas powder will be found more often in the pockets of the white middle- and upper-classes. Clearly, African American youths are perceived as a dangerous class, and according to an actuarial rationality they should be punished more than their white, less dangerous fellows (Beckett & Sassoon, 2000).

[16] A clear example is offered by the treatment of immigrants in Italy. In this country — as in many others in Europe — refusing to show one's Identity Card if requested to do so by a police officer is a crime. However, if this crime is committed by an immigrant, both the fine and the prison terms provided by the law are two times higher than the ones established for an Italian citizen. This provision was introduced by the Italian '1998 Immigration Law' as an amendment to the *Penal Code*.

reversed: no longer is success measured by the number of people who do not re-offend, but (quite paradoxically) by the amount of individuals who are channelled back to prison, as this confirms the correctness of the risk-predictions made about them. In this sense, parole operates as a 'waste management' system and the 'toxic waste' is represented by the 'underclass' communities (Simon, 1993).[17]

Comparable trends can be observed also in other segments of the criminal justice system. For instance, in probation the 'clinical model' for the prediction of dangerousness, based on the study of individual cases, the analysis of subjective variables and the reconstruction of single 'biographies', is put under question by the diffusion of 'actuarial models' for the assessment of categorial risk 'based upon the statistical analysis of data derived from sample groups of the population' (Kemshall, 1996, VI).[18] Finally, signs of a risk-oriented rationality of control can be detected also in the US Juvenile Justice System (Kempf-Leonard & Elicka, 2000). However, it is not only in the field of penality that actuarial rationalities appear to be prevailing over individual-oriented technologies: for example, important signals come also from the field of psychiatry (Castel, 1991). In other words, it seems no longer to be the individual characteristics of subjects that are the object of social control, as instead those social factors which permit to assign some individuals to a specific risk-class: whole categories of people virtually cease to *commit crimes* to *become crimes* (Morris, 1999).

What I am suggesting is that concrete individuals and the social interaction in which they are engaged tend to be replaced by the artificial production of classes and categories that are 'simulacra' of the real. 'Illegal immigrants', 'African Americans from the inner city', 'drug addicts', 'the unemployed': it is toward these discursive categories that postdisciplinary control is exercised. Whereas disciplinary technologies defined a complex of 'laboratories of power' in which the development of control strategies allowed for the production of a new knowledge about the subject, risk-based mass incarceration seems to work differently. The diffusion of a risk-based rationality gives birth to a complex of practices whose aim is to deconstruct individuals; in other words, actuarial technologies do not simply 'represent' individuals, they 'produce' them (Simon, 1987).

---

[17] For a critique of this position, based on ethnographic research in California, see Lynch (1998).

[18] This author suggests that the 'actuarial model' and the 'clinical model' can be used jointly by probation officers. However, actuarial predictions should always precede individual assessments: 'Staff will need to learn and apply the appropriate baseline actuarial knowledge prior to carrying out in-depth interviews aimed at clinically assessing patterns of behaviour and motivations' (Kemshall, 1996: 31). In other words, a person has the right to have his/her own biography considered only after s/he has been actuarially classified.

In the field of criminal justice, the emergence of an actuarial logic shows the diffusion of a managerial rationality: a 'systemic' approach based on the principles of economisation of resources, monetisation of risks, and cost-effectiveness (Taylor, 1999). It should be noted however that *this is an entirely post-Fordist economic rationality*. External as it is to the complexity of the social world and unable to produce a detailed knowledge about its own fields of application, it replaces the disciplinary regulation of social forces with an attempt to reduce human potentialities it can no longer control.

We would argue that it is exactly the increasing difficulty to separate the deviant from the precarious worker, the criminal subject from the 'illegal' immigrant, the hidden worker from the informal one that promotes the regrouping of all human 'diversities' into dangerous classes. In other words, it is as if the difficulty to maintain the traditional distinction between 'dangerous' and 'labouring' classes — as it was inferred from the characteristics of individuals — compelled postdisciplinary institutions of control to perform this function through risk-based classifications.

As is well known, the consolidation of an actuarial logic within the institutions and practices of social regulation is not an absolute novelty in the history of Western societies: indeed, the welfare state can be described as a model of government connecting disciplinary practices for the control of individuals to actuarial systems for the socialisation of structural risks affecting the population as a whole. In that context, actuarial technologies worked as instruments for the social redistribution of risks produced by industrialisation, the labour market, dangerous productions, polluting factors and so on: it was a socialised mechanism for relieving individuals from the risks produced by a complex industrial society. In this sense that 'social version' of the actuarial technology was part of what Michel Foucault defined as a *bio-political* model of government: a 'power over life' whose visible symbols were the national health systems, social insurances, labour legislations, unemployment benefit systems, etc. In all these instances, actuarial rationality informed the bio-political dispositives for the regulation of populations (Ewald, 1986, 1990, 1991).

What has changed, however, is the way in which the actuarial technology meets the new strategies of social control. While in the welfarist version actuarial rationality produced mechanisms of regulation based on the socialisation of collective risks, thus enhancing social interactions inspired by cooperation, empathy and solidarity, contemporary technologies of control lead in the opposite direction: they limit, neutralise and de-structure forms of social interaction now perceived as dangerous. In systematic connection with a political rhetoric which promotes the public perception of fear, insecurity, risk and danger as always posed by 'strangers', actuarial technologies perform both the instrumental role of selecting a surplus labour force suitable for mass confinement, and the symbolic role of de-structuring the social bonds within the post-Fordist labour force (O'Malley, 1992, 2001). Mass incarceration, sustained by a political rhetoric of war, invasion and siege, contributes to the public representation of the 'social surplus' as a new dangerous class, and thus de-socialises the post-Fordist labour force by preventing the formation of stable relationships of cooperation inside it. Thus, empathy is replaced by what O'Malley (2001) defines as 'new prudentialism': a regime of universal diffidence that hinders any reciprocal recognition among individuals as parts of the same labour-force. Just one example: by representing immigrants as dangerous classes and public enemies, the power elite prevent the lowest strata of the national labour force from recognising in their foreign fellows suitable allies in the struggles over work conditions, welfare benefits, etc. Thus, the 'immigrant' becomes either a dangerous competitor on the labour market (as a 'desperate' worker) or a scapegoat for public insecurities and fears (as a potential 'criminal').

The process of constructing 'diversity' — of places, situations, individuals and whole social groups — as synonymous with 'dangerousness', defines new hierarchies and inequalities within society. New 'communities of fear' replace any other form of communal self-identification:

> Threats and dangers, and fears about them, are dealt with by the construction of suitable enemies, and attendant negative labelling, denial, avoidance and exclusion. Solidarity is based on a commonality of fear. In some cases, such as the war on drugs, insecurities are cultivated and focused on unfortunate people to gain political purchase and to offset the endemic insecurity experienced more generally in everyday life (Ericson & Carriere, 1994: 102–103)[19].

As a result, the multiplicity of differences, the mixture of languages, the irreducibility of experiences typical of the 'post-modern condition' are successfully presented by hegemonic public discourses as sources of insecurity, panic and fear of 'strangers' (Bauman, 2000). The preservation of contemporary social order seems to be based on the development of control strategies capable of disarticulating those very forms of socialisation and social cooperation which the Fordist system of production promoted: in fact, they appear now as dangerous interactions to be prevented and neutralised.

---

[19] Gregg Barak makes this point even clearer: 'In television, for example (...) the working class has all but disappeared. As a result, there are basically three kinds of classes constructed by the mass media: the rich classes, the middle classes, and the criminal classes' (Barak, 1994: 134). But the underlying logic is the same: work and exploitation — as common grounds for the construction of a shared sense of belonging — are replaced by fear and insecurity. This analysis is not very distant from the one proposed by David Garland, who suggests that — in our contemporary 'culture of control' — the symbolic role traditionally played by the 'oppressed' in modern society has been taken by the universal 'victim'. In other words, 'victimhood' — more than 'oppression' — has become the common ground for mutual identification and solidarity: feelings which find their most coherent expression in the emerging punitive attitudes (Garland, 2001: 200-201).

CONCLUDING REMARKS

The aim of this contribution was to suggest some theoretical routes toward a new political economy of punishment. My starting assumption was that a materialist approach to social control cannot overlook the deep transformations affecting global capitalism, which are driving Western economies toward a post-Fordist model of production and social regulation.

The crisis of the industrial economy and the disappearance of the Taylorist factory as the main site of production — whose visible result is the emergence of a flexible, mobile, precarious and vulnerable post-Fordist labour force — suggests that the disciplinary technologies of control are losing much of their centrality in contemporary society. Enmeshed as they are in a flexible and deregulated economy — constantly on the border between work and non-work, legal and illegal activities, formal and informal markets — the subjects of post-Fordist production seem to escape the disciplinary logic of individualised knowledge and control. On the one hand, because the triumphant logic of flexibility contradicts the rigidities of the disciplinary society; on the other hand, because it becomes very problematic to draw clear distinctions between 'laborious' and 'dangerous' classes, or 'resources' and 'threats' ('illegal' immigrants are a good example here).

My point of view is that the 'new penology' — as a globalising model of control based on the social construction of 'dangerous others' who must be incapacitated and neutralised — configures a post-disciplinary strategy that is both instrumentally and symbolically connected to the emerging post-Fordist system of production. Instrumentally, because by excluding whole categories of marginal people it contributes to the reproduction of a Marxian 'reserve army' of labour — criminalised immigrants, vulnerable poor, stigmatised minorities — socially perceived as a threatening 'enemy'. Symbolically, because by representing some categories of people as 'dangerous classes', it prevents the formation of stable social bonds and possibly the constitution of political alliances within the contemporary labour force. It is here that a post-Fordist political economy of punishment should play its critical role, by developing theoretical 'counter-strategies' against these new rationalities of control, before they consolidate themselves into a new global 'paradigm of exclusion'.

REFERENCES

Adamson, C (1984) 'Toward a Marxist Penology: Captive Criminal Populations as Economic Threats and Resources' *Social Problems*, 31, 435–58.
Barak, G (1994) 'Between Waves, Mass-Mediated Themes of Crime and Justice' *Social Justice*, 3, 133–47.
Bauman, Z (1998) *Work, Consumerism and the New Poor* (Buckingham, Open University Press).

—— (2000) *Liquid Modernity* (Cambridge, Polity Press).

Beck, U (1999) *Schöne Arbeitswelt. Vision: Welt Burgergesellschaft. Frankfurt am Main* (Campus Verlag).

Beckett, K (1997) *Making Crime Pay: Law and Order in Contemporary American Politics* (Oxford, Oxford University Press).

Beckett, K & Sassoon, T (2000) *The Politics of Injustice. Crime and Punishment in America* (Thousand Oaks, Pine Forge).

Bourgois, P (1996) *In Search of Respect. Selling Crack in El Barrio* (Cambridge, Cambridge University Press).

Box, S & Hale, C (1982) 'Economic Crisis and the Rising Prisoner Population in England and Wales' *Crime and Social Justice*, 17, 20–35.

—— (1985) 'Unemployment, Imprisonment and Prison Overcrowding' *Contemporary Crises*, 9, 209–228.

—— (1986) 'Unemployment, Crime and Imprisonment, and the Enduring Problem of Prison Overcrowding' in R Matthews & J Young (eds) *Confronting Crime* (London, Sage).

Burchell, G (1991) 'Governmental Rationality' in G Burchell, C Gordon & P Miller (eds) *The Foucault Effect* (Chicago, University of Chicago Press).

Bureau of Justice Statistics (1998) *Correctional Populations in the United States 1997* (Washington DC).

—— (2000) *Correctional Surveys* (Washington DC).

—— (2001) *National Crime Victimization Survey* (Washington DC).

—— (2002a) *At a Glance* (Washington DC).

—— (2002b) *Expenditure and Employment Extracts* (Washington DC).

—— (2003) *Report on Education and Correctional Populations* (Washington DC).

Caplow, T & Simon, J (1999) 'Understanding Prison Policy and Population Trends' in M Tonry & J Petersilia (eds) *Prisons. Crime and Justice* (Chicago, University of Chicago Press).

Castel, Robert (1991) 'From Dangerousness to Risk' in G Burchell, C Gordon and P Miller (eds) *The Foucault Effect. Studies in Governmentality* (Chicago, University of Chicago Press).

Dean, M (1999) *Governmentality. Power and Rule in Modern Society* (London, Sage).

Ehrenreich, B (2001) *Nickel and Dimed. On (Not) Getting by in America* (New York, Metropolitan).

Ericson, RV & Carriere, K (1994) 'The Fragmentation of Criminology' in D Nelken (ed) *The Futures of Criminology* (London, Sage).

Ewald, F (1986) *L'état-providence* (Paris, Grasset).

—— (1990) 'Norms, Discipline and The Law' *Representations*, 30, 136–161.

—— (1991) 'Insurance and Risk' in G Burchell, C Gordon & P Miller (eds) *The Foucault Effect. Studies in Governmentality* (Chicago, University of Chicago Press).

Federici, S (1975) *Wages Against Housework* (London, Power of Women Collective and Falling Wall Press).

Feeley, MM & Simon, J (1992) 'The New Penology. Notes on the Emerging Strategies of Corrections and Its Implications' *Criminology*, XXX, 449–474.

—— (1994) 'Actuarial Justice: The Emerging New Criminal Law' in D Nelken (ed) *The Futures of Criminology* (London, Sage).

Foucault, M (1977) *Discipline and Punish. The Birth of the Prison* (London, Penguin).

——(1991) 'Governmentality' in G Burchell, CG Graham & P Miller (eds) *The Foucault Effect* (Hemel Hempstead, Harvester).

—— (1997) 'Security, Territory, and Population' in P Rabinow (ed) *Essential Works of Foucault 1954–84* (New York, New Publishing Group).

—— (2000) 'Truth and Juridical Forms' in JD Faubion (ed) *Essential Works of Foucault 1954–84, Volume III* (New York, New Publishing Group).

Fumagalli, A (1997) 'Aspetti dell'accumulazione flessibile in Italia' in S Bologna & A Fumagalli (eds) *Il lavoro Autonomo di seconda generazione* (Milano, Feltrinelli).

Garland, D (2001) *The Culture of Control. Crime and Social Order in Contemporary Society* (Oxford, Oxford University Press).

Gorz, A (1989) *Critique of Economic Reason* (London, Verso).

—— (1999) *Reclaiming Work. Beyond the Wage-Based Society* (Cambridge, Polity Press).

Greenberg, D (1977) 'The Dynamics of Oscillatory Punishment Processes' *The Journal of Criminal Law and Criminology*, 68, 643–651.

—— (1980) 'Penal Sanctions in Poland: A Test for Alternative Models' *Social Problems*, 28, 194–204.

Greenwood, P (1982) *Selective Incapacitation* (Santa Monica, RAND Corporation).

Hardt, M & Negri, A (2000) *Empire* (Cambridge, MA, Harvard University Press).

Hudson, B (2001) 'Punishment, Rights and Difference: Defending Justice in the Risk-Society' in K Stenson & Sullivan R (eds) *Crime, Risk and Justice* (Devon, Willan).

Human Rights Watch and The Sentencing Project (1998) *Losing the Vote. The Impact of Felony Disenfranchisement Laws in the United States* (Washington DC).

Irwin, J, Schiraldi, V & Ziedenberg, J (2000) 'America's One Million Nonviolent Prisoners' *Social Justice*, 27, 135–147.

Jankovic, I 1977 'Labor Market and Imprisonment' *Crime and Social Justice*, 8, 17–31.

Kempf-Leonard, K & Elicka, SL Peterson (2000) 'Expanding Realms of the New Penology' *Punishment and Society* 2, 1; 66–97.

Kemshall, H *Reviewing Risk. A Review of Research on the Assessment and Management of Risk and Dangerousness: Implications for Policy and Practice in the Probation Service* (London, Home Office Research and Statistics Directorate).

Kuhn, A (2001) 'Incarceration Rates Across the World' in M Tonry (ed) *Penal Reform in Overcrowded Times* (Oxford, Oxford University Press).

Lynch, M (1998) 'Waste Managers: The New Penology, Crime Fighting, and Parole Agent Identity' *Law and Society Review*, 32, 839–871.

Marshall, TH (1992) 'Citizenship and Social Class' in T Bottomore & TH Marshall (eds) *Citizenship and Social Class* (London, Pluto Press).

Matthews, R (1999) *Doing Time. An Introduction to the Sociology of Imprisonment* (London, Macmillan Publishing Group).

Mathiesen, T (1997) 'The Viewer Society: Foucault's Panopticon Revisited' *Theoretical Criminology*, 1, 215–234.

Melossi, D & Pavarini, M (1981) *The Prison and the Factory. Origins of the Penitentiary System* (London, Macmillan).

Melossi, D (1985) 'Punishment and Social Action: Changing Vocabularies of Punitive Motive Within a Political Business Cycle' *Current Perspectives in Social Theory*, 6, 167–197.

—— (editor) (1998) *The Sociology of Punishment* (Aldershot, Ashgate).

—— (2000) 'Changing Representations of the Criminal' *The British Journal of Criminology*, 40, 296–320.

Miller, J (1996) *Search and Destroy. African-American Males in the Criminal Justice System* (Cambridge, Cambridge University Press).

Morris, L (1999) *Dangerous Class. The Underclass and Social Citizenship* (London, Routledge).

Negri, A (1989) *The Politics of Subversion: A Manifesto for the Twenty-First Century* (Cambridge, Polity Press).

O'Connor, J (1973) *The Fiscal Crisis of the State* (New York, St Martin's).

O'Malley, P (1991) 'Legal Networks and Domestic Security' *Studies in Law, Politics, and Society*, XI, 170–190.

—— (1992) 'Risk, Power and Crime Prevention' *Economy and Society*, 21, 252–275.

—— (2001) 'Risk, Crime and Prudentialism Revisited' in K Stenson & R Sullivan (eds) *Crime, Risk and Justice* (Sullivan, Devon, Willan).

O'Malley, P & Mugford, S (1991) 'Moral Technology: The Political Agenda of Random Drug Testing' *Social Justice*, 18, 122–146.

Ohmae, K (1990) *The Borderless World: Power and Strategy in the Interlinked Economy* (New York, Harper).

Palidda, S (2001) *Devianza e vittimizzazione tra i migranti* (Milano, Fondazione Cariplo ISMU).

Parenti, C (1999) *Lockdown America. Police and Prisons in the Age of Crisis* (London, Verso)

Petersilia, J (1999) 'Parole and Prisoner Reentry in the United States' in M Tonry & J Petersilia (eds) *Prisons. Crime and Justice* (Chicago, University of Chicago Press).

Piore & Sabel (1984) *The Second Industrial Divide: Possibilities for Prosperity* (New York, Basic Books).

Piven & Cloward (1972) *Regulating the Poor. The Functions of Public Welfare* (London, Tavistock).

Reich, R (1991) *The Work of Nations. Preparing Ourselves for 21st Century Capitalism* (New York, Vintage).

Rubinstein, G & Mukamal, D (2002) 'Welfare and Housing — Denial of Benefits to Drug Offenders' in M Mauer & M Chesney-Lind (eds) *Invisible Punishment. The Collateral Consequences of Mass Imprisonment* (New York, New Publishing Group).

Rusche, G & Kirchheimer, O (1939) *Punishment and Social Structure* (New York, Columbia University Press).

Sassen, S (1991) *The Global City: New York, London, Tokyo* (Princeton, Princeton University Press).

Sennet, R (1998) *The Corrosion of Character. The Personal Consequences of Work in the New Capitalism* (New York, Norton).

Simon, J (1987) 'The Emergence of a Risk Society: Insurance, Law, and the State' *Socialist Review*, 95, 61–89.

—— (1993) *Poor Discipline. Parole and the Social Control of the Underclass 1890–1990* (Chicago, University of Chicago Press).

—— (2001) 'Fear and Loathing in Late Modernity: Reflections on the Cultural Sources of Mass Imprisonment in the United States' in D Garland (ed) *Mass Imprisonment. Social Causes and Consequences* (London, Sage).

Sparks, R (2000) 'Perspectives on Risk and Penal Politics' in T Hope & R Sparks (eds) *Crime, Risk and Insecurity* (London, Routledge).

Standing, G (2002) *Beyond the New Paternalism. Basic Security as Equality* (London, Verso).

Taylor, I (1999) *Crime in Context. A Critical Criminology of Market Societies* (Cambridge, Polity Press).

Tonry, M (2001) Why Are US Incarceration Rates so High?' in M Tonry (ed) *Penal Reform in Overcrowded Times* (Oxford, Oxford University Press).

Tournier, P (1999) *Statistiques pénales annuelles du Conseil de l'Europe. Enquête 1997* (Strasbourg, Council of Europe).

Travis, J (2002) 'Invisible Punishment: an Instrument of Social Exclusion' in M Mauer & M Chesney-Lind (eds) *Invisible Punishment* (New York, New Publishing Group).

Van Den Haag, E (1975) *Punishing Criminals* (New York, Basic Books).

Vaughan, B (2000) 'Punishment and Conditional Citizenship' *Punishment and Society*, 2, 23–39.

—— (2002) 'The Punitive Consequences of Consumer Culture' *Punishment and Society*, 4, 195–211.

Wacquant, L (1999) *Les Prisons de la misère* (Paris, Raisons d'Agir).

—— (2001) 'Deadly Symbiosis.When Ghetto and Prison Meet and Mesh' in D Garland (ed) *Mass Imprisonment. Social Causes and Consequences* (London, Sage).

Western, B & Beckett, K (2001) 'Governing Social Marginality: Welfare, Incarceration, and the Transformation of State Policy' in D Garland (ed) *Mass Imprisonment. Social Causes and Consequences*, (London, Sage).

Wilson, JQ (1983) *Thinking About Crime* (New York, Basic Books).

Young, J (1999) *The Exclusive Society* (London, Sage).

Part III

Travels of Discourses of Criminology and Crime Prevention

7

Lombroso's *La Donna Delinquente:* Its Strange Journeys in Italy, England and the USA, Including Scenes of Mutilation and Salvation

NICOLE RAFTER

Cesare Lombroso's *La donna delinquente* (Lombroso and Ferrero, 1893) provides an ideal text for discussions of the relationship of criminology to culture because the book exists in three very different states, each reflecting quite different social circumstances. *La donna delinquente* was originally published in 1893 in Italy, where Lombroso produced it to prove that his famous theory of the born criminal applied to women as well as men. This Italian version of the book bears the imprint of the cultural context in which it was written, and one can trace its impact on subsequent Italian theory and practices concerning female crime. Then, in 1895, just two years after publication of *La donna delinquente*, there appeared an English translation, *The Female Offender* (Lombroso & Ferrero, 1895), which differed radically from the original. This translation bears the imprint of Anglo-American culture, and over time it accumulated its own history, which one can compare with that of *La donna delinquente*. A new English version, this one titled *Criminal Woman* (Lombroso and Ferrero, 2004) and translated by myself and the Italian historian Mary Gibson, was recently published by Duke University Press. *Criminal Woman* differs in crucial respects from both of its predecessors. While its impact remains to be seen, I can speak about the circumstances that gave birth to this new edition and what it is like to be personally involved in a 'cultural voyage'.

In what follows, I describe *La donna delinquente*[1] (1893) as a text, examine the cultural circumstances in which Lombroso produced it, and assess aspects of its impact in Italy. Next I turn to *The Female Offender* (1895), describing ways in which it differs as a text, the cultural circumstances in which it appeared, and its cultural impact in England and the United States. In the third section, I go through the same steps for *Criminal Woman* (2004), except that, instead of assessing its impact – an impossibility at this point – I speak a little about the odd experience of participating in the life of a classic text.

LA DONNA DELINQUENTE (1893)

L'uomo delinquente or *Criminal Man* (Lombroso, 1876), the book in which Lombroso first put forth his theory of the atavistic born criminal, was nearly 15 years old when he started working on *La donna delinquente*. Although Lombroso had revised *L'uomo delinquente* several times, critics continued to attack it. Some complained that he had not used a control group; thus he decided to test his born-criminal theory out on a new group — women — and also to compare female offenders with 'normal' women.[2] Lombroso invited Guglielmo Ferrero, a 19 year old law student, to assist him with the book and, with characteristic generosity, credited Ferrero with co-authorship. The book's full title is *La donna delinquente, la prostituta, e la donna normale*.

The original text of *La donna delinquente* consists of 640 pages organised into four Parts with a total of 31 chapters, plus illustrations and a preface in which Lombroso speaks anxiously about the hostile reception he anticipates for this new effort. The book was apparently reprinted in Italian twice, in 1894 and 1903, before being reissued in 1913 in a new edition by his daughter Gina Lombroso-Ferrero.[3] A 1915 edition (perhaps identical with that of 1913) was reissued in 1923 and 1927. Today, there can be few Italians who have seen the original. In the United States, it is now difficult to obtain even a microfilmed copy of the first edition.

---

[1] *La donna delinquente* was translated into German (1894), French (1896, 1906), and Russian (1897, 1902, and 1909) as well as English, but I will be discussing only the original and the two English translations.

[2] Even in the first (1876) edition of *L'uomo delinquente*, Lombroso included data on criminal women as well as criminal men. However, it was not until *La donna delinquente* that he attempted an extended comparison of female with male criminals. *La donna delinquente* also makes a three-way comparison among female criminals, prostitutes, and 'normal' women.

[3] It is difficult to get clear information on the various early editions and reprints of Lombroso's work. This information was derived from a combination of sources: The National Union Catalog, the Library of Congress's WorldCat listing, and Renzo Villa's study (1985) of *Il deviante e i suoi segni*.

In what ways was *La donna delinquente* shaped by the cultural circumstances in which it was written? It shows the impact of a number of nineteenth-century trends and enthusiasms, including the growing prestige of science (especially Darwinism), a reaction against Enlightenment legal theories, and the fondness for consumer-oriented displays that Walter Benjamin (1999) writes of in *The Arcades Project*. Three other influences, which I will examine in more detail, were the movement for female emancipation, the birth of sexology, and the public debate in Italy over prostitution.[4]

La donna delinquente was produced during a period when Italian feminists were starting to establish formal organisations. Activists in the women's movement were demanding access to education, entrance to the professions, equality within the family, and the right to vote. Lombroso, who was politically liberal and a friend of the prominent feminist Anna Kuliscioff, did not oppose all changes in women's legal status. He was profoundly troubled, however, by the prospect of a fundamental restructuring of gender roles, as shown by his decision to allocate the first major section of *La donna delinquente* to proofs of the inferiority of even normal women. Lombroso argued that women are doomed by evolution to be inferior to men — emotionally, intellectually, morally, and physically. By ridiculing intellectual women as masculine and by insisting on maternity as the natural goal of all women, he scientifically affirmed the wisdom of traditional gender roles and contradicted the vision of female emancipationists.

While the women's movement was unsettling the outer world, it was also working mischief in Lombroso's own home. At the time he embarked on *La donna delinquente*, Lombroso's two daughters, Paola and Gina, were both approaching the age of 20 and growing more independent — a particular problem for a father who already relied on Gina as a research assistant. Moreover, while he was working on the book, Anna Kuliscioff spent a great deal of time with Lombroso's family, dining with them almost nightly and slipping the girls a copy of JS Mill's *The Subjection of Women* (Dolza, 1990). Lombroso's family life, together with the women's movement that Kuliscioff represented, probably inspired some of the passages in *La donna delinquente* where he speaks of women with annoyance and even trepidation. The book's biological 'proofs' of female inferiority were part of a reaction against transformations in women's status (Gibson, 1982; Gibson, 1990; Horn, 1995).

The advent of sexology, another aspect of the cultural context in which Lombroso worked, also leaves its mark on the pages of *La donna delinquente*. Although he was never as focused or systematic in his study of human sexuality

---

[4] Mary Gibson's work is my source for most of the material that follows in this section, including her book on prostitution (1986/1999), her book on Lombroso and the impact of his ideas in Italy (2002), her paper on female deviance and sexuality (2004), and material she generated for our introduction to the new edition of Criminal Woman (Lombroso and Ferrero 2004).

as Richard von Krafft-Ebing, whose work he greatly admired, Lombroso was nonetheless a transitional figure between Victorian prudery and the celebrations of sexual freedom that characterised sexology in the early twentieth century. Lombroso shared many views with earlier nineteenth-century moralists. In keeping with the bourgeois ideology of separate spheres for men and women, he points to the movement of sperm and the immobility of the egg to justify male public activity and female domestic passivity. Claiming that 'primitive' women, including born criminals and born prostitutes, are characterised by an unbridled and masculine sex drive, he touts monogamy as one of the treasures of civilisation produced by evolution. He concludes that white European women no longer desire sexual intercourse except for procreation, the defining act of womanhood.

Yet Lombroso resembled contemporary sexologists in his curiosity about a variety of sexual practices and his interest in cataloguing them. *La donna delinquente* devotes sections to adultery, frigidity, lesbianism, masturbation, and premarital sex. One of its chapters is titled 'Sexual Sensitivity (Lesbianism and Sexual Psychopathy)', and elsewhere, too, Lombroso spends a good deal of time discussing female sexuality and sexual deviance. In a long section on the history of prostitution, Lombroso enumerates its many purposes in the past: to celebrate the gods, to entertain guests, and, in the case of Greek and Renaissance courtesans, to unite beauty with learning. Two chapters analyse the causes and characteristics of contemporary prostitution. Even though Lombroso is sometimes prurient and always anxious to reinforce female chastity or monogamy, his approach contrasts with the silence about sexuality of many earlier writers.

A third influential aspect of the cultural context in which Lombroso worked was the Italian debate over whether prostitution should be prohibited or regulated. Rapid growth of the Italian population was causing mass migration to the cities of both North and South, swelling the ranks of the so-called dangerous classes. A central figure in the iconography of the dangerous classes was the prostitute, a woman seemingly no longer bound by family or morality. To middle-class observers, the hordes of homeless and unemployed women on urban streets were indistinguishable from prostitutes. Actual prostitutes, blamed for the spread of venereal disease, were placed under police supervision and required to live in state-regulated brothels. Under these circumstances, it is not surprising that Lombroso found the prostitute even more threatening and atavistic than the criminal woman. Indeed, a central thesis of *La donna delinquente* is that 'prostitution is closer than criminality to woman's primitive behavior' (Lombroso, 1893: Part III, ch 8.)

What was the impact of *La donna delinquente* in Italy? Some historians have dismissed Lombroso as a ridiculous figure whose writings had little impact on larger policy debates, but in fact he was the leader of a large group of lawyers, physicians, and psychiatrists who constituted the so-called Positivist or Italian School of Criminology, and whose theory of the born criminal dominated debates on criminal justice through the fascist period (Gibson, 2002). Moreover, Lombroso wrote for the popular press as well as professional journals. He and his followers were social activists, eager to influence legislation and public policy.

Mary Gibson (2004) argues that *La donna delinquente* had a significant impact on a range of Italian women, including prostitutes, criminal women, 'normal' women, and lesbians. By maintaining that prostitution is the female equivalent of male crime, Lombroso both criminalised prostitution and sexualised female criminality. By raising the spectre of the atavistic born prostitute, his book helped perpetuate the official state policy of restricting prostitutes to licensed brothels. His positions contributed to the defeat of the abolitionist movement, which had worked to free prostitutes from state control. *La donna delinquente* also reinforced the belief that all female behaviour, including female criminal behaviour, is governed by women's sexual organs. Thus, for generations not only prostitution but also offenses like murder and even theft were analysed in sexual terms. Lombroso's arguments led to an emphasis on moral rather than economic training for female offenders. They also undergirded the view that even 'normal' women lose their reason and self-control during menstruation, pregnancy, nursing, and menopause — a sequence that leaves little time for female self-governance. Only lesbians may have been in some ways shielded by Lombroso's book, and that only because he classified them as a subset of prostitutes, thus helping to keep them invisible (Gibson, 2004).

THE FEMALE OFFENDER (1895)

The Female Offender, excerpted and translated by someone who remains unidentified, runs to 313 pages, about half the length of *La donna delinquente*. It does not indicate that it is only a partial translation. Few if any readers could have known that they were reading excerpts from a longer whole.

Nor, of course, could readers have understood *how* the English version related to the Italian original. Organised into 18 chapters, *The Female Offender* covers roughly the same ground as Parts III and IV of *La donna delinquente*. It omits Lombroso's preface, all of Part I on the Normal Woman, all of Part II on Female Criminology, and chapters in Part IV on 'Sexual Sensitivity,' 'The Born Prostitute,' and 'The Occasional Prostitute'. Without notice, *The Female Offender* also omits shorter passages on breasts and genitals, menstruation, sexual precocity, fecundity, female erotism, and virility. In addition (and again without notice), *The Female Offender* shifts Lombroso's final chapter, 'Hysterical Offenders,' to an earlier position in the book.

Taken together, these omissions and changes seriously distort the original. For example, for over a century no one realised that to reach his conclusions about criminal women, Lombroso had in fact used a control group of 'normal' women. (This was one of the first efforts in scientific criminology to construct a control group.) Moreover, *The Female Offender* masks its distortions of

Lombroso's original. The edition's major drawback, however, is that it simplifies Lombroso's arguments, making it impossible for readers to grasp the complexity of his thought.

Where it does cover the original, *The Female Offender* translates Lombroso literally but listlessly into sanitised and sometimes confusing English prose. Lombroso's original, hastily written like most of his works, presents many problems of interpretation; instead of confronting these problems, the translator of *The Female Offender* (who evidently had no criminological background) reproduces them, for example by translating an Italian pronoun of ambiguous referent into an equally ambiguous English pronoun. Worse yet, *The Female Offender* drains even short phrases of sexual content. (In a passage describing a woman referred to as 'MR' for instance, it reports that she 'resisted the profligate designs of her father' (Lombroso & Ferrero, 1895: 198). The original, however, clearly states that MR 'resisted her father, who wanted to rape her' (*stuprarla*) (Lombroso and Ferrero, 1893: 475).) As a result, *The Female Offender* is a pedestrian, bowdlerised, and sometimes incomprehensible text.

Originally published by Unwin in London and Appleton in New York, *The Female Offender* replaced Lombroso's own preface with an introduction by W. Douglas Morrison, an English cleric whose contribution has nothing to do with female offenders. This English edition was reprinted 14 times between 1897 and 1980, after which a New Mexico press brought out a 'new and expanded edition' which was actually one-third the length of the Appleton original (Lombroso, 1983).

In what ways was *The Female Offender* shaped by the cultural circumstances in which it was written? Two circumstances seem particularly relevant: the Anglo-American world's thirst for scientific explanations of crime and its attitudes toward sexuality.

In England and the United States in the early 1890s, a shift away from free will accounts of criminal behaviour and toward positivist explanations created a demand for scientific criminology. Some proto-Lombrosian work was being produced in England (J Bruce Thomson, 1870; Henry Maudsley, 1874) and in the States (Richard Dugdale, 1877; the Elmira Reformatory (Rafter, 1997)). Articles on Lombroso's work were turning up in the popular press, and interest was further stimulated by the 1890 publication of Havelock Ellis's *The Criminal*, the first English-language book on criminal anthropology. However, men and women who read only English as yet had no access to a full-length book by Lombroso, nor would they until 1911 (Lombroso, 1911; Lombroso-Ferrero, 1911). The desire for something substantive by Lombroso himself about the criminal may, ironically, have led to the cuts in *The Female Offender*. The publishers may have simply decided that material on normal women and prostitution would be far less interesting to English and American readers at that point than the hardcore material on anomalies and atavisms.

Moreover, the translator and publishers seem to have been exceedingly anxious to avoid mentioning either normal or deviant sexuality. Krafft-Ebing's

Psychopathia Sexualis was not published in English until 1892, and Havelock Ellis's first book on human sexuality, *Man and Woman*, did not appear till 1894. The reading public in England and America, whatever they might have been doing in private, were not yet ready for Lombroso's anecdotes of nymphomania and saffic prison orgies. The sexual content of his book was a little too advanced for this audience, and hence, no doubt, the decision to delete it.

As for the cultural impact of *The Female Offender* in England and the United States, it is safe to say that no other book can rival its influence on subsequent thinking about women and crime.[5] Lombroso bequeathed four interrelated (albeit sometimes contradictory) concepts to subsequent understandings of female criminality. The first concerned the nature of female crime, which according to Lombroso is fundamentally biological in origin. While he was not the first to equate female deviance with sexuality, he powerfully reinforced the association by confirming it 'scientifically'. The effects reverberated throughout Anglo-American criminal justice systems: female crime such as shoplifting was explained in terms of sublimated sexuality, and in many jurisdictions girls arrested for delinquency were automatically given vaginal examinations to determine their virginity. Related to Lombroso's emphasis on the biological nature of female criminality is the notion that female criminals are less evolved than both male criminals and law-abiding women, an idea that throughout the twentieth century reinforced infantalising disciplinary modalities for women offenders, leading them to be treated as errant children.

A second major part of Lombroso's legacy to the Anglo-American world is the idea that criminal women are more masculine than law-abiding women. This concept reemerged with considerable fanfare in the 1970s with the publication of Freda Adler's *Sisters in Crime* (1975), a work arguing that women's crime rates are on the rise because women (especially women of colour) are becoming more like men. Closely related to the masculinity thesis is the criminological tendency to conceptualise female criminality as what Frances Heidensohn (1996: 114) calls 'a beauty contest,' with the prize of being deemed 'reformable' awarded to the most feminine (meaning, among other things, Caucasian) offenders.

A third facet of Lombroso's legacy in English-speaking countries is the idea that not only criminal women but also 'normal' women are inherently deviant, walking bundles of pathology that can at any moment explode or dissolve into criminality. This pathologisation of ordinary womanhood authorised physicians and other normalisers to intervene more frequently and deeply in women's lives than in those of men. Additionally, it made female sexuality automatically suspect.

Fourth and finally, Lombroso's work on the female offender helped establish 'normality' itself as a standard for conceptualising law-abiding behaviour in English-speaking countries (see also Horn, 1995). This standard has been applied to male behaviour as well, but there remained alternative ways of

---

[5] Much of what I say here applies to Anglophone Canada and Australia as well.

thinking about male deviance (heroic rebellion, for example, or the sowing of wild oats). Female deviance, by contrast, almost always ran the risk in England and the United States of being labelled abnormal and hence pathological. This put law-abiding women, too, in peril, for any woman who challenged the status quo could be deemed abnormal.

In many respects, *The Female Offender*'s legacy in English-speaking countries paralleled the impact of *La donna delinquente* on Italian thinking about women's nature and female criminality. This gives us an example of two disparate versions of a single text having a similar impact in disparate cultures. In Anglo-American countries, much more so than in Italy, Lombroso became a whipping boy for feminist criminologists in the 1970s and 1980s. Dorie Klein (1973), Carol Smart (1976), and others used Lombroso's pronouncements on women to expose the sexist biases in criminology in general. In Italy, the reaction against Lombroso was more muted, but this probably had less to do with differences between the two texts than with international differences in the women's movement and in the goals of criminology itself (Rafter and Heidensohn, 1995; Pitch 1995).

CRIMINAL WOMAN (2004)

The purpose of the new edition of *Criminal Woman*, as of its companion edition of *Criminal Man* (Lombroso, 2006), is twofold: to provide, for the first time, adequate English translations of Lombroso's criminological work, and to lay foundations for an emerging new generation of Lombroso scholarship. The new editions aim at facilitating Lombroso scholarship in fields as diverse as anthropology, art history, criminology, and rhetoric; Italian and European history; the history of science, medicine, and psychiatry; law and legal history; studies of race and ethnicity; and gender studies. Our introduction to *Criminal Woman* (Lombroso and Ferrero, 2004) examines in-depth one of the issues I have looked at briefly here: the impact of Lombroso's work on subsequent theory and practice in the area of women and crime. However, Mary Gibson and I are much less interested in trying to answer questions than in providing materials for others to use in answering long-standing questions and formulating new ones.

To select material for inclusion in the new edition, we developed three criteria:
1. complete coverage of Lombroso's arguments and adherence to the order in which he presented them;
2. clear representation of Lombroso's procedures, including his use of tables, illustrations, and citations;
3. reduction in bulk of the original to make the new edition readable and affordable.

About half of the new edition is given over to previously untranslated material from *La donna delinquente*, while the other half consists of a compressed and retranslated version of the material covered by *The Female Offender*. We have included Lombroso's own preface and added explanatory footnotes, a glossary, and an index. Fully translating Lombroso's original title, we have titled our edition *Criminal Woman, the Prostitute, and the Normal Woman.*

Many of our key translation decisions followed from an assessment of differences between Lombroso's goals and ours. In writing *La donna delinquente* Lombroso's goal was to advance his theory of criminal anthropology by applying it to criminal women. In translating *La donna delinquente* our goal was to give English-speaking scholars and students access to the book's text — not just the bits and pieces translated by *The Female Offender* but all four of its Parts. While we were interested in Lombroso's methods of proof and types of evidence, we did not consider it crucial to present every one of his hundreds of examples. Moreover, our interest in accessibility meant that our translation had to be a good deal shorter than the 640-page original. It followed that we had to boil down the original while preserving its meanings, procedures, and key examples.

Reducing *La donna delinquente* to manageable size while retaining the original Parts and chapter structure involved cutting pages, paragraphs, and — within single sentences — words that seemed unnecessary. Our edition runs to 300 pages, over 200 of them translations of Lombroso's text. We eliminated two sorts of material: repetitions and examples. Lombroso was untroubled by repetitions and indeed, he often presents material repeatedly, approaching it from new angles or combining it in new ways with other topics. We did away with most of his overlaps.

We also eliminated many of the examples Lombroso presents in support of his positions. To Lombroso as a scientist, a wealth of examples was important because it signified a wealth of scientific evidence for his theory. The sheer quantity of evidence mattered less to us, however. From today's point of view, moreover, the 'science' of Lombroso's examples is often dubious or even ludicrous. (Some of his contemporaries shared this opinion.) Our policy for each of Lombroso's new points was to translate one or two of the more vivid or clarifying examples but to omit the rest.

Our cuts created two 'translation effects'. First, they minimise Lombroso's long-windedness. In this respect, our translation somewhat distorts the original. Second, by cutting some of the book's outlandish examples, our translation may, ironically, make the text seem more rational and scientifically sound that it in fact was. In this respect, too, our cuts may slightly skew Lombroso's original. However, without them the book would have remained inaccessible to most contemporary readers. We identify these translation effects in our introduction, warning readers of their impact.

Lombroso wrote in formal, scholarly Italian, using medical and scientific terms that are today obsolete. To twenty-first century Italians, Lombroso's language is old-fashioned, difficult, and at times even incomprehensible. Its datedness is in part an effect of the passage of time. To educated contemporaries, Lombroso's language would have seemed appropriately learned, and among non-scientists, his obscure terminology might have had a credentialing effect, increasing his credibility.

Because one of our goals was to make Lombroso's work accessible, we translated obscure words into more familiar terms. We also tried to relax his prose style, making it slightly more colloquial. Our rule-of-thumb was to write for our audience, not his. By contrast, we did not aim at entirely colloquial English. We attempted to make his prose comprehensible to modern readers while preserving some of its formality.

In working on this translation we occasionally flinched at reproducing Lombroso's gaffs and missteps — his sloppy use of numbers, uncritical examples, unsophisticated generalisations, internal contractions, and overall incoherence. Our temptation here was akin to what translation theorists call 'ennoblement' — the temptation, confronted most often by poetry translators, to make translated material more flowery or elevated than it was originally. If our temptation was similar to that of ennoblers, however, it was certainly not identical: few translators can have had to cope as we did with outright foolishness on the part of the source-author.

In our view, Lombroso's work is historically valuable despite its scientific and logical naïveté. In fact, it is valuable partly *because* it so clearly reveals scientific and scientistic vulnerabilities, making them available for study. For better or worse, moreover, one outstanding quality of Lombroso's work is its magnificent tangle of brilliance and nonsense, the way it combines what a recent biographer calls Lombroso's 'encyclopedic ambition, his characteristically extreme mental adventuresomeness, and his titanic failures' (Guarnieri, 2000: 14). Our key concern was to produce a full (if abbreviated) and accurate translation, a concern that led us to explicitly resolve to include the warts. We still flinched, but having recognised the temptation to hide Lombroso's faults, we were better able to resist it.

What cultural circumstances encouraged Mary Gibson and me to prepare this new edition? One was the growth, over the past 35 years or so, of an interest in the history of crime and of criminology. Another was the growth of interest in Lombroso himself.[6] Europeans, especially, have started realising that although he was a wretched scientist, even by the standards of his own day, Lombroso was a great myth-maker. Moreover, as a writer he worked along major intellectual faultlines, in the contested areas where various trends in social thought about gender, race, and deviance collided. A third cultural factor that helped prepare

---

[6] Between 1975 and 2003, at least eight books on Lombroso were published in Italian and another six books in languages other than Italian and English (Baima Bollone 1992; Bulferetti 1975; Ch'en 1992; Colombo 1975; Dolza 1990; Drapkin 1977; Frigessi 2003; Gadebusch Bondio 1995; Guarnieri 2000; Leschiutta 1996; Mella 1999; Lombroso (Reig and Reig) 1975; Quiroz 1977; Villa 1985). In another sign of the renewed interest, a thousand-page collection of extracts from various Lombroso works (including but not limited to the criminological studies) appeared in Italian in 1995 (Lombroso 1995). Also see Becker and Wetzell 2006; Gibson 2002; Horn 2003; Pick 1989; Mucchielli 1994; Rafter 1997; and Wetzell 2000.

the ground for the new translation of *La donna delinquente* was the upsurge of interest over the previous several decades in gender and crime, and in the gendering of criminology.

On the personal level, Mary Gibson and I had a selfish reason for undertaking translations of Lombroso's work. While working separately on Lombroso's work and influence, we had been repeatedly frustrated by impediments to tracing the development of his ideas over time. *La donna delinquente* was all but inaccessible in the Italian original, and we knew that the 1895 English translation was misleading. The situation was even worse regarding *L'uomo delinquente*, which went through five Italian editions, the last of them four volumes long (Lombroso, 1876, 1878, 1884, 1889, 1896–1897). No one knew how the two partial English translations of *L'uomo delinquente* (Lombroso, 1911; Lombroso-Ferrero, 1911) related to Lombroso's originals. How could we hope to make intelligent generalisations about a body of work so large and inaccessible? We were also frustrated by the misstatements about Lombroso that appeared in many standard criminological texts. (For a review of these errors, see Rafter, 2006.)

Another personal ingredient in this cultural stew was the fact that Mary and I, as feminists teaching the history of criminology, were frequently exposed to materials generated by feminist criminologists on the basis of reading *The Female Offender*. We were eager to provide other feminists with better tools for their research. We decided to work on *La donna delinquente* before translating *L'uomo delinquente*, not only because the former would be easier to condense than the five editions of *L'uomo delinquente* but also because we were especially intrigued by Lombroso's pronouncements on women and anxious to set the record about them straight.

What has it been like to be part of this cultural journey? The process of translating *La donna delinquente* and writing hundreds of explanatory footnotes was long and sometimes tedious, but it was also very pleasurable. Much of the pleasure came from working with Mary Gibson, from whom I learned a great deal about the history of Italian women, Italian criminology, and the Italian language. For me personally, as well as for the text, this has been a cultural journey, one that has taken me into new areas of inquiry and brought me intellectual joy. Another part of the pleasure came from my odd sense of colleagueship with Lombroso himself. Although I disagreed with him at almost every turn, I enjoyed the intimacy with his thought processes. I came to know the structure of his ideation and his intellectual habits, including his tendency to go limp and vague when he sensed that he was approaching a logical contradiction. Lombroso cared passionately about his work, and he would have loved knowing that this book is still of interest over a century after he produced it.

While I undertook this project for myself, not Lombroso, over time I developed a sense of mission, a desire to save him from misunderstandings, to correct the misrepresentations of his work and somehow resurrect him as a thinker. Lombroso was very much 'there' for me as we worked. Mary and I sometimes grew irritated with the obscurities of his prose and impatient with his troglodytic views about women. But at the same time, we became fond of him and felt a sense of companionship as we struggled to complete the latest transformation of his book on criminal women. There were always three of us on this cultural journey.

REFERENCES

Adler, F (1975) *Sisters in Crime* (New York, McGraw-Hill).
Becker, P & Wetzell, R (eds) (2006) *Criminals and Their Scientists* (Cambridge, Cambridge University Press).
Benjamin, W (1999) The Arcades Project, H Eiland and K McLaughlin (trans) (Cambridge, Mass, The Belknap Press of Harvard University Press).
Bollone, B & Luigi, P (1992) *Cesare Lombroso: ovvero, il principio del'irresponsabilità* (Turin, Societa editrice internazionale).
Bulferetti, Luigi (1975) *Cesare Lombroso* (Turin, Unione tipografico-editrice torinese).
Ch'en, H (1992) *I ch'uan yu fan tsui* (Pei-ching,Chun Chung ch'u pan she).
Colombo, G (1975) *La scienza infelice: Il museo di antropologia criminale di Cesare Lombroso* (Turin, P. Boringhieri).
Dolza, D (1990) *Essere figlie di Lombroso: Due donne intellettuali tra '800 e '900* (Milan, Franco Angeli).
Drapkin, I (1977) *Cesare Lombroso: el creador de la moderna criminología científica* (Buenos Aires, Congreso Judío Latinoamericano).
Dugdale, RL (1877) *The Jukes: A Study in Crime, Pauperism, Disease and Heredity; also Further Studies of Criminals* (New York, G.P Putnam's Sons).
Ellis, H (1890) *The Criminal* (London, Walter Scott).
—— (1894) *Man and Woman: A Study of Human Secondary Sexual Characters* (London, Scott).
Frigressi, D (2003) *Cesare Lombroso* (Turin, Giulio Einaudi).
Gadebusch Bondio, M (1995) *Die Rezeption der kriminalanthropologischen Theorien von Cesare Lombroso in Deutschland von 1880–1914* (Husum, Matthiesen).
Gibson, M (1982) 'The Female Offender and the Italian School of Criminal Anthropology' *Journal of European Studies* , 12, 155–165.
——(1990) 'On the Insensitivity of Women: Science and the Woman Question in Liberal Italy, 1890–1910' *Journal of Women's History*, 2, 11–41.
——(1986/1999) *Prostitution and the State in Italy, 1860–1915* (Columbus, OH, Ohio State University Press).
——(2002) *Born to Crime: Cesare Lombroso and the Italian Origins of Biological Criminology* (Westport, CT, Praeger).
——(2004) 'Labeling Women Deviant: Heterosexual Women, Prostitutes, and Lesbians in Early Criminological Discourse' in P Wilson (ed) *Gender and the Private Sphere in Italy* (London, Palgrave Macmillan) 89–104.

Guarnieri, L (2000) *L'atlante criminale: vita scriteriata di Cesare Lombroso.* (Milan, Mondadori).

Heidensohn, F (1985/1996) *Women and Crime* (London, Macmillan).

Horn, DG (1995) 'This Norm Which Is Not One: Reading the Female Body in Lombroso's Anthropology' Ch4, 109–128 in J Terry and J Urla (eds) *Deviant Bodies* (Bloomington, IN, Indiana University Press).

—— (2003) *The Criminal Body: Lombroso and the Anatomy of Deviance* (New York, Routledge).

Klein, D (1973) 'The Etiology of Female Crime' *Issues in Criminology*, 8, 3–30.

von Krafft-Ebing, R (1892) *Psychopathia Sexualis* (Philadelphia, F A Davis).

Leschiutta, P (1996) *Palimsesti del carcere: Cesare Lombroso e le scritture proibite* (Naples, Liguori).

Lombroso, C (1876) *L'uomo delinquente studiato in rapporto alla antropologia, alla medicina legale ed alle discipline carcerarie,* 1st edn (Milan, Hoepli).

—— (1878) *L'uomo delinquente in rapporto all'antropologia, giurisprudenza e alle discipline carcerarie.* 2nd edn (Turin, Bocca).

——(1884) *L'uomo delinquente in rapporto all'antropologia, giurisprudenza ed alle discipline carcerarie. Delinquente-nato e pazzo morale.* 3rd edn (Turin, Bocca).

—— (1889) *L'uomo delinquente in rapporto all'antropologia, alla giurisprudenza ed alle discipline carcerarie.* 2 vols. 4th edn (Turin, Bocca).

—— (1896–1897) *L'uomo delinquente in rapporto all'antropologia, alla giurisprudenza ed alle discipline carcerarie.* 5th edn: 4 vols, including *L'atlante* (Turin, Bocca).

——(1911) *Crime: Its Causes and Remedies* (Boston, Little, Brown).

—— (1975) (Joe Luis Peset Reig and Mariano Peset Reig) *Lombroso y la escuela positivista italiana* (Madrid, CS de I.C).

——(1983) *Basic Characteristics of Women Criminals. New and Expanded Edition* (Albuquerque, The Foundation for Classical Reprints).

——(1995) *Delitto, Genio, Follia: Scritti scelt I* D Frigessi, F Giacanelli & L Mangoni (eds) (Turin, Bollati Boringhieri).

—— (2006) *Criminal Man* (translated and with a new introduction by Mary Gibson and Nicole Hahn Rafter) (Duke University Press).

—— & Ferrero, G (1893) *La donna delinquente, La prostituta e la donna normale* (Turin, Roux) 640.

—— (1895) *The Female Offender. With an Introduction by W Douglas Morrison* (London, Unwin; New York, Appleton) 313.

—— (2004) *Criminal Woman, the Prostitute, and the Norman Woman* Translated and edited by N Hahn Rafter and M Gibson (Durham, NC, Duke University Press).

Lombroso-Ferrero, G (1911) *Criminal Man, According to the Classification of Cesare Lombroso, Briefly Summarised by His Daughter Gina Lombroso-Ferrero* (New York and London, GP Putnam's Sons).

Maudsley, H (1874) *Responsibility in Mental Disease* (New York, D Appleton and Company).

Mella, R (1999) *Lombroso e os anarquistas* (Vigo, Edicions Xerais de Galicia).

Mucchielli, L (ed) (1994) *Histoire de la criminologie française* (Paris, L'Harmattan).

Pick, D (1989) *Faces of Degeneration* (Cambridge, Cambridge University Press).

Pitch, T (1995) 'Feminist Politics, Crime, Law and Order in Italy' in N Hahn Rafter and F Heidensohn (eds) *International Feminist Perspectives in Criminology: Engendering a Discipline*. (Buckingham, UK, Open University Press).

Quiroz Cuaron, A (1977) *Homenaje a Cesar Lombroso* (Mexico, Secretaria de Gobernación).

Rafter, NH (1997) *Creating Born Criminals. Champaign* (Ill, University of Illinois Publishing Group).

——(2006) 'Cesare Lombroso and the Origins of Criminology: Rethinking Criminological Tradition' in S Henry and MM Lanier (eds) *Essential Criminology Reader* (Boulder CO, Westview Press).

—— & Heidensohn, F (eds) (1995) *International Feminist Perspectives in Criminology: Engendering a Discipline* (Buckingham, United Kingdom, Open University Press).

Salvatore, RD & Aguirre, C (eds) (1996) *The Birth of the Penitentiary in Latin American: Essays on Criminology, Prison Reform, and Social Control, 1830–1940* (Austin, University of Texas Press).

Smart, C (1976) *Women, Crime, and Criminology: A Feminist Critique* (London, Routledge & Kegan Paul).

Thomson, JB (1870) 'The Psychology of Criminals' *Journal of Mental Science*, 17, 321–350.

Villa, R (1985) *Il deviante e i suoi segni: Lombroso e la nascita del'antropologia criminale* (Milano, Franco Angeli).

Wetzell, RF (2000) *Inventing the Criminal: A History of German Criminology, 1880–1945* (Chapel Hill, University of North Carolina Press).

8

The Governance of Crime in Italy: Global Tendencies and Local Peculiarities

ROSSELLA SELMINI

INTRODUCTION

One of the most prominent phenomena of the last decades in the field of crime control policies is probably the development of new strategies to address the generalised processes of increase in crime rates and in levels of insecurity in communities. Under the titles 'new crime prevention measures' or 'security policies', or 'community safety' we find a growing body of scientific research and literature, of policies and programmes, of discourse and languages which share the common attempt to single out new approaches to crime prevention and control in many Western democracies. This new approach has already been well analysed and described in a rich comparative criminological literature,[1] and is characterised by some — at least apparently — common features, which can be summarised as follows:

- the quest to identify strategies and measures different from the traditional penal intervention;
- the attention towards victims of crime;
- the attempt to combine different kinds of measures;
- the focus on the local level;
- the responsibilisation of new actors in the field of crime control and consequently the need for cooperation, under the title of 'partnership' or 'multi-agency approach';
- the attention paid to research on crime and prevention and to evaluation.[2]

---

[1] For Europe, see for instance Hebberecht & Sack (1997: 21), which notes how 'several European countries have developed new discourses and new practices and structures with regard to crime prevention in the 1980s. This change in orientation of crime policy in Europe came close on the heels of a very similar trend in North America'.

[2] See, among the many who analysed these features, Robert (1991a).

All these features have been, during recent years, well investigated under many different perspectives, including — as already mentioned — the comparative, which is a particularly fruitful one, given the intensification of processes of exchange and 'policy transfer' characterising this field.

Starting from this increasing evidence of the diffusion and convergence of ideas, languages and practices of crime control (Garland, 2001), it seems more and more interesting to investigate this process for a better understanding of the mechanisms of and reasons for such flows and transfers, which are, as has been noted, 'both more complex and less well elucidated empirically and theoretically than is commonly assumed' (Newburn and Sparks, 2004:3).

In this essay I will try to explore these processes in the particular field of security and crime prevention policies developed in Italy in the last decade. The type of 'transfer' in question is related to some specific issues: the way to define the same policies under different titles in different contexts, the influence of certain ideas and practices in a particular socio-political context, and how this context adopts and re-shapes those ideas and practices. At the same time, I will offer a very sketchy framework about the development of an Italian way to security and prevention. I will focus on some specific issues in contemporary Italian security policies, such as the use of the word 'security'; the model of crime prevention emerging from the convergence between the national context and the external influences; the idea of partnership (a *leit-motif* of the security policies, as we currently understand them) and the involvement of community organisations in crime prevention.[3]

These issues are the prevailing ones because they show, probably much more clearly than others, how the general process of policy transfer is subjected to a complex mix of variables which go from cultural aspects to structural factors, from the features of institutional and political context to the relationships among some criminologists, and so on. As has been clearly noted: 'the emergence and adoption of crime control practices, policies and technologies are subject to a much more complex mix of structural, subjective and simply serendipitous influences' (Newburn and Sparks, 2004: 6).

Some Preliminary Remarks About the Word 'Security': Or the New Meaning of an Old Word

The development of security policies, as we currently understand them, is a recent phenomenon in Italy. It is only at the beginning of the 1990s,[4] in fact

---

[3] Other interesting fields of observation of the policy transfer processes will remain outside this article: the issue of police, for instance, which is, in my opinion, one of the most affected by these dynamics.

[4] This late origin is rather common in Southern European countries (see Recasens & Brunet (2001) for Spain, Da Agra, Quintas & Fonseca (2001) for Portugal & Vidali...

that we can see the emergence of a social reaction against ordinary crime, a growing interest of institutions towards citizens' fears and concerns about crime, and consequently the development of a body of policies and of a related new vocabulary about crime and crime prevention.

The key word of this new vocabulary is, paradoxically, a very old one in the Italian context, ie the term security (*sicurezza*) which is however now used without its traditional adjective of public (*pubblica*). It is with the phrase 'security policies' that we name, since the beginning of the 1990s, a set of practices, strategies and policies both of crime prevention and of social reassurance adopted by local authorities[5] and often different from the traditional measures of the criminal justice system. The concept of security, which is given, at least apparently, a similar meaning by different actors, is notwithstanding much more complex and problematic than it was in the past. Once separated from its usual adjective of 'public' (which immediately recalls the interventions of criminal justice apparatus), and once entered in the political arena, security has became an *omnicomprensivo* word, whose content is defined time by time, according to the different interests of the actors involved. Taking in mind this vagueness and ambiguity of the concept, I will try nonetheless to clarify the meaning and the use of the concept, starting from the specific Italian socio-political and cultural context.[6]

First of all, the abandonment of the adjective 'public', clearly shows the rejection of an idea of security merely confined to the protection of the public from certain crimes. In Italy 'security' is now intended as a general condition which implies strategies directed not only to the prevention of certain behaviours, but also to a positive strengthtening of public perceptions of safety (Zedner, 2000: 201).

The attempts to explain what is 'new' in the use of the old word security wavers between a delimitation of its meaning and the attempt, only superficially contradictory, to enlarge it.

(2001) for Greece). Nonetheless, in the last decade, in Italy the security policies have rapidly assumed the features they already have in other European contexts of the North and the Centre. The delay, which might be very interesting to analyse in the perspective of 'cultural travels' and which is related to the specific socio-political and cultural Italian context, is better investigated in Selmini (1999). About the origin of security policies in Italy see also Pavarini (1994).

[5] With the term 'local authority' I mean local governments, ie Municipalities, Provinces and Regions.

[6] It worth noting that, speaking of an 'Italian context', I do not consider, here, the great difference, also in the development of security policies, existing between Northern and Southern Italy, where these policies are not as wide-spread or advanced as they are in the rest of the country. I could not embark, here, on the issue of 'domestic' travels of ideas and policies about security, which would be a very interesting analysis in the Italian case, considering the multiple differences between the North and the South. My remarks will mainly consider the security policies developed in Northern and Centre Italy, and especially in some regions of the North.

In the first case, the favourite adjectives accompanying the word security are 'local' or 'urban', to highlight the fact that the place where these policies can better be implemented and show their effects is the city or the neighbourhood; secondly, this also means that those who are responsible for the citizens' safety at a local level are the local governments' representatives.[7]

The second approach — the extension of the meaning of security, which is not at all alternative to the first one — replaces the word 'public' with the adjective 'integrated'.[8] 'Integrated security policies' is now a wide-spread and successful slogan in the political and administrative discourses. Once again, the intention is to give security policies a wider meaning, emphasising how different approaches can converge to guarantee not only the absence of threats, but also the positive attempts to promote social inclusion and a more general well-being of the citizens. From this point of view, what needs to be integrated are the various local projects and the local policies with the national ones. The word 'integrated', especially in political discourse, recalls the idea that the 'new' security policies should be able to deal with the symptoms of crime and its causes, namely to combine social and situational measures, or, in other words, to combine crime prevention and social reassurance with crime control and disuasion.[9]

The issue of integration has to do also with the question of partnership: if the way to promote citizens' security lies in a mixture of different actions, policies, and strategies, — as recommended in Italy and elsewhere — various actors need to develop a new way to work together.

If the adjectives local/urban and integrated share the attempt to modernise the concept of security policies, they differ in the idea of who is the main actor of this process of redefinition of security and in the kind of the relationships between the two main actors involved: local and central governments. In the case

---

[7] In Italy there are twenty regional governments, established in 1970, which, over three decades, have increased their responsibilities and competencies, especially after a recent administrative and constitutional reform (Vandelli, 2003). About the origin of regional governments and, above all, about the great differences existing among regions of the Centre-North and of the South, in terms of economic development, social welfare and civic traditions, see Putnam (1997). The same occurred for the Municipalities, which already had a substantial body of competencies especially in social policies at a local level.

[8] The same word is used in some other European countries to qualify those approaches to security able to combine social/structural measures together with administrative/situational prevention. For a comparative analysis on this point, see Hebberecht & Duprez (2001: 371).

[9] A mixture which, even if rather successful in the political discourses and rhetoric, is however the expression of a paradox and of an inherent contradiction of these policies, namely the fact that they represent, at the same time, an 'actuarial' and a more structural approach to crime problems (Van Swaanningen, 1998: 145). For a deep analysis of the crossing and overlapping of these two approaches, see also Cartuyvels (1996).

of the local/urban security policies, the role of local government (regions and municipalities, as already mentioned) is emphasised. In the idea of integrated security, what emerges is the necessity of balancing powers and responsibilities between local and national institutions.

I will go further into these issues in the following pages. What is probably now clear is the fact that, from the outset, in the Italian context the word security has always been used, by different actors and in different places, to qualify a new way of thinking and acting around crime issues comprehensive of both crime reduction and prevention and of social reassurance.

As distinct from what happened in other contexts,[10] crime prevention policies in Italy are considered part of a general strategy for citizens' security, and the concept of prevention is not so important as it is in other European countries. Not even the concept is used to describe those measures and policies addressed at a more general intervention on the social level, as it is in France, or in Belgium, where, on the contrary, and rather interestingly, the word 'sécurité' is mainly referred to formal control and public order practices.[11]

This can be explained by the fact that Italian criminal justice system is strictly based on a formalistic concept of prevention as a function of the criminal law, and that consequently 'prevention' itself never received a great deal of attention in Italian criminological discourse or in control and policing practices.

The preliminary question here, however, concerns the emergence of crime as a feature of public discourse. Under what conditions precisely does such discourse emerge, and why? The answer we can give is of course, only tentative, and is linked with the more general structure of social relationships and dynamics of Italian history in recent decades.

The Emergence of Crime and Fear of Crime[12]

In recent Italian history, the emergence of 'crime' as a central question of public debate coincided with a crucial transition from a society strongly divided along class and political lines (or anyway so perceived and described by its members)

---

[10] I refer here especially to the British experience, in which one can distinguish two phases of development, from a strategy mainly, if not exclusively, based on crime prevention to a wider policy based on the concept of 'community safety', comprehensive of both prevention and reassurance at a local level. For a thorough analysis see Crawford (1997).

[11] For this distinction between 'sécurité' and 'prévention' see Hebberecht & Duprez (2001). About how these two words have been used to indicate the move from a social prevention approach to a more repressive and situational one in the content of the 'contrats de sécurité' see, for France Roche (1999) and for Belgium Cartuyvels and Hebberecht (2001).

[12] An earlier — and partially different — version of this section has already been published in Melossi & Selmini (2000).

to a society where the central sections of the working-class became incorporated within the established system of governance. From this perspective, a crucial protracted transition took place in the 1970s, when a number of social processes began to unfold. First, the role of the police started changing from being a public order force engaged in the control and repression of the Left and the working class to a force that is more and more supposed to deal with 'ordinary' crime (Della Porta & Reiter, 1994). Second, crime (as represented in official statistics) increased dramatically, especially the kind that Garland has recently termed a 'criminality of the self' (ie property crime (Barbagli, 1995)). Third, socio-economic change brought 'to power' the organised working-class but also at the same time its nemesis, 'post-Fordism' (decline of the factory, decline of work ethics, etc.). Fourth, a general process of class fragmentation ensued that marked both a deep decline in the self-understanding of large sectors of the population as 'working class', and increasing symptoms of social disorganisation especially among working class youth (such as the sudden and huge creation of a drug culture and market after the mid-1970s).

Until recently, however, phenomena of fear and 'moral panic' have not been very relevant in the public arena or the political agenda. In the second half of the 1970s and in the 1980s, institutions, public opinion and political parties directed their attention towards the Mafia — and related forms of organised crime — and political terrorism. In both cases, Italy experienced the outbreak of a widespread moral panic and the emergence of a law and order campaign, accompanied by a strong law enforcement tendency in criminal policies.[13] Only in a few cases, however, did the Mafia and political terrorism give rise to a community-based reaction, except of course for the most politicised sectors of the public opinion, especially on the Left. Even then, public opinion did not orient its requests towards more punishment, the death penalty, and so on. The alarm surrounding events involving the Mafia and terrorism neither extended to other less serious forms of crime, nor gave rise to a widespread feeling of lack of safety, such as we have experienced latterly.

According to Massimo Pavarini's view (1994), both concern about crime and demands for safety remained low because demands for political change and democratic participation channelled whatever may have existed of feelings of fear and lack of security. Consistent with such views one should note that in Italy there have been two strong increases in the recorded crime rate, the first in the 1960s and the second in the 1990s (Barbagli, 1995). A rise in fear of crime and social alarm[14] developed however only around the second of these, together

---

[13] If one analyses the articles appeared in the journal that marked the appearance of a 'critical criminology' in Italy & La Questione Criminale (1975–81), one will find that topics of 'law and order' are very present — they are however never coupled with so-called 'common' crime but always with 'political' repression.

[14] In Italy, studies about fear and concern about crime, feelings of lack of safety and also victimisation, have been conducted only recently and in most cases they refer...

with a decrease of political and social participation, as we will see in a section below.

The most recent — and also the most updated and reliable — source of information about these issues is however the first national victimisation survey conducted for the first time at the end of 1997 and repeated in 2002, by the Italian National Institute of Statistics (ISTAT). The sample used in this research is rather substantial (50,000 families) and we can consider the results more reliable than any other information gathered until now. The study's authors come to the conclusion that 'in our country too, the feeling of lack of safety not only exists, but has become a serious social phenomenon, the importance of which cannot be neglected' (Barbagli, 1998: 50). In fact, 29 per cent of Italians say they feel unsafe walking alone at night in the area where they live (ISTAT, 1999:131). In the more recent survey of 2002, this percentage is of 27 (ISTAT, 2003: 118).

A further result, which should be taken carefully into consideration, is the difference emerging between the typical victim of crime, and the typical individual who expresses feelings of lack of safety. Risk of victimisation (generally, but above all for predatory crimes) is higher in the middle/upper classes, while fear of crime is more widespread among disadvantaged people (workers, unemployed and people with low education (ISTAT, 1999:131) and ISTAT, 2003:116). However, the survey points out also that what mainly affects fear of crime is the perceived presence of disorder in the area in which one lives: social disorder seems to be strictly related to fear of crime, and especially fear of crime outside the home (Barbagli, 1998: 67; ISTAT, 2003:129). Related to this last point, a further aspect of safety issues in Italy is the kind of social groups that are considered primarily responsible for crime and disorder: the immigrants, and especially undocumented immigrants. These groups, sometimes together with urban and marginalised homeless, are frequently associated with forms of 'soft' crimes, such as the 'spectacle' of drugs, prostitution and various 'incivilities'. An almost irrelevant role is played instead — contrary to what happens in other contexts, such as France, or the United Kingdom — by juvenile delinquency, and, specifically, by violent behaviour of young people: an absence which deserves to be deeply analysed.[15]

to sections of the country. We have therefore to rely upon a very fragmented type of research that mainly concerns the last decade. What seems to be rather indisputable is anyway the fact that, during the 1990s, demands for safety increased dramatically. This is proved by forms of social reaction to crime and disorder, such as, on the one hand, citizens' complaints to the Mayors (Barbagli, 1999) or to the police and, on the other, the constitution of many community organisations which have reached a strong visibility, as we will see in a section below.

[15] Killias (2002: 273) explains the low crime rates for young people in Italy with reference to structural and cultural factors related to the features of Italian families and to the persistence of the attachments between generations.

FROM A JOURNAL TO A PROGRAMME:
THE STORY OF THE 'SAFE CITIES' REGIONAL PROJECT

The emergence, and the perception of, these phenomena converged with the rise of an institutional conflict about the issue of federalism, or better, about the redistribution of competencies and responsibilities among three different level of governments: the central state, the regional administrations and the municipalities, within a political and legal system traditionally based on national centralisation. This conflict was led by the Left Parties and especially by local Left governments. From its very beginnings, matters of safety were strictly related to the aim of extending principles of autonomy for regions and cities vis-a-vis the central State and they became part of a more general struggle for federalism.[16]

In 1992, the Democratic Party of the Left (PDS) in Bologna decided to launch a magazine, promoted by researchers, academics, politicians and local administrators, called *Sicurezza e territorio* (Safety and Territory). It was through the pages of this journal that the concepts of safety and of a 'new' crime prevention policy developed and spread, at least in Northern Italy, but above all in the Regione Emilia–Romagna. In the first issue of the magazine we find all the key-words of the new strategies for tackling crime and safety issues, in a fashion similar to that spurred by so-called 'Left realism'[17] in the United Kingdom: the need, for instance, to take crime and fear seriously, the attention to victims (a category which has traditionally been neglected in the Italian legal system), the search for communitarian mobilisation, the importance of the 'local' against the 'central'.

These considerations, and more generally the development that safety policies have experienced in Italy, lead us to qualify Garland's concept of 'responsibilisation strategies'.[18] What is central in the Italian case is that the

[16] As clearly stated in those years by the President of Regione Emilia-Romagna: '[safety issues] are strictly and increasingly related to the new functions that Regions and Municipalities may assume in many fields, in the general framework of a federalist reform of the State, which gives pre-eminence to the role of the Regions' (Braccesi, 1994: 5, interview with Pier Luigi Bersani).

[17] Basic assumptions of 'Left realism' appeared for the first time in Italy in 1986, thanks to an essay by Jock Young (1986), published in the review 'Dei delitti e delle pene'. The academic world, however, remained silent — when not critical — until the 1990s, when the issue was strongly reintroduced by Massimo Pavarini (1994). On the contrary, the institutional and political world assumed quickly the main theoretical assumptions of this 'new' criminological trend.

[18] As Garland (1996: 452) clearly stated: 'The responsibilization strategy involves a number of new techniques and methods whereby the State seeks to bring about actions on the part of 'private' agencies and individuals...'. In Garland's words, this strategy focuses on the move of crime control — promoted by the public sector — from the public to the private. But, more generally, we see also a move from the State — as central government — towards different public authorities (the local ones), never involved before in crime control strategies.

redistribution of competencies and responsibilities is strongly demanded by new actors (local governments) that directly ask to play a role in criminal policies. Institutions that have never been involved in crime control strategies begin to struggle for the recognition of new fields of intervention, and the central state opposed and resisted this tendency for many years, at least until the beginning of this decade.

In 1994, *Sicurezza e Territorio* ceased publication: times were fit for the move from a strategy of sensibilisation of new actors to the implementation of local strategies for safety. In fact, the regional government of Emilia-Romagna, in that same year, started a programme called *Città sicure* (Safe cities), specifically devoted to issues of urban safety. *Città sicure* was the first Italian attempt to develop a general programme about urban safety and crime prevention, through research, promotional activities, and coordination and elaboration of new strategies for reduction of fear and crime prevention.

Therefore, according to the principles of *Città sicure*, the place for safety policies is to be found partly in an existing framework of competencies (which we could term social prevention) and partly in a new area of intervention for local authorities, in which the right to live safely is considered a public good akin to other citizens' rights, and the responsibility for which belongs with local government (a better quality of life, a better environment, etc.). However, as already mentioned, the conceptualisation of this new field of work remains uncertain, especially with respect to the difficulty of distinguishing between safety policies and crime prevention, and between safety and public order. The main actor in safety policies should be, according to *Città sicure*, the Mayor, who, after the electoral reform of 1991, is now elected directly by the voters.

Other guidelines elaborated by the Scientific Committee (Comitato scientifico) of *Città sicure* (1995) recall directly, once again, some of those basic principles of 'Left Realism' already imported in Italy by the criminologists involved in the Sicurezza e territorio enterprise and already mentioned before.

During the following years, the programme has been developing along these lines:

- a great deal of research about crime and related social phenomena;
- a strong impulse towards projects managed directly by cities;
- the training of new professionals of safety (coordinators, mediators, etc.), of local and national police, and of social workers;
- the mobilisation of community participation in safety policies and crime prevention (as we shall see better below);
- the development of networks and relationships both in the country, among cities and other local governments, and outside, with other European countries and cities.

The programme also played a central role-even if not always successful — in stimulating the national public bodies (police, ministers, prefects) towards introducing the new vocabulary of safety and the new strategies if crime prevention in their everyday work. During 10 years, the project — which is now a well-structured department of the Regione Emilia-Romagna — extended its activity of coordination and funding of many local security programmes, of research and sensibilisation for the rest of the country, and has enlarged its activity in the field of coordination of local polices forces.

This story tells us how our experience of safety policies is strongly influenced by an emphasis on the role of local authorities and especially of cities as the favourite sites for the attempt to develop an alternative model of social order and of regulation of conflicts, and by a consequent political struggle for the acknowledgement of new tasks and responsibilities in the issue of safety on the part of local governments.

In Italy we have witnessed and are still witnessing a great inability of the state to respond to local demands for safety, which is cultural, professional and political and, without doubt, is also a consequence of the traditional weakness of the Italian state apparatus and of the culture and organisation of our national polices forces, rather distant from a relationship with the local demand for safety and ill-equipped to work within a preventive approach. In recent years, national governments have been forced by local institutions to face the new configuration of urban unsafety. Subsequently, the process of redistribution of responsibility in the field of prevention and unsafety has been promoted entirely by local authorities.

Accordingly, the achievement by the regions and cities of legitimacy in managing prevention has been the result of an informal praxis, of the increasing growth of administrative programmes, of the activism of these local authorities, despite the formal denial of their role. In fact, from a formal or legal point of view, competencies on security and public order remain at the state level (police, the judiciary, etc.).

This absence of the national State has created what I think is a really peculiar situation, in which local governments are behaving — at least in part — as national governments usually do elsewhere. I refer, here, especially to the role played by the regional governments: in Italy these actors, following the example of the already quoted *Città sicure* project, have developed the first programmes on urban safety, have spread knowledge and techniques, and, finally, are supporting municipalities in realising safety projects through technical support and, above all, also by providing funding. Moreover, seven regional governments have enacted laws about safety and prevention.

An Italian Way to a 'New' Prevention: a Mixed Model

Since 1995, many Italian cities have been developing programmes to improve safety and to reduce crime and incivilities. Most of these programmes were inspired by the principles of integration among different preventive measures, and especially between social and situational prevention.[19]

---

[19] For a comprehensive overview (even if limited to the last 5 years of the Nineties) of the local security programmes developed in the main Italian cities see Martin & Selmini (2000).

All these measures nowadays comprise the content of the Italian security policies and their features are a further example of the circulation of practices which is part of the travelling process in the field of criminal justice. Originally, indeed, the concepts and practices of social and situational prevention arrived through the academic relationships both with the already quoted British Left realism, and with some French sociologists and criminologists.[20] *Città sicure* was the main actor in this process of importation of policies and in its subsequent diffusion in the rest of the country. In doing so, *Città sicure* offered an answer to those local politicians who — under the pressure of a growing social reaction to the emerging crime problems — were in search of 'new' solution and of a new vocabulary to face the increasing feelings of unsafety.

An important role in this process of transferring policies was also played by a well-known network of cities, the European Forum for Urban Safety. The relationship of the Italian local governments with this association stressed the connections with the French-speaking world and other continental countries, offering a partial counterweight to the Anglo-American origins of prevention discourse. In 1996, the foundation of an Italian section of the Forum (*Forum Italiano per la sicurezza urbana*)[21] gave a further and strong contribution to the spreading of ideas, programmes, and languages about security, especially in Northern and Central Italy.

Whereas the set of practices defined as 'social prevention'[22] was already known and applied in many cities (as already belonging, at least partially, to the field of competencies of the municipalities in the area of social policies), the situational crime prevention measures represented a true novelty. Here (as elsewhere) these measures were enthusiastically[23] adopted in many cities, and not always with the necessary adaptations to our local contexts.

We find, for instance, a significant number of measures based on the intensification of formal control, but the agent of such control at the city level

---

[20] One of the most well-known documents on the matter was the 'Scientific Report. Researchers and Prevention Policies' by Philippe Robert (1991b) reporting the conclusive remarks of the International Conference on Urban safety, Drugs and Crime Prevention, held in Paris in the same year, in which the general recommendations for a scientific approach to crime prevention and security were outlined.

[21] The association counts now almost 80 Cities, 8 Regional administrations and also some Provinces. Its work gave a strong impulse both to the domestic circulation of ideas and practices and to the enlargement and intensification of the external relationships with other European Cities.

[22] Some of the activities of the Municipality in the field of social policy are now oriented towards an aim for safety, but the content of the measures does not diverge from rather traditional ones (eg professional training for young people 'at risk' and for people released from prison, shelters for battered women and for immigrants, harm reduction programmes, etc).

[23] For some interesting remarks about the wide-spread favour of many different institutional and political contexts towards situational crime prevention, see Hope & Sparks (2000).

is, in Italy, above all, municipal police, which, despite its territorial limits and its administrative competencies,[24] is nonetheless becoming an important agent of formal control, through various means: a widespread presence in some areas of the town, a stronger professionalisation in prevention tasks, a different organisation of work (for instance presence at night, new services to victims, etc). In most cases, as we will see, these activities go far beyond the formal competencies of the municipal police thanks to an extension of the boundaries of some administrative tasks.

The absence of national police gives a different dimension also to the organisation of new forms of informal control. This is managed by municipal police or by the municipality, and is oriented much more towards a general environmental management than towards control of deviant or criminal behaviours, as we will see further below.

A last dimension of situational prevention in Italy, which is worthy of note, is represented by the approach based on using administrative orders for deterrent purposes. Once again, we are witnessing a distortion caused by the lack of partnership with the national agencies strictly responsible for compliance and crime reduction. In the Italian context, the ambiguous overlapping of prevention and dissuasion which often characterises these new strategies of crime control (Hebberecht & Sack, 1997:20) means that local authorities transfer the dissuasive powers and instruments they have in other fields (for instance, 'public hygiene') into security policies. Local authorities have the power to control people, to close businesses, to keep some activities under control, but only for reasons unrelated to 'public order' and with limited powers of criminal enforcement. Under the pressure of the public, more and more frequently the mayors of many Italian cities have tried to apply their own administrative instruments to different ends. An example of this tendency have been the so-called *ordinanze sindacali* (mayors ordinances), adopted in many Italian cities since the second half of the 1990s to control behaviours and to manage crime and incivilities at a local level. As a result of these administrative orders, we have experienced a substantial intervention of local police especially against street prostitution, but also disorder, incivilities, nuisance related to undocumented immigrants, etc. These ordinances are not grounded in criminal law powers, but in administrative ones and the tendency towards their use (or misuse) is not only increasing but also creates a sort of vicious circle, giving the public the impression that the Mayor can actually do something and so reinforcing the demand for safety and the growing responsibilisation of local authorities for crime problems.

[24] The municipal police, which depends on the Mayor, has an exclusive competency in the general field of administrative police, but it has also the status of a public security police, even if with auxiliary tasks. When municipal police acts in the field of crime control, it is submitted to the Prefects' orders, namely the local representative of the national government. It is clear how this situation provokes many conflicts of competencies and a lot of problems in defining the identity of this police, which is, in any case, one of the main actors of the 'new' local security policies.

From the point of view of the 'content' of the safety policies, what seems to emerge is a 'mixed' model of crime prevention, in which social and situational crime prevention activities are combined within the programmes in a more or less well balanced way, even if we note a tendency, under the pressure of public opinion and of political competition, to the search for fast solutions and, consequently, to develop more and more the situational approach.

The Multi-agency Approach: 'Partnerships' and 'Protocols'

The idea and the emphasis on the so-called multi-agency approach is another example of how some concepts, approaches and strategies travel from one country to another and how they partially change their meaning and content according to local peculiarities.

The idea of partnership is a basic component of the new strategies of crime prevention all over Europe, and it landed in Italy together with other principles of Left Realism. During its development, however, the idea assumed a 'French' flavour, well expressed by the adoption of the words *contratti di sicurezza*, an evolution from the French *contrats de sécurité*, to define the agreements between different actors involved in security policies.

Despite the 'British' origin and its French development, the Italian way to partnership cannot completely be assimilated to these ways of governing the cooperation of actors in the field of security. Our *protocolli*, or *contratti di sicurezza*, are rather different from the British audits, or the French *contrats de sécurité*. They represents a formal way to collaborate, are subscribed only by the mayors and the prefects and are aimed to regulate some activities at a local level. The first protocol was stipulated in Modena, once again a city located in Emilia-Romagna, in February 1998. At the end of 2003, data of the Ministery of the Interior shows that more than 200 cities all over the country have undersigned some formal agreement of this kind. Moreover, this way to collaborate is extending: starting from 2001 — and once again following the example of Regione Emilia-Romagna — five Italian Regions have signed with the Ministry of Interior a so called *accordo di programma*, namely a general agreement for the implementation of some activities in the field of security[25] at a regional level.

In almost all cases, municipalities and regions were the ones to initiate the procedure for cooperation, once again confirming their central role in launching

---

[25] These agreements represent an administrative instrument to govern partnership and crime problems at a macro level. They usually regulate the general cooperation among Regions and State and especially these activities: (1) the joint management of formal control and surveillance among national police, 'carabinieri', and local police; (2) the joint professional training of the three police forces mentioned above; (3) the institution of a regional centre for the collection of data about crime, incivilities and disorder.

the issue of safety policies. What is important to point out is the fact that protocols are used in pursuit of many different goals. First, they are adopted with the aim of compelling agencies of the central government to collaborate in local projects managed by municipalities. The need for partnership does not respond only, however, to the principle of a multi-agency approach. It depends also on the fact that, in the last few years, mayors have become the most important point of reference for many complaints and demands by citizens also in the field of safety, and some of these complaints concern matters in which municipalities have no competencies. The protocols, then, meet both the requirements of collaboration (especially with respect to the exchange of data and information about crime problems at a local level) and the need for a distribution of responsibilities between different agencies. Ironically, however, such protocols often restate the traditional boundaries between prevention and crime control, ie between local and central governments. Given that it was just those boundaries that local institutions were trying to blur in the first period of their activity, protocols therefore represent also a retrenchment in the attempt of local administrations to acquire a greater autonomy in the field of criminal policies. Under the growing pressure of public opinion and the media about 'sky-rocketing crime', many mayors reacted by abandoning the struggle for more incisive powers, and found it politically expedient to go back to reaffirmation of the traditional framework of competencies and functions.

This practice for cooperation met, on the one hand, with a very formalistic approach to collaboration, which gave the multi-agency approach a strong institutional fashion. By contrast, it was shaped and re-defined according to the different purposes of the actors involved. Even if also in other European context the partnership expressed through formal agreements could be considered also a way to regulate institutional conflicts, this seems to be the main scope of Italian *protocolli* or *contratti di sicurezza*.

Until now, any evaluation of the efficacy of these agreements, nor from the point of view of their impact on phenomena and neither of the changements they are provoking in the institutional relationships, has been conducted. In any case, and notwithstanding their diffusion all over the country, they never reach the intensity of cooperation or the range of activities which emerge from similar agreements in other European countries.

THE INVOLVEMENT OF COMMUNITY

Until the beginning of the 1990s the word 'community' was a very unusual one in discourses about crime and in practices of crime control in Italy, and our criminal justice system was both ill-equipped and culturally remote from the idea of an involvement of community in crime control strategies.

This fact is related to the specific relationship established in Italy between the State and civil Society. On the one hand, for a long time the state has conceived of this relationship as a mere imposition of a soverein state over its subjects, in a context, however, of a weak idea of the state itself, both in the citizens' opinion and in most of the main political parties's ideology. From the other hand, civil society itself has kept rather low its expectations toward the state and its institutions, and has strongly limited its capacity of reaction and civic mobilisation (La Spina, 1993: 58).[26]

In this climate, where structural weakness and inefficiency of state apparatus and agencies met with a culture of low-expectations and low activism of civil society, citizens' role in the process of policy making has been denied for a long time, whereas political parties have often assumed the role of intermediary between the State and the civil society.

In my opinion, the issue of the involvement of community in policy making, and also in the field of crime control policies, cannot be understand if it is not related to this peculiarity: the weakness of the relationship between state and civil society on the one hand, and the role of political parties on the other. Some few remarks can make these points clearer and can help in understanding the recent forms of community involvement in crime prevention strategies.

Not only have political parties re-interpreted social demands and expectations towards state institutions: they also have been promoters of collective identity in civil society, offering those symbols, which serve to give identity to the members of a community and to communicate among them. Collective action and mobilisation of citizens was for a long time channelled towards political system and this kind of 'mediate' participation has had a socialisation function, favouring the sharing of the rules and the prevention of conflicts. This action was particularly important in those areas of the country already characterised by a stronger tendency towards social and political participation, ie Northern Italy and especially some of the regions.

At the beginning of the 1990s, however, the crisis of the whole Italian political system, after the events of Tangentopoli,[27] and the generalised decline of political parties and of citizens' participation in the political and social life, reached their peak. These events gave rise to a widespread crisis of the institutional trust, to the emergence of 'localism' (often related to intercultural and racial conflicts), and to a search for new collective identities and new forms of citizenship for those groups formerly represented by political parties and once more involved in social and political life.

---

[26] With some differences, as already mentioned in this paper, among the regions of the North, where civic and social participation have always been strong and rather widespread, and the South of the country.

[27] 'Tangentopoli' is the name given to the wide-spread system of political corruption which was discovered at the beginning of the 1990's all over Italy, but above all in the North. The reaction to these events, led by a group of magistrates in Milan, brought to the collapse of some of the most important Italian political parties (first of all the Socialist Party and the Christian Democracy), to the sentencing of many famous Italian political leaders and also businessmen, and to a strong social reaction.

As Diani (1999:7) wrote, in the Italy of the 1990s the definition of collective identities emerges as a core issue, together with the widening of conflicts around some basic concepts as citizenship an its related rights. As a consequence of these processes, at the beginning of the decade and especially in the towns of the North of the country, new forms of spontaneous collective mobilisation emerged, and in many cases they were related to the perception of the menace of crime and disorder.

According to the results of some studies, the community mobilisation expressed by the so-called 'comitati di cittadini' (citizens' committees)[28] has appeared especially in those areas undergoing deep changes in terms of urban renewal and socio-economic development. Inner cities, the old working-class neighbourhoods and the new middle-class suburbs are the areas in which this kind of reaction to crime seems to emerge most frequently.[29] For inner cities, the major problems are decline, poverty and disorder; for traditional working-class districts, the lack of security perceived with the arrival of immigrants and the consequent difficulty in working towards new ways of life in common; for new suburbs, problems usually related to transports and services.

Especially in traditional working-class areas in the North, the community organisations active 'against' crime generally belong to the cultural and political field of the Left and frequently they seem to privilege the discourse of rights and social justice rather than that of defensiveness and victimisation (della Porta, 1996: 334; Selmini & di Città, 1997).

The attention of these communitarian groups focuses particularly on crime and deviance among recent immigrant groups and their visibility in the everyday life of the neighbourhood. At the core of the problem there no longer seems to be simply a threat to one's property or personal safety, but rather a generalised risk for the whole society, for a well-established idea of order. We can see here how the discourse is not so much about crime but seems to be about disorder, incivilities, and, finally an anxiety about lack of safety related more to a newly perceived distance from local institutions than to the presence of 'crime' as such — almost the feeling of being 'abandoned' by local institutions that have traditionally been 'the people's' institutions.

The fast and deep change in the social and economic structure of some cities and districts, the de-industrialisation of those same areas, the crisis of a 'work ethic' and of work as a means to promote social progress and personal dignity, the disappearance of traditional urban social networks — often related to political participation — and the consequent fragmentation of social identities (Belluati, 1998: 9), all of this creates a context in which new images of disorder

---

[28] So are called in Italy those groups of citizens of a neighborhood who acquire visibility and who organise themselves against crime or other local problems.

[29] This is especially true for Emilia-Romagna (Selmini , 1997; Chiodi, 1999) but similar outcomes emerge also from other studies in Milan (AASTER, 1996), Turin (Ires, 1995), and Florence (della Porta, 1999).

tend to emerge, often related, as we have seen, to the presence of immigrants and, more rarely, of groups of young homeless (who are considered responsible for a new 'decay' in the city, and are perceived as opposite to the values and ideals of the former working-class rather than for committing crime as such). So, what is clearly emerging is the question of 'rules', of civic rules.

Starting from these very sketchy remarks, we can note that the community mobilisations in crime prevention activities in Italy is deeply affected by the cultural and social context I have tried to describe before. In my opinion, these features of the community involvement in crime and prevention issues in Italy during the 1990s shows clearly how the matter is here, much more the attempt to redefine social identities and forms of citizenship than protecting coming themselves from a perceived menace from crime and victimisation. The same features bring us to contextualise Italian community involvement in crime and prevention strategies in those approaches which see the development of community governance as an attempt to formulate a new model of democratic participation (Hughes & Edwards, 2002:4) in Western democracies, and as an example of a new attempt to take part to political decision making process from below.

In these experiences, citizens' reaction and mobilisation does not assumes the features of private defensiveness and of community's direct responsibilisation in crime control and surveillance, as it occurred elsewhere and, first, in the well-known Anglo-American experiences of Neighbourhood Watch Scheme. In most cases, and also during the period of greater conflict among citizen committees, groups of immigrants, police and local institutions, community organisations engaged themselves in crime prevention activities mainly based on regeneration of urban spaces, mediation of conflicts, rivitalisation of neighbourhoods through social and cultural initiatives, in which the control, surveillance and crime report activities remained backstage.

These characteristics of community crime prevention in Italy have also been supported by the response given by local institution and by the strategy they developed to react to communities' protests. In fact, Italian local security policies are characterised by a moderate involvement of community organisations in crime prevention activities, and emphasis on community, which surely is present in public discourses, has remained anyway low during the past years, and also nowadays. In most cases, municipalities have tried to bring community mobilisation inside the institutional framework, giving the committees a visibility inside the safety local project through an involvement in the field of social regeneration of neighbourhoods.

Many new forms of collective participation were supported by the local administration, and new opportunities for the groups involved were singled out. In these cases, the crisis initiated by the community reaction became an opportunity and a factor of change for all those involved.[30]

---

[30] See for instance the cases of Turin (Allasino, Bobbio & Neri, 2000; Belluati, 1998) and Modena (Poletti...). We also have to notice that the absence, at least until now, of national...

If this remains the prevailing model to foster community's participation in crime prevention local strategies, nonetheless we are now also witnessing the emergence, albeit limited to a very few cases, of a different approach based on municipal support for organised groups of citizens whose activities focus on the control of some areas of the cities. One example of this strategy is offered by the constitution of the so-called *assistenti civici* (civic assistants), a project of community involvement which represents a direct emulation of the British experience of the wardians.[31]

Differently from the experiences of 'Neighbourhood watch', these groups work only on the public spaces and are trained and organised by local institution or local police, and never by national police forces. The overall philosophy of citizens' involvement is rather similar.

SOME CONCLUSIONS

From the sketch of security policies in Italy that I have outlined here, it is nonetheless clear that the origin and development of these policies are the result of some convergent processes and sociopolitical dynamics and that the context in which 'transfer' occurs is important (Newburn and Sparks, 2004: 6).

One point to note is the relevance assumed in the adoption of policies by institutional conflict among different levels of government and the struggle of local authorities to acquire new competencies and responsibilities. This is probably the main factor influencing the shape and style of the policies developed in the last decade. The choice to name these policies as *politiche di sicurezza* is an example of the importance of this conflict: the word *sicurezza* recalls the responsibility of the state and its penal institutions in maintaining order, and for the world of local autonomies it would have been reductive to refer to these strategies as 'preventive policies' or 'community safety policies', etc. On the contrary, to define this intervention in the field of crime control as 'security' symbolically re-affirms the intention of local public institutions to legitimate their role in this field. From this point of view, the Italian context shows clearly how contemporary crime control practices are at the core of an

police forces from this picture has surely favourished this kind of 'soft' community involvement in crime prevention.

[31] The civic assistants are volunteers usually belonging to preexisting associations or, very often, also retired policemen, who have been trained and involved in control activities in some areas of the city, especially parks, schools and overcrowded area (bus stops, public events, etc). They are described as a friendly presence in the city, they can't stop people or intervene on behaviours, the only should give assistance to citizens, point out risks and problems, and call the police when necessary. They are invited to pay attention to these phenomena: drugs, presence of suspected people, disturbing juvenile behaviours, decay, incivilities, lack of lighting, vandalism, etc.

ambiguous process of re-distribution of responsibilities among the sovereign state, the local centres of powers, and civil society. This process, well analysed in the recent literature about changes in crime and social order strategies,[32] in the European context, and in the Italian one above all, is deeply marked by the crisis of the national state and its traditional form of government and the search for a new role and legitimacy of the regional and municipal administrations.

Some further issues I have tried to expand are the peculiarities of community involvement in crime prevention strategies, the reasons for which can be summarised as follows. First, the relationship historically established between the state, the civil society and the political system (reminding, however, the differences existing among the different areas of the country). Second, the loss of hegemony of some social groups and the subsequent fragmentation of identities deriving from the crisis of the working-class in Italy and of political parties in the past years. I have also tried to explain how this social, cultural and political climate affected both community mobilisation and institutional practices of citizens' involvement, helping in avoiding the development of a community approach mainly based on defensiveness, vigilantism and victimisation.

I have also tried to outline how the model of crime prevention strategies emerging after 10 years from the first implementations of safety projects at a lo-cal level is a very mixed one, in which situational and social measures are com-bined in a more or less balanced way and I have argued that this model is the result of the contemporary influence of British and of French experiences. The first one landed in Italy through the relationships among part of the Italian criti-cal criminology with the British Left realism at the end of the 1980s. Together with the main principles of this approach to crime preventions we have 'import-ed' a pragmatic style, which, in some cases, become simply a search for 'fast solu-tions'. So, the overall approach of local safety projects is based not only on the attention to crime victims', to fear of crime and anxiety as signs of social vulner-ability and to social disadvantaged groups, but also on enhancement of formal control, through police and video surveillance, and on all the measures aimed at reducing crime through the modification of physical contexts and of behaviours.

But, at the same time, the contacts existing also with some French sociologists and criminologists, and the establishing of a relationship with the preexisting European Forum for Urban Safety, both of them engaged — in very different way and contexts — in developing safety policies mainly based on social prevention or on a 'new' prevention approach, affected Italian local safety projects. The outcome, as I have already argued, is a mixed model of crime prevention. We can single out some reasons why the specific Italian local context was rather ready to accept both these external influences. Situational and social approach met the needs and interests of local political figures in different ways. No different from what occurred and is occurring in other contexts, the success of situational

---

[32] Especially in the anglo-american world (Garland, 1996; 2001).

crime prevention lies in its capacity to offer to those who are responsible for the government of urban life, ie the mayors and other local politicians, a pragmatic and quick political response to manage crime and disorder problems. What is interesting is the fact that in Italy this approach to crime prevention has been accepted enthusiastically without any diffusion of the kind of criminological knowledge on which it depends, namely the theory of opportunities and the routine activity approach, which are, apart from the recent interest of some academics, largely unknown and also unfamiliar to our scientific discourse on crime and crime prevention.

The social prevention approach, on the contrary, has a solid tradition both in academic thinking and in institutional practices; nonetheless, we have to remark how social prevention, once included in local safety projects, is increasingly at risk of losing its traditional features. More precisely, measures of social prevention adopted in local safety projects clearly show a shift from radical intervention in the causes of crime through social reforms to a less ambitious plan to offer humanitarian solutions to some disadvantaged groups. A 'taking care' philosophy (Pavarini, 2000) which is also more consistent with the limited instruments that local governments can adopt in the field of social inclusion, labour, education, house policies, immigration policies, etc. and which is characterised, rather paradoxically — by a certain 'short-termism' sometimes not very different from that one typical of situational crime approach.

I would like finally to mention a further factor which can explain the mixed features of this model of crime prevention which is related to Italian criminological culture. The absence of a well-established criminological community, the prevalence, until a few years ago, of an obsolete clinical and forensic approach to criminology, the academic difficulties of the more advanced 'critical' criminologists in developing alternative categories and paradigms — together with the great delay of social research in this field — have led to the strong influence of ideas about security and prevention developed in other countries. The criminological thinking underling the development of security policies and local crime prevention projects is in fact deeply influenced, as already mentioned, by Left realism in its origin — and in some cases, simply criminological realism in its subsequent development — and by French theoretical framework about crime and crime prevention.

As we have seen, many concepts, ideas and practices around safety policies travelled around Europe during the last decades: some of these have been adopted with light changements in their meaning and content, most have been adapted to specific local contexts, some remained outside the scientific discourse and institutional practices of Italian security policies. I have tried to enlighten the most evident of these policy transfer processes, but surely many of them have remained on the backstage, or are less consolidated and comprehensible.[33]

---

[33] For instance, 'import processes' related to police strategies, which are actually occurring in Italy, already mentioned in note 3, but which are also so vague, ambiguous and unknown that any remarks would be approximative and untimely.

REFERENCES

AAS TER (1997) 'Dalla comunità rinserrata alla comunità possibile' *Metronomie* IV, 10, 1–35.

Allasino Pietro, A, Bobbio Luigi, B & Neri Stefano, N (2000) 'Crisi urbane: che cosa succede dopo? Le politiche per la gestione della conflittualità legata ai problemi dell'immigrazione' *Polis*. XIV, 3; 431–449.

Barbagli, M (1995) *L'occasione e l' in uomo ladro. Furti e Rapine in Italia* (Bologna, Il Mulino).

——— (1998) 'Reati, vittime, insicurezza dei Cittadini', paper presented at the seminar *La sicurezza dei Cittadini*, ISTAT, Rome, 22 September (unpublished).

——— (ed) (1999) *Egregio Signor sindaco. Lettere dei Cittadini e risposta dell'istituzione Sui problemi Della sicurezza* (Bologna, Il Mulino).

Belluati, M (1998) 'Un quartiere in protesta' in *Il Caso San Salvario Tra rappresentazioni Socialis e immagini mediali* (Doctoral thesis, University of Milan, unpublished).

Braccesi, C (1994) 'La Political regionale dell'Emilia — Romagna in Tema di sicurezza. Interview with Pier Luigi Versani' *Sicurezza e Territorio*, 15, 5–10.

Cartuyvels, Y (1996) 'Insécurité et prévention en Belgique: Les ambigüités d'un modèle globale intégré entre concertation partenariale et intégration verticale' *Déviance et Société*, 20, 153–171 [DOI: 10.3406/ds.1996.1602].

Cartuyvels, Y & Hebberecht P (2001) 'La Politique fédérale belge de sécurité et de prévention de la criminalité' *Déviance et Société*, 25, 403–426 [DOI: 10.3917/ds.254.0403].

Chiodi, M (1999) 'Immigrazione, devianza e percezione d'insicurezza: analisi del quartiere Crocetta a Modena' *Dei delitti e Delle Pene*, I, 115–140.

Comitato Scientifico di Città sicure (1995) Il Comitato scientifico di Città sicure raccomanda al governo della Regione Emilia-Romagna in *La sicurezza in Emilia-Romagna, First Annual Report*. Quaderni di Città sicure 2. (Bologna, Regione Emilia-Romagna).

Crawford, A (1997) *The Local Governance of Crime. Appeals to Community and Crime Prevention* (Oxford, Clarendon).

Da Agra, C, Quintas, J & Fonseca, E (2001) 'De la sécurité démocratique à la démocratie de sécurité: Le cas portugais' *Déviance et Société*, 25, 479–497.

della Porta, D & Reiter, H (1994) 'Da "polizia del governo" a "polizia dei cittadini"? le politiche dell'Ordine pubblico in Italia' *Stato e Mercato*, 48, 433–465.

——— (1996) 'Polizia e Ordine pubblico' *Polis*, 10, 333–336.

——— (1999) 'Immigrazione e protesta' *Quaderni di Sociologia*, 21, 14–44.

Diani, M (1999) 'La società Italiana: protesta Senza movimenti? Presentazione' *Quaderni di Sociologia*, 21, 3–13.

Garland, D (1996) 'The Limits of the Sovereign State' *British Journal of Criminology*, 36, 445–465.

——— (1997) 'Governmentality and the Problem of Crime: Foucault, Criminology, Sociology' *Theoretical Criminology*, 1, 173–214 [DOI: 10.1177/1362480697001002002].

——— (2001) *The Culture of Control. Crime and Social Order in Contemporary Society* (Oxford, Oxford University Press).

Hebberecht, P & Sack, F (editors) (1997) 'La prévention de la délinquance en Europe' *Nouvelles strategies* (Paris, L'Harmattan).

Hebberecht, P & Duprez, D (2001) 'Sur les politiques de prévention et de sécurité en Europe: réflexions introductives sur un tournant' *Déviance et Société 25*, 371–376.

Hope, T (1995) 'Community Crime Prevention' in M Tonry & D Farrington (eds) *Building a Safer Society* (Chicago, University of Chicago Press).

Hope, T & Sparks, R (2000) 'For a Sociological Theory of Situations (or How Useful is Pragmatic Criminology?)' in A von Hirsch, D Garland & A Wakefield (eds) *Ethical and Social Perspectives on Situational Crime Prevention* (Oxford, Oxford University Press).

Hughes, G & Edwards, A (2002) *Crime Control and Community. The New Politics of Public Safety* (Cullompton, Willan).

IRES (1995) 'Un caso al microscopio: Conflitti e prospettive in un quartiere Urbano' in *Relazione annuale Sulla situazione socio-economical Del Piemonte* (Torino, Rosenberg and Sellier).

ISTAT (1999) *La sicurezza dei Cittadini. Reati, vittime, percezione Della sicurezza e sistemi di protezione* (Roma, ISTAT).

——— (2003) *La sicurezza dei Cittadini. Reati, vittime, percezione Della sicurezza e sistemi di protezione* (Roma, ISTAT).

Killias, M (2002) 'La criminalità in Italia: Uno sguardo Dall'esterno' in B Marzio & U Gatti (eds) *La criminalità in Italia* (Bologna, Il Mulino).

La Spina, A (1993) 'Le Strategise informali di autotutela del Cittadino: significato, presupposti e linee di tendenza' *Quaderni di Sociologia*, 4, 42–62.

Martin L & Selmini R (editors) (2000) 'Le politiche di sicurezza nelle città e nelle regioni italiane. 1995–1999' *Quaderni di città sicure* 20b (Bologna, Regione Emilia-Romagna).

Melossi, D & Selmini, R (2001) 'Social Conflict and the Microphysics of Crime: The Experience of the Emilia-Romagna *Città sicure* Project' in T Hope and R Sparks (eds) *Crime, Risk and Insecurity* (London, Routledge).

Newburn, T & Sparks R (eds) (2004) 'National Justice and Political Cultures' in *Criminal Justice and Political Cultures. National and International Dimensions of Crime Control* (Cullompton, Willan).

Pavarini M (1994) 'Bisogni di sicurezza e questione criminale' *Rassegna Italiana di Criminologia*, 4, 436–462.

——— (2000) *'La questione criminale Nell'emergenza sicuritaria'* (Note teoriche sul caso italiano, unpublished).

Putnam, R (1993) *Making Democracy Work* (Milano, Mondadori).

Recasens Brunet, A (2001) 'Politiques de sécurité et de prévention dans l'Espagne des années 1990' *Déviance et Société*, 25, 479–497 [DOI: 10.3917/ds.254.0479].

Robert, P (1991a) 'Les chercheurs face aux politiques de prévention' in *AA VV: Les Politiques de prévention de la délinquance à l'une de la recherche. Un bilan international* (Paris, L'Harmattan).

—— (1991b) 'Researchers and Prevention Policies' (Scientific Report) in *International Conference on Urban Safety, Drugs and Crime Prevention* (Paris).

Rochè, S (1999) 'Le nuove tematiche Della criminalità e Della sua prevenzione in Francia' *Polis XIII, 1*, 99–120.

Selmini, R (1997) 'Il Punto di Vista dei comitati di Cittadini' in *La sicurezza in Emilia — Romagna* (Third Annual Report); *Quaderni di Città sicure* 11 (Bologna: Regione Emilia-Romagna).

—— (1999) 'Sicurezza Urbana e prevenzione Della criminalità: Il Caso Italiano' *Polis XIII, 1*, 121–142.

Vandelli, L 'Devolution e *altre* Storie' in *Paradossi, ambiguità e rischi di un progetto. Politico* (Bologna, IL Mulino).

Van Swaaningen, R (1998) 'Quale Political per una città sicura?' *Dei delitti e Delle Pene*, 2, 143–173.

Vidali, S (2001) 'Politiques de prévention et de sécurité en Grèce: Le controle politique passé et présent, quelles perspectives?' *Déviance et Société*, 25, 479–497.

Young J (1986) 'Il fallimento Della criminologia: per un realismo radicale' *Dei delitti e Delle Pene*, 3, 387–415.

Zedner, L (2001) 'The Pursuit of Security' in T Hope & R Sparks (eds) *Crime, Risk and Insecurity* (London, Routledge).

9

Cultural Travels and Crime Prevention in Argentina

MÁXIMO SOZZO[1]

INTRODUCTION

The presence of cultural travels pervades the history of the government of crime in Argentina as well as in the rest of Latin America. Different elements originally produced in other cultural contexts, in the 'centre' — a sort of multiple and heterogeneous 'there', which in different moments and situations was located in North America or in Europe — were 'translated' into our cultural context by different actors — intellectuals, prison administrators, police officers, etc — through different procedures, with the aim of devising local rationalities and technologies. Although this is a fundamental feature of this history it should not be considered unalterable or unaltered, as the cultural imports themselves have been successively transformed in their modalities and characteristics.

At the beginning of the 1970s in Latin America a critical discourse began to be elaborated on the government of crime — a 'radical' criminology, a 'criminology of emancipation' — that articulated a first interpretation of these 'cultural travels'. Within this frame these cultural translations were considered, mainly, as instances of the cultural and political 'colonialism' and 'neo-colonialism' of the 'centre' over the 'periphery', the 'North' over the 'South', and hence as a complement to, economic 'colonialism' and 'neo-colonialism'.

Rosa del Olmo, one of the founders of this Latin American critical tradition, pointed out that the Latin American criminologist 'depends on the foreign criminologist', adopting issues and the latest trends typical of developed countries' criminologies — which is an expression of 'cultural colonialism'

[1] I would like to thank all the participants in the Oñati workshop for their helpful comments and specially Richard Sparks for all his help with my written English.

(1975, 24). Their criminology does not correspond with their social reality. This 'indifference towards social reality' and the 'adoption of techniques from other places' are the fundamental reasons why 'there is no Latin American criminology'.

'What we have is a not very well assimilated use of foreign theories ("we copy and translate what has been produced for other realities") that, when applied, are only useful to distort our reality' (1975, 25).

At the beginning of the 1980s Lola Aniyar de Castro — another founder of this perspective in the region — made specific reference to crime control policies:

> all the internal policies are designed on the basis of the knowledge produced in central developed countries. Imitation, generally out of context, is the basis of reforming initiatives... cultural dependence also exists in this sphere (1981–82, 51).

And, in this respect, by the middle of that decade, she had denounced:

> ...the deficient and ahistorical imitations of European political models, which was part of a larger cultural dependence that imposes lifestyles, laws and institutions that have very little to do with the anthropological or social Latin American reality (Aniyar, 1986, 4).

Setting the theme of cultural translations related to the government of crime in the broader context of economic, political and cultural colonialism/neo-colonialism, in this way seems often to have resulted in subsuming it under the simple idea of transplanting, in which the 'cultural artefact' was transferred from 'there' to 'here', without thereby undergoing any fundamental modification (see, among others, Bergalli, 1982, 280–284; 1983, 199).

This kind of reading had strong political implications. The 'cultural trip', as an expression of colonialism/neo-colonialism and mere transplant or transfer, was rejected from a normative stance, strongly committed to the production of a critical criminology and an 'alternative' crime control policy, each of which had to have as a principal quality — apart from being the expression of the subordinate classes' interests — being truly Latin American even though this claim was paradoxically based on the realisation of new cultural translations of a new criminological and political vocabulary also produced in North America and Europe (Del Olmo, 1985, 138–9; 1988, 209–211; Sozzo, 2001).

In fact a fuller analysis of the accounts of these cultural translations shows us a rather different image from that one of mere transplant or transfer.[2] The local actors translated elements of the rationalities and technologies for the government of crime produced in other cultural contexts, but in so doing

---

[2] Rosa del Olmo, probably one of the sharpest analysts in this tradition had already expressed her dissatisfaction with the simple idea of transplant or transfer, highlighting that the 'assimilation' of European or North American discourses was always 'distorted and artificial' to 'meet local needs' 'discarding what didn't correspond with' the context of 'our dependent and undeveloped societies' (1981: 125, 155; see more recently, Del Olmo, 1999: 26).

they altered their character considering both the 'empirical' elements (which referred to their own context) and the 'non-empirical' elements created by the translator's own theoretical and political inventiveness. The 'rejections', and 'adaptations' of elements of these cultural artefacts that travel between 'here' and 'there', produced by local actors in the local context, lead us to think of these translations — bearing in mind the expression 'traduttore traditore' — as true 'metamorphoses' of the thing translated (Sozzo, 2001).[3]

From this point of view, the history of the government of crime in Latin America, although pervaded by cultural travels that have played a fundamental role in the configuration of local rationalities and technologies, has at the same time a strong 'cultural embeddedness' (Melossi, 1997, 2001), as every cultural translation has been surrounded by rejections supplements and adaptations with regard to its own cultural context, which have produced a kind of 'indigenisation' of the transported cultural devices (Van Zyl Smit, 1989; Salvatore & Aguirre, 1996b; Karstedt, 2001). To think of cultural travels as metamorphoses provokes a series of question: what is culturally imported? How is it culturally imported? Who imports culturally? What are the effects brought about by the cultural importation in the local context? And so on. At the same time, it allows us to look again afresh at the connection between crime control and the broader context of economic, political and cultural colonialism/neo-colonialism — we will go back to this in the third section of this essay.

In the following sections we will look closely at the emergence from the second half of the 1990s in Argentina of initiatives and actions directed to the ideal of 'crime prevention', within the frame of processes of cultural translation. We will try to use this field as a case in point of the conceptual issues so far discussed.

THE REBIRTH OF 'CRIME PREVENTION' IN ARGENTINA

Since the 1960s there has been a widespread growth of interest in crime prevention. There have been projects and innovations in this field in the United States, Great Britain, Canada, Australia, New Zealand, France, Belgium, Holland, Italy, among other countries. Such initiatives and actions have sometimes been termed the 'new prevention' to distinguish them from crime

---

[3] We construct this metaphor of the metamorphosis inspired by the use of this concept by Robert Castel. This French sociologist uses this expression to deal with the 'dialectic of what is same and different' in time, in the processes of change, as a key to the 'history of the present', questioning the relationship between persistence and transformation (Castel, 1997: 17–18). But here it is used to question such dialectic in space. I believe the clearest illustration of the implications of thinking in terms of metamorphosis –in time as well as in space — is precisely present in an analogy drawn in a text of the same Castel: 'Zeus converted into an ox is still Zeus. He is/isn't Zeus and it is necessary to be fully alert to recognise him' (1980: 18).

prevention through legal punishment. The expression 'community safety' has also gained currency — to connote the appeal to 'community' as one of the actors involved in a 'partnership' between state and non-state actors and the importance of 'locality'. These terms have often been confused and conflated.[4]

The field of 'crime prevention' has been 'internationally' developed, nurtured by an increasing flow of travels between different cultural contexts involved, promoted by governmental (eg the National Council for Crime Prevention of the United States), non-governmental (eg the National Association for the Care and Resettlement of Offenders in Great Britain) or 'hybrid' (eg Crime Concern in Great Britain) national actors. But also by the increasing activity of governmental and non-governmental international organisations whose aim is to promote the cultural circulation of this kind of initiatives and actions from the International Centre for the Prevention of Crime with its headquarters in Montreal (www.crimeprevention.intl.org) to the United Nations Centre for International Crime Prevention with its headquarters in Vienna (www.uncjin. org/CPIC), through the European Forum for Urban Safety (www.urbansecurity. org/fesu) with its headquarters in Paris.

This is not a homogeneous field, however, since it is possible to distinguish different 'crime prevention strategies', which assemble some conceptions of what crime is and how to prevent it and certain intervention techniques: 'social prevention', 'community prevention', 'situational-environmental prevention' (cf for a fuller analysis of these strategies, Sozzo, 2000).[5] At the same time, in many of the initiatives and actions carried out in recent years in these cultural contexts the aim was to combine elements from different preventive strategies within the frame of an increasing appeal to what is called 'integrated prevention' (Robert, 1991; Baratta, 1993; Pavarini, 1994; Selmini, 1999, 2003).

However, it is possible to outline some minimum common features which characterise this field of preventive action:

1. The importance given to state and non-state actors that were traditionally in a marginal position or outside the area of crime control — in France and Italy, for example, local governments or, internationally, the 'commercial sector'.

2. The relevance attached to the co-ordination and articulation of efforts between public agencies and their alliance and co-operation with private actors — the language of 'partnership'.

---

[4] For a general overview of these developments, see Robert (1991); Baratta (1993); Pavarini (1994); Graham & Bennet (1995); Tonry & Farrington (1995); Hebberecht & Sack (1997); Gilling (1997); O'Malley (1997); Crawford (1997, 1998); Hughes (1998); Rosenbaum, Lurigio & Davis (1998); Selmini (1999, 2003); laboratory, 2000; Hughes, McLaughlin & Muncie (2002).

[5] Multiple variations can be found in the literature on the names of these strategies and about whether it is a bipartite or tripartite classification, of which we cannot give an account here. See instead references of note 3.

3. The importance given to 'locality': starting from the recognition of the local specificity of crime and fear of crime, the construction of answers which take into account such local specificity is promoted.
4. The significant role of scientific knowledge about crime and fear of crime, on the levels of diagnosis, intervention and evaluation.

The domain of 'crime prevention' has been claimed to be a 'novel' concept in those diverse cultural scenes. However, it is possible to find some precedents of these rationalities and technologies of government of crime in the history of modern discourses on the criminal question from Colquhoun's ideas about the role of the police in crime prevention to Prins' ideas about pre-criminal security measures against 'dangerous' individuals (Hughes, 1998: 25–57; Gilling, 1997: 31–42). That is why it is more appropriate to think of the emergence of this field as a 'rebirth' (Crawford, 1998: 32–33).

During the second half of the 1990s in Argentina, a variety of initiatives were launched aimed at preventing crime without resort to punishment. These initiatives were fostered by provincial and local governments and drew extensively upon the vocabulary of 'community prevention' or 'community safety'. In some cases they turned out to be no more than rhetorical exercises: an official announcement or the production of a policy instrument — a provincial law or a municipal ordinance. In others, they became fairly developed practices, albeit for fairly limited periods thanks to political ups and downs, changes of government, the lack of sustainable funding and the poor quality of the implementation processes (see Sagarduy-Rosua, 1999; Croccia-Eilbaum-Lekerman-Martinez, 1999; Sozzo, 1999; Saín, 2002). Two rather different initiatives could be considered as the main experiences in this field, tacking into account its extent and durability. We will analyse them more in-depth.

'PLAN ALERTA': NEIGHBOURHOOD WATCH AND COMMUNITY INVOLVEMENT IN BUENOS AIRES

At the beginning of 1997 in Saavedra, a neighbourhood in the City of Buenos Aires, a group of neighbours worried about urban safety got together. This area had suffered a series of crimes against property with resort to violence against people — burglary and car-stealing. This group of people called themselves 'JUVESA' and they voiced a series of complaints to the relevant public authorities — Police Station 49 of the 'Policia Federal Argentina' ('Federal Police of Argentina', henceforth PFA), the 'Secretaria de Seguridad Interior' (national Secretary of Interior Security, henceforth SSI), the 'Dirección Nacional de Política Criminal' ('National Directorate for Crime Control Policy', henceforth, DNPC), etc.

Their original complaints were oriented to the adoption of traditional measures of crime control, such as calling upon the police and penal system to take tougher action. However disagreement emerged over the development of their position and they split into two subgroups, one of them with the new name

'Vecinos Solidarios' ('Neighbours for Solidarity', henceforth, VS). VS continued complaining to public authorities, but at the same time, it started to look for alternative means of producing urban safety through practices generated within civil society. According to one of the founder members of this group (Daniel), by 'chatting' with an Argentinian woman living in London, he learnt about different experiences of mobilisation of residents to generate, through citizen participation, a device aimed at 'being protected against crime'. Later, this neighbour set out to construct an electronic forum exchanging e-mails with different people who appeared on the Internet as experts on the subject. A Colombian technician told him about the programme called 'Neighbourhood Watch' (Finquelevich-Vercelli-Saguier, 2002: 7).

As is well known, the first experiments with Neighbourhood Watch began in the United States in the 1970s, following the pioneering experience of the Community Crime Prevention Programme in Seattle (Hope, 1995: 44). In the early 1980s, it was imported into Great Britain — the first scheme was set up in Cheshire in 1982 (Gilling, 1997: 144). It soon grew bigger, reaching a very important rate of diffusion: in 1998 there were 140 000 NW schemes in England and Wales covering 6 million households (Crawford, 1998: 148). Simultaneously, this device started to be internationally diffused (Graham-Bennett, 1995: 79).

NW is one of the prevention techniques which has dominated the 'community crime prevention' sphere for the last 25 years (Rosenbaum-Lurigio-Davis, 1998, 42). Rosenbaum, one of the first academics to evaluate this kind of scheme in the United States, has defined them as:

> citizens coming together in relatively small groups (usually block clubs) to share information about local crime problems, exchange crime prevention tips and make plans for engaging in surveillance ('watching') of the neighbourhood and crime reporting activities (Rosenbaum, 1987: 104).

Their members can be involved in other activities as well — for example, adopt collectively a common self-protection course of action — though empirical research on these experiences have shown that in practice members do little more than put stickers or posters in their windows (Graham-Bennett, 1995: 79–80; Hope, 1995: 49; Gilling, 1997: 143).

The main idea behind Neighbourhood Watch is that by extending informal surveillance, reporting to the police and the number of arrests increases, the number of offenders in the streets declines and other potential offenders are deterred. And by coming together to fight a common problem, the frequency and quality of social relations among residents improve, community bonds are enhanced and, therefore, the capacity for informal surveillance grows and, accordingly, the neighbours' feeling of fear and anxiety decreases. Besides, by establishing a special co-operation system between the 'community' and the police, NW aims to improve substantially this bond of trust and communication (Graham-Bennett, 1995: 79; Hope, 1995: 43).

Initially, NW was put into practice by police institutions and was one of the key elements that led to 'community policing' in different cultural contexts, as a way of making people 'responsible', in alliance with police officers, for the production of urban (Graham & Bennet, 1995: 91–96; Crawford, 1998: 147–8). The clearest example is the emergence of Neighbourhood Watch in Great Britain, about which Daniel Gilling says:

> Neighbourhood Watch is presented as a solution to a police problem. Investigating opportunistic crime brings the least reward in terms of clear-up rates, and thus there is a pressure to limit the deployment of scarce resources in this area. Neighbourhood Watch offers a way out of this difficulty, with the added bonus that it routinises and formalises the collection of low level intelligence from the public, acting as the 'eyes and ears' of the police (Gilling, 1997: 144).

During a second phase, from the latter part of the 1980s, NW schemes started to be developed directly by the public (Gilling, 1997, 145). Nevertheless, this did not mean that the role of the police lost importance, as it continued to be essential to the organisation and maintenance of these schemes. However, this new situation is also a symptom of the problem it caused for the police institutions, which promoted it within the frame of a 'responsibilising strategy', to 'devolve' activities to the civil society through 'partnership' language (O'Malley, 1992, 1997), but found themselves facing the perverse effect caused by its propagation: a growing demand for police assistance from the public, which may lead to progressive distrust of the police if it is not satisfactorily answered — contradicting one of the basic goals of its creation (Gilling, 1997: 149).

Let us return to Saavedra. Having been advised to consider the NW alternative Daniel started to search for information on the Internet about NW. He accessed the Scotland Yard web page, which offered a series of instructive documents on how to set up an NW scheme. Together with other members of the group, he downloaded these documents and translated them into Spanish. Daniel later pointed out: 'This project was born out of the Internet...' (Finquelevich-Vercelli-Saguier, 2002: 7). A series of meetings were held by VS to discuss the possibilities of putting this project into practice in Saavedra. Later these neighbours started to spread the news around. At the same time, they contacted an officer from Scotland Yard, again via Internet, to ask for other details concerning the installation and functioning of NW.

An NW scheme was put into practice in different blocks in the neighbourhood under the name of 'Plan Alerta' ('Alert Plan'). One of the promoters pointed out — expressing the ambiguity of this intervention technique (see above) — in an interview:

> It is a type of collective situational prevention through which neighbours are socialised. So, by having a common goal, we revive the bonds among the members of the community (Revista *Estrategias*, June, 2000, 'Buenos Aires kills me').

All the residents of a block — a 'functional unit' in the organisational jargon of 'Plan Alerta' — were requested to participate in the first meeting. The attendants were instructed in how NW worked, received a series of documents written by VS and were asked to set up a scheme in their own blocks. The residents who adhered to the initiative — it was made clear that the participation was voluntary — exchanged names and phone numbers and designed a 'block plan' where all this information would appear and which they had to put next to their phones. During the same first meeting, a co-ordinator of each functional unit was appointed and they decided on what were the 'critical times' for each block, at which the neighbours were more vulnerable to becoming victims of a crime — the examples given in the instructions were 'going into or out of the garage or home, school and work timetables, holidays'.[6]

Participants were expected to alert by phone the rest of the residents in the block and the police in case of 'suspicious signs of imminent criminal activity (strangers hanging around, unknown vehicles driving past the block repeatedly, etc)'. The installation of 'community alarms' was also promoted, using 'inter-neighbours sounding alarms', 'intelligent lighting', or whistles, in each functional unit. They identified 'suspicious attitudes' considering whether they were present or not within the 'critical times' previously defined. If they were out of such times the participants would communicate among themselves to corroborate the 'suspicion'. By contrast, if they occurred within the 'critical times' the members would be immediately on the alert, considering it a situation of 'imminent danger'. The same happened in the case of a crime being committed, when it was specifically recommended 'not to be physically involved in it by fighting against the criminals', but assisting, in every sense, the member who had suffered the crime.

The instructions pointed out:

> The neighbour does not become a police officer or an informant. He will be only playing his part as a citizen of a Republic, in its strictest sense, working in defence of his life, his family and his property. The members of the project are not expected to assume the control of security, which is the State's unavoidable responsibility; the citizens will only assume their constitutional rights and duties.

The instructions specifically excluded the possibility of putting into practice 'citizen patrols':

> Preventive patrolling, similar to the ones made by armed police officers or custodians, is considered to be highly prejudicial, as it is physically dangerous and may bring about serious legal problems. However, the information everybody could get in the street (e.g. while walking the dog) will be very useful; it will help to co-ordinate surveillance and ways of communication within each respective functional unit.

Mutually protective actions among the members of a functional unit were also promoted. Normally, when one of the neighbours was away for a long time, the rest of the members would try to make it pass unnoticed, doing things, such as frequently sweeping his pavement, picking up his newspapers

---

[6] The instructions can be consulted at tripod.com.ar/planalerta.

or accumulated post, and so on. The instructions pointed out that 'sharing activities in the street improves safety, as it dissuades anyone who would try to take advantage of a possible victim being alone'. And recommended: 'it is necessary to agree on times for sweeping the pavement and washing the car, walking the dog and any other activity which makes the neighbours recover their blocks and enjoy them, instead of hiding and caging themselves up behind a fence'.

The residents were also encouraged to ask the local authorities to improve street lighting by installing new lamps or pruning street trees. At the same time, stickers and notices indicating the existence of 'Plan Alerta' were put all along the block, on telephone and lamp posts, as a warning to potential offenders to dissuade them from committing crimes: 'Plan Alerta. Block Controlled by its Neighbours in Direct Contact with the Police'.

As regards the relationship with the police, VS recommended that a representative group of each functional unit — or many of them from the same zone — should have an interview with the police officer of the highest rank in the competent police unit. The instructions said about this:

> In this interview you should explain clearly: that the neighbours of the block have decided to come together to improve their safety; that they want to share this responsibility with the police; that the neighbours will co-operate with the police as regards the observation of movement in the block and will contact them in case they have a doubt; that, at the same time, they ask the police to answer all their calls as soon as possible, as the Plan is based on mutual trust and on both parts assuming their roles; if the police department does not have an emergency phone number, the neighbours could pay for the installation of an input telephone line, which will allow direct access to the station at a very low cost and with the guarantee that it will not be possible to use it for anything else; to reach agreement with the officer about having regular meetings, in which they should check the general functioning of the Plan, discuss what can be improved and supervise every one in doing their jobs. The neighbours should tell the police about detected irregularities (e.g. that they were called and nobody answered, or that there was a 30-minute delay in getting to the place, etc) and co-ordinate what can be done to improve. It is important not to be highly critical but try to understand they are doing a co-operative job that will benefit everyone, as the neighbours become the Police's eyes and the latter the armed branch of the former; always handle the relationship as a co-operative enterprise and not as a constant complaint; take into account the fact that you are likely to get the Police's assistance, as the directives issued by their superiors contemplate the use of these plans which imply fluid contact with the Community, if by any chance you don't get support from the police station or they are not as disposed or supportive as you wish, don't think twice about getting in contact with a higher rank officer and explain to him your problems.

The first functional units of Saavedra started to work with the assistance of Police Station 49 of the PFA — the competent police institution in the City of Buenos Aires. When the first 'functional units' started to work, the VS group were trying to get the official support of the PFA and the DNPC. The Plan was formally set in motion in March 1998, with the support of both these agencies. But the change produced by the official support of this police institution did not mean a transformation of the way in which 'Plan Alerta' conceived this relationship, promoting the autonomous creation of 'functional units' from civil society. An individualised, direct relationship between the constituted functional units and the pertinent organisational segments of the police institution has thus been established, which presents certain variability. In some cases there has been a very good reception by the police.[7]

Early in October 1997 VS in Saavedra created a web page for 'Plan Alerta' in which the instructions to offset up a 'Plan Alerta' scheme were made known (http://tripod.com.ar/~Daniel_E_Cantón/base.htm). From this web page many connections were established with groups of neighbours and public institutions in the City of Buenos Aires as well as in different provinces of the country. At the end of 1999 VS drew up an e-mail list as a new space for virtual exchange of ideas with the aim of promoting 'Plan Alerta' (http://grupos.yahoo.com/group/PlanAlerta). Another member of this group pointed out: 'Most of what we have achieved as a group is due to the Internet. The Internet strengthens the experience we are carrying out' (Finquelevich-Vercelli-Saguier, 2002: 9). So much so that in 2001 a new 'Plan Alerta' web page was created (http://tripod.com.ar/planalerta).

From that moment, 'Plan Alerta' began to be 'imported' to other neighbourhoods in the city of Buenos Aires — Flores, Núñez, Palermo, etc and to some 'partidos' ('districts') in the Province of Buenos Aires–Almirante Brown, City Bell, La Plata, etc (see 'Proliferan los Planes de Seguridad Vecinal', *La Nación*, 24/9/02). One of the most important examples was the one in Ituzaingo, where the group which promotes it has its own web page (www.vecinosalerta.empre.com.ar). It was also extended to other provinces, such as La Pampa, Córdoba, Entre Ríos and Neuquén.

Today, the original group from Saavedra has established a Civil Association and is working together with the SSI on the creation of a 'Red Nacional de Seguridad Comunitaria' ('National Network for Community Security', henceforth RENASECO) through a cooperation agreement. Resolution (n) 556 of the National Ministry of Justice, Security and Human Rights of 27 November 2003 through which the RENASCO is formed, establishes that RENASECO is coordinated by the SSI and has been conceived as an instrument aimed at articulating and promoting even more the development and diffusion of this kind of initiative at national level, with the original format produced by VS,

---

[7] Superintendent Daniel Moreno, in charge of Police Station 45 in Villa Devoto in the City of Buenos Aires recently declared in an interview that 'Plan Alerta': 'is very useful to us because the neighbours become the police's eyes. As they live there and see everything, they can call us if something happens. It is impossible to say how many crimes are prevented with this system, but what is certain is that it prevents marauders from knowing whether a house is unprotected and, this is a good way of avoiding burglary. It is necessary to promote the creation of these nets.' (*Clarín*, 24/9/03).

which is the actor that, according to the terms of the agreement 'will provide the contents' of RENASECO (see www.planalerta.gov.ar and www.renaseco.gov.ar).

'PLAN NACIONAL DE PREVENCIÓN DEL DELITO': PARTNERSHIP, CITIZEN PARTICIPATION AND 'INTEGRATED PREVENTION' IN BUENOS AIRES

The 'Plan Nacional de Prevención del Delito' ('National Plan of Crime Prevention') was announced by the National Government of President de la Rúa, as a joint initiative of the national Ministry of Justice and Human Rights and the national Ministry of the Interior in August 2000 (Res. MJDH N. 768/00 and Res. MI N. 56/00). The PNPD was designed by a commission involving officers from both ministries, lead by the DNPC (Ministry of Justice and Human Rights) and the National Directorate of Security Policies (Ministry of the Interior).[8]

The PNPD sets as fundamental objectives: 'to reduce street or predatory crimes'; 'to decrease the fear of crime' and 'to promote the active participation of non-governmental actors and constitute a network of commitment, co-operation and articulation with governmental actors aimed at crime prevention' (PNPD, 2000). Initially, the PNPD is presented as an initiative of national scope, which is going to adjust its forms of preventive intervention to the concrete manifestations of urban insecurity in different regions, cities and areas of implementation, but in its design some 'strategic outlines' are drawn. The PNPD explicitly adopts the model of 'integrated prevention'. 'Integrated prevention' proposes in each preventive intervention a blending of techniques that are characteristic of 'social crime prevention' strategies — 'one intended to work on the social causes of crime' — and the 'situational environmental prevention' strategy — 'one intended to reduce crime opportunities'. The PNPD design states:

> ...both make important contributions towards the objective of reducing crime and fear of crime, but it is necessary to recognise that whilst the situational-environmental strategy has a greater degree of effectiveness in the short term it does not generate lasting effects in the medium and long terms. This strategy should, therefore, be articulated with the social strategy since its scope is extremely limited. The Plan favours medium and long term interventions, and in this respect, subordinates the situational-environmental strategy to the social strategy (PNPD, 2000).

For the development of 'integrated prevention' PNPD design proposes a structure of decentralised and multi-agency administration that combines national, provincial and municipal state actors through a series of formal agreements. Along with this, the PNPD promotes the development of 'commitment, co-operation and articulation schemes' with other state agencies, apart from the PNPD structure of administration, which at national, provincial and municipal levels are carrying out actions and initiatives connected to crime prevention.

In the same direction, the PNPD design makes a strong appeal to 'citizen participation', as a 'fundamental engine of the plan', stating that it is thought that: 'the problem of urban insecurity is an unavoidable responsibility of the State, although it is necessary to recognise the limits of governmental action' and that '... the interventions must be constructed with the active participation of the citizens in its different modalities in local communities, contributing to the democratisation of public policies and increasing their effectiveness and efficiency' (PNPD, 2000). When the PNPD design appeals to 'citizen participation' it explicitly moves away from 'community' language, which as we have seen had been promoted in different recent experiences in our country.[9]

The implementation process according to the PNPD design comprises different stages: (1) the selection of regions, cities and areas where preventive interventions can be developed; (2) a scientific, quantitative and qualitative diagnosis of the state of urban safety in the areas of implementation; (3) drawing a socio-demographic, economic and infrastructural map of the area of implementation; (4) drawing a map of the civil organisations in the area of implementation; (5) creating a mechanism of formal and permanent citizen participation through periodic 'assemblies' in sub-areas within every area of implementation to determine through debate an 'agenda of problems', of 'proposals of viable solutions within the frame of crime prevention strategies promoted by the Plan', 'co-operation in the development of preventive interventions' and their 'evaluation'; (6) 'designing the interventions, the articulation with other governmental actors and the development of the interventions'; (7) monitoring of the implementation process (PNPD, 2000). Finally, the PNPD design proposes a mechanism of annual evaluation of the implementation processes which combines a 'results evaluation' or 'quantitative' with a 'procedural evaluation' or 'qualitative' (PNPD, 2000).

From the moment it was put into practice, the PNPD has been primarily implemented in the City of Buenos Aires with a formal agreement between

---

[8] This initiative was somewhat related to the birth and development of Plan 'Alerta', as one of the two public organisms that conducted its design — the DNPC — was, as mentioned above, connected to that experience.

[9] 'Certain political and academic discourses circulate in our country in which the expression "local communities" makes reference to a group of individuals who share a territory and a "community sense" or "sense of belonging" which means they have interests, values and identities in common — a "moral consensus". This mythical view sees the community as a homogeneous and harmonious group which defends itself against "strangers", conceived as potential criminals, installing an "us against them" attitude. Nowadays, local communities are complex social assemblages, pervaded by multiple sources of social differentiation, power, age, gender, class, religion, etc. These social differences generate diverse voices which produce manifest or latent friction within the community. Consensus about what is good and what is wrong, in this sphere, is the product of intricate and complex negotiations and many times turns out to be unattainable' (PNPD, 2000).

the National Government and the Government of the City of Buenos Aires. Evidently, the implementation process of the PNPD suffered a number of 'deviations' from its original design in different issues — something that, by contrast, is always, to a certain extent, inevitable. But there have also been a series of 'innovations' to mitigate gaps in the original design, which was set at a general and abstract level. The procedural evaluation of the implementation in the City of Buenos Aires during the 2000–01 period shows the fundamental features in the 'life' of the PNPD (Sozzo, 2003).[10] In extreme synthesis, it can be highlighted:

a. As regards the PNPD operators there was in the Argentinian context a lack of 'crime prevention specialists', so this specific competence was replaced by competences in adjacent areas — especially in the area of social work. However, the selection of the PNPD operators at the Government of the CBA level was not led by the prescriptions of the PNPD design but by political convenience and patronising interests. The only criteria used for the creation of the Regional Technical Unit — henceforth, UTR- and the Local Implementation Teams — henceforth, EIL (two people for each of the 16 zones of the city) — was that the members must belonged to one of the political parties of the governing coalition in equal quantities. An interviewed operator called it 'the "partydisation" of the practices' —which began, however, to be neutralised as the implementation process advanced and such coalition started to be decomposed.

b. As regards the establishment of co-operation schemes at national level, the results were remarkably limited, only a few formal relations being generated towards the end of 2001 with: (1) the 'Consejo Nacional de Niñez, Adolescencia y Familia' ('National Council for Childhood, Adolescence and Family') with the objective of articulating prevention actions, sharing information and improving resources connected to young people who leave institutions for minors — especially those who were on a sort of 'parole'; (2) and the Ministerio de Trabajo, Empleo y Seguridad Social de la Nación ('National Ministry of Labour, Employment and Social Security') through which the distribution of Labour Emergency Plans was established, with 100 beneficiaries, to be used within the frame of the PNPD, for the development of social prevention interventions in sectors of 'high social vulnerability'—we will come back to this later. At the local level there was no co-operation schemes between the PNPD and the pertinent local state agencies. Only 'informal' relations were created based on direct 'personal contacts' in regard to particular problems and with a 'favour request-favour concession' dynamics, the potential 'combined actions' between local state agencies associated to the 'partnership' idea being transformed, in one of the EIL members' words, into 'casuistry'.

---

[10] This procedural evaluation was based on focus groups and in-depth interviews held with every crime prevention operator within the PNPD administration structure, both from the national and local level.

c. In particular, it was not possible to establish a co-operation scheme with the PFA, especially from the moment the Ministry of the Interior –from which it formally depend — 'retreated' from the PNPD implementation because of changes in the cabinet in March 2001. Also here there was a series of 'informal', 'casuistry' relations that varied according to the 'personal' aptitudes of the EIL members to establish liaisons with police superintendents, in the different police stations.

d. There was no scientific diagnosis of the state of urban safety in each zone letting the creation of the 'agenda of problems' depend exclusively on the performance of the participatory mechanism, with all kinds of deviations as regards the representation of the citizens who participated in it and the interpretations of those debates made by crime prevention operators.

e. The participatory mechanism became the centre of the PNPD implementation, even displacing the development of preventive interventions. The participatory mechanism in practice, has been fundamentally oriented towards the search for a quantitative result: the greatest number of assemblies with the greatest number of participants in every area. These quantitative data became the 'effectiveness' indicators and, in most of the cases, the 'democratising' objective of the promotion of the citizens' participation was lost. Such citizen participation was extremely 'selective': adults — mainly over 50 years old — with a certain preponderance of women over men and belonging to the middle class. The participatory mechanism neither include young people, nor the poor, nor other 'difficult to reach' groups (prostitutes, homeless, etc). (Newburn and Jones, 2000).

f. The participatory mechanism was not aimed at establishing an 'agenda of problems' but a list of 'demands', of these citizens who selectively participated in the assemblies, who could hardly be considered democratically representatives of the population of the implementation area. The idea of 'demand' refers back to a definition of the intervention to be carried out, exclusively performed by the citizens who take part in the participatory mechanism, with the role of activating the 'answer' left to the state actors. This 'demand-answer' dynamics has a clear 'populist' logic that is based on 'popular' claims, intended to produce and reproduce political consensus. The demands which were 'received' — this expression implies the idea that the role of crime prevention operators is absolutely passive in the assembly space, although this was not true in many cases — by the PNPD during 2001 were connected to — according to the operators' 'occupational language' — 'police intervention': 57 per cent — police presence and patrolling in public spaces—, 'public works': 15 per cent — requests for lights to be installed or reinforcement of the existing ones –'environmental intervention': 12 per cent — requests for tree pruning and the maintenance of parks and squares, contravention: 8 per cent — requests for punishing intervention towards minor offenses, such as prostitution or alcoholic drinks expenditure to minors-and 'apparent squatting': 3 per cent — requests for eviction of squatted houses or estates. Only in a few cases are these demands 'received' through the participatory mechanism expressly or exactly connected to 'problems', expressing in multiple cases a feeling of insecurity and 'moral indignation'.

g. In the 'demand-answer' dynamics associated to 'populism' with which the PNPD implementation process has worked, the pseudo-preventive interventions have been those demanded by the 'public' — the social groups that have been selectively present — in the participatory mechanism, mainly inscribed in a pretended 'situational-environmental prevention strategy'. They have been only pseudo-preventive interventions as they have not been connected to 'problems' but to 'popular' claims and requests and they have not been, therefore, rationally designed to fulfil the objective of reducing the dimensions of a 'problem' but to satisfy the 'demand'. As a result of this there is no unit of analysis of 'preventive interventions' in the PNPD database, but information is given about the 'demands' which have received an 'answer' and those which have not: out of 1309 'received' demands during 2001, 39 per cent of them have been 'answered'. It is difficult to consider these 'answers' as 'preventive interventions', but if that would be the case, the original PNPD design would have been inverted with an absolute preponderance of 'situational-environmental prevention' measures (police presence and patrolling in public spaces, pruning, illumination). To this can be added actions that would hardly be considered 'preventive', such as the eviction of 'squatted houses and estates'.

h. Since the middle of 2001 the creation of 'Redes Solidarias de Prevención del Delito' ('Networks of Solidarity for Crime Prevention', henceforth, RSPD) has been promoted — an innovation as regards the original design. This was a device for the mobilisation of individuals and families so that they could develop certain self-protective actions. In 2001, 40 networks were formed. According to the document 'Redes Solidarias. Cómo conformar una red de vecinos' ('Networks of Solidarity. How to constitute a network of neighbours') the networks have as their principal tool: 'being on the alert for situations of real or potential risk, in which case the neighbours should call the police immediately saying you are neighbours who participate in the Plan for Crime Prevention' (PNPD, 2001). The source of inspiration of the RSPD has evidently been 'Plan Alerta' of Saavedra, previously analysed. A member of the DNPC pointed out: 'the networks of neighbours turn out to be defensive mechanisms adopting the worst of "Plan Alerta"'. In fact, it is not by chance that the word 'alert' is used to define its fundamental tool. Another member of the UTG characterised these 'networks of solidarity' as 'unions caused by terror' constructed under the motto 'let's form the network to defend ourselves'.

i. Facing the almost complete annulment of any kind of reference to the 'social prevention' strategy, in October 2001 the 'Programa de Comunidades

Vulnerables' ('Programme for Vulnerable Communities', henceforth, PCV) was created at national level to try to reverse, at least partially, this tendency — another innovation as regards the original design. This Programme was intended to take actions to reduce 'social vulnerability' through the promotion of 'insertion to the labour market, job training, educational and health assistance and leisure facilities' (PCV, 2001). This programme is oriented to the members of 'vulnerable communities' defined as 'a group of interrelated people within a territorial unit, who share a situation of significant non-fulfilment of essential human rights, such as housing, health, education, etc' (PCV, 2001). It is therefore the PCV goal, according to its design: 'to reduce social vulnerability by preventing violence and dealing with social conflicts in different everyday aspects in a vulnerable community, in order to improve the community's quality of life, from the point of view of the minimum intervention principle' (PCV, 2001). According to the PCV original design, there are four dimensions in this type of intervention: the 'individual dimension' (the capacity to retain the most vulnerable members within their reference groups or the groups they belong to), the 'group dimension' (the capacity of the reference groups to answer the community's needs), the 'socio-community dimension' ('community constitution and construction process') and the 'socio-institutional dimension' (the capacity of the State and non-governmental institutions to assist') (PCV, 2001). The first person to be in charge of the PCV direction pointed out: 'It is the land to thresh in a crime prevention plan that shouldn't reproduce marginal groups.'

An analogous PCV was simultaneously created at the CBA Government level. Both programmes had to function as a single work team but a conflict rapidly emerged due to the availability by the local PCV of a series of 'personal benefits' — labour Emergency Plans and analogues — to use in different 'villas miserias' (shanty towns) of CBA. Those personal benefits were administered under a patronage system, according some members of the national PCV, without any kind of connection with the objective of preventing crime. As a result of this, the national PVC started to work directly in several 'villas miserias' of CBA and Greater Buenos Aires. This work was supported through the agreement before mentioned with the Ministerio de Trabajo, Empleo y Seguridad Social de la Nación, which made it possible to have from January 2002 Labour Emergency Plans to facilitate the task — a monthly personal benefit of 150 Pesos for four to six months. This has been the only type of financial resources that this PCV obtained, until today. Six projects were set up, with this financial help. For example: determining the needs and resources of the vulnerable community, including the reconstruction of their history, and setting up a workshop where they produced handmade candles in order to generate sustainable micro-enterprises — 'Ciudad Oculta', Buenos Aires, 20 beneficiaries —; or organic manure production through worm cultivation from household solid waste (organic rubbish) collection, selection and processing and the reconstruction of the vulnerable community's history and determination of their central problems through a video (a workshop was set up for the beneficiaries to learn how to make it) – 'Villa Tranquila', Avellaneda, 10 beneficiaries–; and so on.

The creation of the PCV sanctioned another inversion of the original PNPD design: the 'integrated prevention' model was turned into 'dissociated prevention'. The preponderant strategy of situational-environmental 'pseudo-prevention' connected to the 'demand-answer' dynamics of the participatory mechanism, ruled by populism, was developed in certain middle and upper class urban areas, whereas an incipient and shy 'social prevention' strategy started to be developed in the most precarious lower class urban areas, without any type of articulation between them and with different and even opposing assumptions and logics. A member of the DNPC said about it: 'The plan was certainly transformed into two plans, of situational-environmental prevention and social prevention... the integrated prevention never existed... In practice, I see social prevention and situational prevention as dissociated, and on the other hand, I'm worried that we go on dissociating them...'.

Despite the dramatic events of December 2001 and the abrupt fall of the National Government of President de la Rúa, the PNPD continued to be implemented in CBA during 2002 with similar characteristics to the ones observed during 2001, with less emphasis on the assemblies and stressing the importance of holding 'inter-assemblies meetings' and the constitution of many RSPD.[11] All this combined with an absolute distance between the activity of the national and local operators. During 2002 all the members of the DNPC focused completely on the PCV and totally abandoned any monitoring or assisting role connected to the participatory mechanism and the situational-environmental prevention, which was left in the hands of local operators. The activity of the PCV progressively multiplied the intervention spaces as well as the volume of direct beneficiaries. In January 2003 the number of young people involved grew to 300 and since September that year, it has grown to 400.

CULTURAL TRAVELS, METAMORPHOSIS AND CRIME PREVENTION IN ARGENTINA

As we said before, these present cultural travels in the field of the government of crime, are not identical to those of the past. Different transformations proper to the process of globalisation have multiplied and speeded up in an amazing way the traffic of elements of rationalities and technologies (Kartstedt, 2001, 2002; Sparks, 2001). There exists nowadays a global network of frantic activities which not only include the travels of discourses, but also the travels of experts. These 'new experts' in the crime control field, frequently have little

---

[11] According to the GCBA there are now 300 organised Networks, which involve about 20 000 neighbours (*La Nación*, 11/11/03).

or no connection to the traditional sources of academic legitimisation. They are the 'consultants' and 'advisors' from companies, foundations and non-governmental organisations, who become the new 'counsellors to the Prince' on the subject (Wacquant, 2000; Haggerty, 2002). This frantic global traffic has to do — as we pointed out with respect to the more specific field of 'crime prevention' — with the development of initiatives and actions taken by different international, governmental and non-governmental organisations which are particularly concerned with the promotion of these cultural imports — UN, IDB, World Bank, etc (Cohen, 1982; Karstedt, 2002).

The installation and functioning of 'Plan Alerta', first in the City of Buenos Aires and progressively in other jurisdictions, as a cultural importation of Neighbourhood Watch, is a clear example of these transformations. As the members themselves of the VS group recognise, the Internet had a fundamental role in their fast translation of this peculiar intervention technique within the field of crime prevention. This velocity introduces a sharp contrast with past experiences. The cultural importation 'here' of these devices developed 'there' used to take decades. A clear example is the birth of the 'modern' prison in Argentina, with the inauguration of the National Penitentiary of Buenos Aires in 1877, quite out of synch with the emergence of penitentiary imprisonment in Europe and North America a century earlier (cf Caimari, 2002). The contemporary developments in Argentina also present another novelty: the fundamental actors in this process of cultural importation, from 'here', are radically different from the ones involved in past cultural travels. They are not 'experts' working in the state sphere — within or outside the academic world-any more, but 'neighbours', 'volunteers', members of 'civil society', worried about urban insecurity, who adopt a technique picked up from somewhere else and who promote its installation and functioning in their own context, carrying the agencies of the state along in their wake — in this case, the PFA, the DNPC and more recently, the SSI.

In the case of the birth of the PNPD, the characteristics of the actors of the cultural importation are closer to the ones of those who traditionally played this role in the past, as they are and were, basically, public servants. Now, within the designing commission of the PNPD, although there were people who had a certain level of specialisation in the subject, connected to academic activity or the design and development of public policies in this field, there was also a strong presence of rather 'political' elements, which could hardly be described as displaying 'expertise' in the subject — even by the permissive standards of the 'new expertise' mentioned above. In addition to this, in the emergence of the PNPD we can also see the influence — though not determinant — of these international entities before mentioned. Specifically, one of the public bodies directly involved in the design and implementation of the PNPD — the DNPC — maintained frequent contacts with the Latin American Institute of the United Nations for Crime Prevention and Treatment of Offenders and the Commission for Crime Prevention and Penal Justice of the United Nations — of which it held the vice-presidency, representing Argentina, in 1996 (DNPC, 1997, 237–8; DNPC, 1999, 161–3). Since 1998, it has also maintained a strong connection with the International Centre for Crime Prevention set up in Montreal — as mentioned above — adopting its descriptions and recommendations in its annual publication of 1999 as well as translating into Spanish its 'Crime Prevention Digest' (cf DNPC, 1999, 37–44).

But, like the cultural travels from the past, beyond their differences, the present ones also imply, substantially, a metamorphosis of the imported cultural objects.

I. The most noticeable peculiarity of 'Plan Alerta', as a cultural translation of NW, is the type of connection maintained with the police. The NW schemes constructed by 'Plan Alerta', owing to the way the importation process of this cultural device was produced, having been initiated by a group of neighbours and only subsequently received the police's support, are put into practice as a 'property' of the groups of neighbours who are formed around them. This is revealed in the constant assertion of the autonomy of these groups of neighbours, who refer to the NW scheme as 'our work' or 'our labour'. Obviously, this assertion of their 'property' does not lack ambiguities, as expressed in the notion of NW as the 'eyes of the police'. even in the schemes promoted by 'Plan Alerta' the role of the police is still a fundamental one — as witness the key phrase in the notices announcing a functional unit: 'block controlled by its neighbours in direct contact with the police'.

Nevertheless, these NW schemes are initially constructed by civil society and only then is a relationship with the police considered. This inverts the dynamics with which this type of intervention technique has functioned, in their original cultural contexts. This is why in the document of the instructions produced by VS a series of steps are suggested to establish the relationship with the police and the possibility of failure is contemplated. This autonomy with regard to the police has been ratified, trough the recent creation of the RENASECO, which promotes the creation of NW schemes of 'Plan Alerta' all over the country, beyond police institutions and giving VS its 'technical control'.

This inversion of the original dynamics of NW, as to its relationship with the police, turns out to be, evidently, an adaptation to a local context. There are two intertwined variables that influence this configuration. On the one hand, the deep public distrust of the police institutions in Argentina, based in the extremely high rates of violence, corruption and inefficiency of the police activity — especially, in the cases of the Police of the Province of Buenos Aires and the Federal Police (Tiscornia & Oliveira, 1998; Tiscornia, 2000; Sozzo, 2002). By contrast, the absence of a strong reforming movement within police institutions which would itself import 'community policing' and 'problem oriented policing' strategies and thus make intervention techniques like NW a structural part of police practices — apart from some slight manifestations, mostly rhetorical, developed in the last years (cf. Sagarduy & Rosua, 1999; Saín, 2002; Gonzalez, 2003).

II. The PNPD has a series of local particularities with regard to its design as well as its implementation.

a. In the first place, there is a local specificity as regards the constitution and functioning of that which the PNPD language calls its 'participatory mechanism'. This device aimed at promoting citizen participation is constituted, in its design as well as in its implementation, by the administrative structure of the PNPD and it is governed by 'crime prevention operators'. In some cases during the first phase of the implementation process there were senior police officers present at the meetings with the neighbours — 'assemblies' according to the PNPD language. This caused several conflicts with the crime prevention operators about the conduct of the dialogue with and among the neighbours. These conflicts resulted in a systematic attempt, on the part of the PNPD to exclude the police from the assemblies, except in those cases in which the neighbours' claims made impossible to avoid it. Meetings of this kind have been, in English-speaking contexts since the 1970s, largely initiated by the police, in the context of internal reform movements favouring 'community policing' and 'problem oriented policing' strategies (Rosenbaum-Lurigio-Davis, 1998: 173–200). This way of acting is adopted by the PNPD in Argentina and adapted to the local context, initiated by crime prevention operators, who not only are not police officers but have a tense — in some cases conflictive-relationship with the police, not only within the frame of the assemblies but also when they seek 'answers' by the police to the 'demand' revealed by the participatory mechanism.

Perhaps some of these local, contextual peculiarities — public distrust of the police in Argentina and the absence of an internal reform movement — enable us to understand the emergence of this 'participatory mechanism', beyond the police institution in the PNPD implementation process, as a political decision based in these evidences relative to the police in Argentina. But it is also possible to consider another reason. The PFA had already held similar meetings with the public since 1997, under the name of 'Centros de Prevención Comunitaria' ('Community Prevention Centres', henceforth, CPC) around the 53 Police Stations of the CBA. However, this initiative was not enthusiastically developed by the police and nor did it find any echo among the neighbours as to the volume of participation — in fact, nowadays there are only a few surviving CPC functioning with very small groups of neighbours. Therefore, the participative mechanism of the PNPD was always part of a political challenge directed towards the police institution in the CBA, as a way of disrupting their traditional monopoly in the field of 'crime prevention' (Sozzo, 2000, 2004). Furthermore, there was a series of conflicts in some PNPD 'assemblies', between the operators and the members of the residual CPCs. After the national Ministry of the Interior 'retreated' from the PNPD implementation process in in March 2001 — when the PFA still depended of it —, the constitution of this participative mechanism was also part-and-parcel of, on one hand the political conflicts in the National Governments of that period — the Government of President De la Rúa and the Government of President Duhalde — about who was in charge of articulating public policies on urban safety within this territory and, on the other, the political conflicts between some sectors in these National Governments and the Government of the City of Buenos Aires, primarily about the problem of 'transferring' a segment of the PFA or the creation a new police by the Government of the City of Buenos Aires (Marteau, 2002).

    b.   In the second place, it is possible to point out another local specificity in regard to the dynamics of this participatory mechanism in the PNPD implementation process, which has functioned, as we said, on the basis of a demand/answer logic connected to a patronage system. In contrast to its original design, the participation of citizens in the PNPD implementation became a way of expressing demands that have to be answered by crime prevention operators, whatever the state agency to give the answer might be, laying emphasis on the satisfaction of the participants. This could be translated into a 'popular' acceptance of the state actors involved, not only the operators in direct contact with the neighbours but, in general, the Government of the City of Buenos Aires.

This demand/answer logic based on a populist way of thinking and acting may have originated, on the one hand, in the 'partydisation' which accompanied the construction of the PNPD administration structure at the local level mentioned above. The fact that the selected crime prevention operators had as a central characteristic an active political militancy could have implied ways of thinking and acting typical of 'playing politics' in the everyday functioning of the PNPD implementation process.

But another element which characterises the present panorama of the government of crime in Argentina has had, certainly, some influence in this peculiar construction of the process of implementation of the PNPD. During the 1990s Argentina witnessed the emergence of high crime and fear of crime rates as a 'normal' social fact. This coincided with a series of economic and cultural transformations which seal the country's transition to a 'peripheral' late modernity. This emergence also implies an 'emergency'. It is embodied in the demands for safety of the residents of large and medium-sized cities aimed at the political sphere. In response, political actors at all levels of the polity lay symbolic claim to take seriously citizens' demands and expectations (Sozzo, 1999). Thus, urban insecurity is progressively transformed into an object of political exchange, into a 'political merchandise', through which the production of political and electoral consensus is sought (Pavarini, 1994, 2003a). This contemporary 'politicisation' that accompanies the emergence/ emergency of urban insecurity implies, primarily, the birth of a need to legitimise crime control strategies 'from the bottom up', a growing requirement for the 'democratic' validation of policies (Pavarini, 2003b). This 'politisation' of urban insecurity reached its peak in Argentina during the Presidential and provincial Gubernatorial election campaigns of and the Mayoral elections in the City of Buenos Aires in 2000. At this time the phenomenon that Bottoms (1995) has defined as 'punitive populism' began to emerge. Populist politics clearly aims at gaining political and electoral consensus, resorting to an 'emotive and ostentatious' display of the moral vocabulary of guilt, responsibility and punishment, stirring feelings of anguish and anger, inhospitable to rational forms of thought and judgement, articulating them with proposals and measures constructed in their image and which open the field of the government of crime to the resurrection of an 'economy of excess' (Foucault, 1989, 2000; Hallsworth, 2000; Pratt, 2000; Pavarini, 2003b).[12]

The demand/answer logic based on a patronage system around which the implementation of the PNPD participatory mechanism was put into effect can be understood as another manifestation of this same 'politisation', characterised by the need for bottom-up legitimation of crime control policy. A sort of 'preventive populism' seems to emerge around it: once crime has become a basic object of political exchange, the idea would be to seek political consensus. But this time the appeal is less towards punishment as such but rather towards prevention, expressed in terms of 'social defence' — the defence of the 'respectable classes' from the 'dangerous and criminal classes', of 'us against them', through situational-environmental measures. It is a game consisting in the submission of demands and the production of answers, which reinforces a 'fortress mentality' and social exclusion. This, in turn, is perfectly articulated with the diffusion of the Networks of Solidarity for Crime Prevention and the 'appeal to "community"' they involve. And at the same time, it is easily compatible with the manifestations of 'punitive populism' that are so pervasive in our present.

c.   In the third place, it is possible to observe another local specificity around the peculiar indexation that the 'social prevention' strategy acquired within the frame of the PNPD implementation with the creation of the Vulnerable Communities Programme. The way of thinking and acting which has been put into practice at a clearly micro-physical level by the PCV are different, to a certain extent, from those proposed within the dominant paradigm of 'social prevention' in English-speaking cultural contexts: 'developmental crime prevention'. Tonry and Farrington define this as:

> interventions designed to prevent the development of criminal potentials in individuals, especially targeting risk and protective factors discovered in studies of human development (1995, 2–3).

This way of thinking and acting social prevention is based, in part, on David Farrington's neopositivist sociopsychological research and also, on Gottfredson

---

[12] Carlos Ruckauf, then Vice-president of the Nation and candidate for Governor of the Province of Buenos Aires for the Justicialismo Party, said: 'We mustn't feel pity for the murderers who kill our people, I want to see them dead. I'm going to be absolutely tough with crime. Between a defenceless citizen and an armed criminal, the one who has to be beaten is the criminal. I have no doubts. We have to choose between people and criminals' (*La Nación*, 6/8/99).

and Hirschi's control theory and specially promotes the development of interventions aimed at the first stages of the individual's development – childhood and adolescence–focusing on the family and the school, trying to address risk factors, generating protective factors (Tremblay-Craig, 1995; Crawford, 1998, 109–124; Rosembaum-Lurigio-Davis, 1998: 203–210).

The way of thinking and acting promoted by the PCV seem to be more connected to other theoretical and political sources. Links could be established with the ideas that fostered experiences, such as the Mobilization for Youth Programme in New York in the 1960s, more recently taken up in the United States by the Eisenhower Foundation in the 1980s, which had a certain elective affinity with Robert Merton's anomie theory and Cloward and Ohlin's ideas about crime and blocked opportunities (Hope, 1995: 34–41; Crawford, 1998, 106–108; Rosenmbaum-Lurigio-Davis, 1998: 210–216). And still we can find more solid points in common with the social prevention initiatives which have been carried out since the 1980s in France: initiatives related to young people who are socially excluded — who are out of the labour market and the school system, generally members of ethnic minorities — which focus on the creation of opportunities of job training, employment, education and leisure facilities — and which in turn have been promoted from theoretical and political views which had some influence of the critical criminologies of the 1980s (Robert, 1991; Baratta, 1993; Pavarini, 1994; Duprez, 1997; Roché, 1999; Selmini, 1999, 2003).

However, according to what its operators coincidentally said, the PCV discourses and practices were structured to a lesser extent by direct processes of cultural importation of these different sources — even though it could be hypothesised that some of them were in a way present in the constitution of their intervention techniques — and to a greater degree by a local tradition of social intervention in impoverished urban areas, especially in the 'villas miserias', not only constructed by state agencies but also by volunteers and civil society. On this basis, less connected in its origin to 'crime' than to the 'social' sphere, it is possible to observe that there is a perspective of the PCV on criminal issues which is to a certain extent connected to elements of the vocabulary of Latin American critical criminology of the 1980s. This is manifested in its operators' discourse in different ways: the negation of the influence of 'psychological factors' on the production of crime, an explicit rejection of any idea about 'treatment of offenders', a strong connection of their practice to the reduction of social injustice and inequality and strong criticism of the criminal justice system — especially, of the police. This influence can be seen graphically expressed in the name of the programme itself, which takes up a very well diffused notion in the critical criminological vocabulary in Latin America from the late 1980s, the concept of 'vulnerability', presented in its most complete form in some texts written at that time by Raúl Zaffaroni to define the social groups which are 'good candidates for criminalisation' and to advocate a transformation of the 'criminological clinic' into a 'vulnerability clinic' (Zaffaroni, 1988: 24–28; 1989: 274–287).

In the way of thinking and acting put into practice by the PCV it is possible to visualise two elements which turn out to be local particularities, even when this experience is compared with those which are more related in other cultural contexts.

On the one hand, the use of 'personal benefits' which, as we said, consist of monthly money subsidies directly aimed at the beneficiaries and which function as a payment for their participation in the programme. The reasons for using these 'personal benefits' lie, in part, in the fact that, in general, a great number of the social policies promoted by the last National Governments — De la Rúa, Duhalde — are structured in relation to this type of device, which makes it difficult to articulate the government funding of programmes and interventions connected to the 'social' sphere though an alternative scheme. By contrast, the funding of the PCV interventions does not, in the strict sense, 'belong' to it. Through the agreement before mentioned with the national Ministry of Labour, Employment and Social Security, this organism 'hands over' to it a portion of 'personal benefits' to elaborate 'projects'. Apart from this funding, the only resources the PCV can count on are those which are used to pay its operators' salaries. In fact, the absence of a budget of its own to finance the intervention is one of the most important obstacles to the development of this social prevention strategy, as it is unanimously recognised by the PCV operators. At the same time, these operators keep an ongoing discussion about the advantages and disadvantages of using these 'personal benefits'. On the one hand, it is asserted that they facilitate contact with the beneficiaries and their commitment to the tasks to be developed. On the other, it is believed that they generate an initial association in the beneficiaries, which later has to be painfully reverted, with the practices based on a patronage system typical of many social policies and also raise the problem of the continuity of the beneficiaries' insertion in the tasks once the period of receiving this 'personal benefit' is over.

By contrast, the recourse to 'social micro-enterprises' serves as a device to generate a new type of insertion in the world of work for the socially excluded young people involved. In a context of high levels of unemployment in the legitimate labour market, as regards regular forms of employment, even in their most precarious and flexible forms, a different connection with work is promoted with the creation of a productive or service activity which has as its primary target the daily economy of the 'vulnerable community'. The aim is to make these 'social micro-enterprises' viable and profitable, in the sense that they establish themselves, in the long run, as income producers for the beneficiaries involved. It is also possible to observe here the impact of the ways in which many of the programmes of social policies are usually structured, fostered by the National Governments, which have tried, especially over recent years, to promote the development of this sort of device. But, at the same time, the compatibility of this type of initiative with the most general theoretical and political premises of the PCV is clear.

COLONIALISM/NEOCOLONIALISM AND THE GOVERNMENT OF CRIME

Over 20 years ago Cohen (1982) wrote an article about the export of models of crime control from the central countries to those of the third world. He distinguished in that text two models of cultural importation of rationalities and technologies for the government of crime: the 'Benign Transfer' and the 'Malign Colonialism'. Both models defined by Cohen were constructed on the basis of a combination of a way of conceiving crime control and a way of understanding the nature of underdevelopment (Cohen, 1982: 90). According to the 'malignant colonialism' model, the colonialism and neo-colonialism born of the globalisation of capitalist relations of production, and the economic dependence of the peripheral countries on the central countries, was translated into cultural colonialism and neo-colonialism, which in our field of knowledge/ power meant 'mimetic reproduction' (Cohen, 1982: 102). Not in vain, Cohen quoted among the examples of 'Malign Colonialism' he used, the work of some Latin-American 'contemporary radical criminologists' and two texts in particular: Del Olmo's (1975) and Riera's (1979). This kind of argument is at the root, as we said in the first section of the present essay, of all Latin American critical criminologists' readings about the history of the government of crime in the region, with the exception, needless to say, of their own intellectual and political production — even when some of these intellectuals, self-critically, extended it to their own critical tradition, as in the case of Rosa Del Olmo. Even the most heterodox authors, who avoided a strong Marxist commitment in their intellectual production, had this common starting point, as in the case of Raúl Zaffaroni, who, furthermore, converted it into the central axis of his vision and proposal —the 'marginal criminological realism' (Zaffaroni, 1988, 1989). As Cohen pointed out, in 'malignant colonialism' 'the importance of the ideas and intentions is frequently obscured' (1982: 102). This argument generated an automatic and simple link between economic and cultural processes. This model considered culture as a dependent variable, even though there will be attempts, in the subtlest versions, to make that dependence more complex.

This approach is rather simplistic. Throughout this essay, via the particular example of the recent cultural travels of crime prevention discourse in Argentina, we have tried to show the elements that call upon another reading of the processes of cultural importation. Departing from the 'malignant colonialism' model does not imply embracing the alternative 'benign transfer' model also analysed by Cohen (1982: 90–8), which turns out to be the 'common sense' of those who are fully involved in these activities of cultural translation — even under the moderate cloak of 'reluctant imperialists' (Cohen, 1982: 96) — and which is infinitely less plausible. It rather aims at installing a different form of understanding, which in our case does not share the hope of founding an alternative 'model' — which is Cohen's political rather than heuristic intention in the proposal of the 'paradoxical damage' model (Cohen, 1982: 103 and ff.)

Cultural travels have been a constant element in the history of the government of crime in Latin America and in Argentina but they have not been mere transplants, transpositions, transfers. They have been real metamorphoses, in which the local actors have made use of the culturally imported devices to face the numerous problems in their local contexts, generating cultural objects 'here', through their political and theoretical inventiveness, which were at the same time different and the same as those from 'there' like Robert Castel's Zeus-Ox. Cultural translation has not excluded creativity or innovation. Rather these, to a certain extent, have been made viable by it, even though the range of options is not infinite if the intention is to keep certain identity among the actors and objects connected through the cultural travel. But it has not excluded either, needless to say, repetition, imitation and mimesis. All along the lengthy run of the analytic description of the constitution of the field of 'crime prevention beyond punishment' in the present in Argentina, we tried to show how these alternatives work.

Seen in this light, 'cultural dependence' looks like a complex phenomenon in itself, which on occasion admits some important degrees of variation on the travel of the cultural devices from 'there' to 'here'. In this sense, the idea of 'dependence' loses the strength of an absolute determination, since cultural translation always opens a certain field of possibilities for the local translators. And it creates the need to observe the amount and form of the influence, in every case, tracking thoroughly the discursive and non-discursive practices generated 'there' and 'here' (cf Newburn & Jones, 2002). By contrast, the cultural processes appear in this way of reading, consequently, autonomised with regard to economic processes and distant from the traditional idea of 'ideology' (Cohen, 1982, 1988). This, of course, does not imply the absence of connections, but rather the need to understand them beyond a strong idea of causality, trying to observe what in Weberian terms could be defined as 'elective affinities', confluences or adaptations which do not let the elements involved lose their autonomy or their potential capacity to become strange or antagonistic (Marteau, 2003, Melossi, this volume).

I have tried in this essay to emphasise the specificity of cultural contexts and, thus, collaborate in rethinking the issue of comparison in the field of the government of crime. As Dario Melossi has recently pointed out: 'If, on the one hand, we can observe conceptualisations about how to organise the world emerging more or less at the same time in very different and distant parts of the world... on the other hand, the use of identical words frequently obscures the degree in which they are entrenched/rooted in the different histories of different places, as well as the way they are articulated through at least partially different discourses' (Melossi, 2001: 405). Besides cultural translations, the construction of rationalities and technologies of government of crime were and are always unyieldingly local, 'native', as they were and are rooted in their own historical and cultural context (Melossi, 1997, 2001; Karstedt, 2001, 2002; Sozzo, 2001).

This does not necessarily involve asserting that the comparison of different cultural contexts is impossible –except if it was constructed out of 'ethnocentrism' — as seems to be the direct consequence of a radical epistemological relativism (Beirne, 1983: 381). But it does entail that the comparative task recognise the multiple local particularities of crime prevention in Argentina with regard to other cultural contexts, as these ways of thinking and acting acquired — at least in part-different meanings in the different cultural and historical *milieux* in which they were articulated. The genealogy of the rationalities and technologies of government of crime cannot be other than local (Melossi, 1997, 2001).

Only with a 'thick description' (Geertz, 2000) of the particularities in the diverse local contexts it is possible to start to construct comparative tools among them, bridges for a 'conversation', for an 'exchange' (Bernie, 1983: 385; Karstedt, 2001: 297). Only with that intense encounter with the 'empirical moment' 'here' and 'there' — avoiding, of course, 'parochialism' (Karstedt, 2001) — it is possible to consider what is 'convergent' or, even 'globalising' (Sparks, 2001). But in this wandering between difference and convergence, there should be no room for all-encompassing discourses that aim at painting a universal panorama of the field of the government of crime, or the *soi-disant* discovery of uniform trends (cf O'Malley, 2002).

Finally, this involves, as Clifford Geertz states, assuming an uncomfortable and sometimes not very coherent position, but at the same time the 'only one that can be effectively defended': 'the differences have reached greater depth than the easy type of humanism "men are men" allows us to see and the similarities are too substantial to be dissolved by an easy type of relativism "other savages", "other customs"' (Geertz, 1994: 57).

REFERENCES

Aniyar de Castro, L, (1981–82) 'Conocimiento y orden social: Criminología como legitimación y criminología de la liberación' *Capítulo Criminológico* 9–10; 39–65.

—— (1986) 'Origenes, fundamentos, aportes y límites de desarrollo futuro de una criminología de la liberación en América Latina como aporte a la teoría critica del control social' in L Aniyar de Castro (ed) *Hacia una teoría crítica del control social* (Maracaibo: Universidad del Zulia).

Baratta, A (1993) 'I Nuovi Orizzonti della Prevenzione' *Sicurezza e Territorio*, 2, 9–14.

Beirne, P (1983) 'Cultural Relativism and Comparative Criminology' *Contemporary Crises*, 7, 371–391 [DOI: 10.1007/BF00728670].

Bergalli, R (1982) 'La cuestión criminal en América Latina ("Origen y empleo de la criminología")' in R Bergalli (ed) *Crítica a la criminología* (Bogotá, Temis).

—— (1983) 'El pensamiento crítico y la criminología' in R Bergalli, J Bustos & T Miralles (eds) *El pensamiento criminológico* (Temis, Bogotá).

Bottoms, A (1995) 'The Politics and Philosophy of Sentencing' in C Clarkson & R Morgan (eds) *The Politics of Sentencing* (Oxford, Clarendon Press).

Caimari, L (2002) 'Castigar civilizadamente. Rasgos de la modernización punitiva en la Argentina (1827–1930)' in G Kessler and S Gayol (eds) *Violencias, delitos y justicias en la Argentina* (Buenos Aires, Manantial/Universidad Nacional de General Sarmiento).

Castel, R (1980) *El orden psiquiátrico* (Madrid, Las Ediciones de la Piqueta).

—— (1997) *Las metamorfosis de la cuestion social* (Buenos Aires, Paidos).

Cohen, S (1982) 'Western Crime Control Models in the Third World: Benign or Malignant?' *Research in Law, Deviance and Social Controlled*, 4, 85–119.

Crawford, A (1997) *The Local Governance of Crime* (Oxford, Clarendon Press).

—— (1998) *Crime Prevention and Community Safety. Politics, Policies and Practices* (Harlow, Longman).

Croccia, M, Eilbaum, L; Lekerman, V and Martínez, J (1999) 'Consejos de Seguridad Barriales y Participación Ciudadana: los miedos y las libertades' in M Sozzo (ed) *Seguridad urbana: Nuevos problemas, nuevos enfoques* (Santa Fe, Editorial UNL).

del Olmo, R (1975) 'Limitations for the Prevention of Violence. The Latin American Reality and its Criminological Theory' *Crime and Social Justice*, 21–29.

—— (1981) *América Latina y su criminología* (México, Siglo XXI).

—— (1990a, Original edition, 1985) 'Un reencuentro con América Latina y su criminologia' in R del Olmo (ed) *Segunda Ruptura Criminological* (Caracas, Universidad Central de Venezuela).

—— (1990b) 'La criminología de América Latina y su objeto de estudio' in R del Olmo (ed) *Segunda Ruptura Criminological* (Caracas, Universidad Central de Venezuela). Original edition, 1988.

—— (1999) 'The Development of Criminology in Latin America' *Social Justice*, 26, 19–45.

Dirección Nacional de Política Criminal (1997) *Hacia un Plan Nacional de Política Criminal II* (Buenos Aires, DNPC).

—— (1997) *Hacia un Plan Nacional de Política Criminal III* (Buenos Aires, DNPC).

Duprez, D (1997) 'Le modèle francais de prévention de la délinquance: La recherche d'un second souffle' in P Hebberecht, F & P Sack (eds) *La Prévention de la délinquance en Europe: Nouvelle strategies* (Paris, L'Harmattan).

Foucault, M (1989) *Vigilar y castigar. Nacimiento de la Prisión* (México, Siglo XXI) [PubMed: 2627149,2627148,2662313,2735803].

—— (2000) *Los anormales* (Buenos Aires, Fondo de Cultura Económica).

Geertz, C (1994) *Conocimiento local. Ensayos sobre la interpretación de las culturas* (Barcelona, Paidos).

—— (2000) *La interpretación de las culturas* (Barcelona, Gedisa).

Gilling, D (1997) *Crime Prevention. Theory, Policy and Politics* (London, UCL Press).

Gonzalez, G (2003) 'Las Reformas policiales en la Argentina: Hablando de las Estatuas de Naipol' (unpublished paper).

Graham, J & Bennet, T (1995) *Crime Prevention Strategies in Europe and North America* (Helsinski, Helsinski United Nations Institute).

Haggerty, K (2002) 'Displaced Expertise: Three Limitations on the Policy-Relevance of Criminological Thought' (unpublished paper).

Hallsworth, S (2000) 'Rethinking the Punitive Turn: Economies of Excess and the Criminology of the Other' *Punishment and Society*, 2, 145–160 [DOI: 10.1177/14624740022227926].

Hebberecht, P & Sack, F (editors) (1997) 'La prévention de la délinquance en Europe' in *Nouvelle Strategies. Paris: L'Harmattan*.

Hope, T (1995) 'Community Crime Prevention' in M Tonry & D Farrington (eds) *Building a Safer Society* (Chicago, University of Chicago Press).

Hughes, G (1998) *Understanding Crime Prevention. Social Control, Risk and Late Modernity* (Buckingham, Open University Press).

Hughes, G, McLaughlin, E & Muncie, J (2002a) *Crime Prevention and Community Safety. New Directions* (London, Sage).

Karstedt, S (2001) 'Comparing Cultures, Comparing Crime. Challenges, Prospects and Problems for a Global Criminology' *Crime, Law, and Social Change*, 36, 285–308 [DOI: 10.1023/A:1012223323445].

—— (2002) 'Durkheim, Tarde and Beyond: The Global Travel of Crime Policies' *Criminal Justice*, 2, 111–123.

Marteau, JF (2002) 'Azul casi Negro. La Gestión policial en Buenos Aires' in R Briceño Leon (ed) *Violencia, sociedad y justicia en América Latina* (Buenos Aires, CLACSO).

Melossi, D (1997) 'La radicación (embeddedness) cultural del control social (o de la imposibilidad de la traducción)' *Delito y Sociedad*, 9–10, 65–84.

—— (2001) 'The Cultural embeddedness of social Control: Reflections on the Comparison of Italian and North-American Cultures Concerning Punishment' *Theoretical Criminology*, 4, 403–424 [DOI: 10.1177/1362480601005004001].

Newburn, T & Jones, T (2000) *Widening Access: Improving Police Relationships with 'Hard to Reach' Groups* (London, Home Office).

—— (2002) 'Policy Convergence and Crime Control in the USA and the UK: Streams of Influence and Levels of Impact' *Criminal Justice*, 2, 173–203 [DOI: 10.1177/1466802502002002718].

O'Malley, P (1992) 'Risk, Power and Crime Prevention' *Economy and Society*, 21, 252–275 [DOI: 10.1080/03085149200000013].

—— (1997) 'The Politics of Crime Prevention' in P O'Malley & A Sutton (eds) *Crime Prevention in Australia* (Sydney, The Federation Press).

—— (2002) 'Globalizing Risk? Distinguishing Styles of Neoliberal Criminal Justice in Australia and the USA' *Criminal Justice*, 2, 205–222.

Pavarini, M (1994) 'Bisogni di Sicurezza e Questione Criminale' *Rassegna Italiana de Criminología*, V, 435–462.

—— (2003a) 'La Emergenza Della Sicurezza Urbana en Italia' (unpublished Paper).

—— (2003b) 'Lo grotesco de la penología contemporanea' (unpublished Paper).

PCV (2001) 'Programa de Comunidades Vulnerables' in *Buenos Aires: Plan Nacional de Prevención del Delito.*

PNPD (2000) *Plan Nacional de Prevención del Delito* (Buenos Aires, Ministerio de Justicia y Derechos Humanos and Ministerio del Interior de la Nación).

—— (2001) 'Redes Solidarias' in *Como conformar una red de vecinos Buenos Aires.*

Pratt, J (2000) 'Emotive and Ostentatious Punishment. Its Decline and Resurgence in Modern Society' *Punishment and Society*, 2, 417–439 [DOI: 10.1177/14624740022228088].

Riera, A (1979) 'Latin American Radical Criminology' *Crime and Social Justice*, 71–76.

Robert, P (1991) 'Les chercheurs face aux politiques de prévention' in P Robert (ed) *Les Politiques de prévention de la délinquance à L'une de la recherche* (Paris, L'Harmattan).

Roché, S (1999) 'Le nuove tematiche della riminalità e della sua prevenzione in Francia' *Polis*, XIII, 99–120.

Rosenbaum, D (1987) 'The Theory and Research Behind Neighbourhood Watch: Is It a Sound Fear and Crime Reduction Strategy?' *Crime and Delinquency*, 33, 103–134 [DOI: 10.1177/0011128787033001007].

Rosenbaum, D, Lurigio, AJ & Davis, RC, (1998) 'The Prevention of Crime' in *Social and Situational Strategies* (Scarabourgh, West /Wadsworth).

Rosua, F, Sagarduy, R (1999) 'La seguridad en el estado de derecho. Algunas medidas posibles desde provincias' in M Sozzo (ed) *Seguridad urbana: Nuevos problemas, nuevos enfoques* (Santa Fe, Editorial UNL).

Saín, M (2002) *Seguridad, democracia y reforma del sistema policial en la Argentina* (Buenos Aires, Fondo de Cultura Económica).

Salvatore, R & Aguirre, C (1996) 'The Birth of the Penitentiary in Latin America: Toward an Interpretative Social History of prisions' in R Salvatore & C Aguirre (eds) *The Birth of the Penitentiary in Latin America* (Austin, University of Texas Publishing Group).

Selmini, R (1999) 'Sucrezza Urbana e Prevenzione della Criminalitpa: il Caso Italiano' *Polis*, XIII, 121–144.

—— (2003) 'Le Politiche di Sicurezza: Origini, Sviluppo e Prospettive' in M Barbagli (ed) *Rapporto Sulla Criminalità in Italia* (Bologna, Istituto Cattaneo-Il Mulino).

Sozzo, M (1999) 'Seguridad urbana y gobierno local: Debate, consenso y racionalidades políticas en la Ciudad de Santa Fe' in M Sozzo (ed) *Seguridad urbana: nuevos problemas, nuevos enfoques* (Santa Fe, Editorial UNL).

——(2000) 'Seguridad urbana y tácticas de prevención del delito' *Cuadernos de doctrina y jurisprudencia penal*, 10, 17–82.

—— (2001) '"Traduttore Traditore" Importación Cultural, Traducción e Historia del Presente de la Criminología en America Latina' *Cuadernos de Doctrina y Jurisprudencia Penal*, 13, 353–431.

—— (2002) 'Usos de la violencia y construcción de la actividad policial en la Argentina' in G Kessler & S Gayol (eds) *Violencias, delitos y justicias en la Argentina* (Buenos Aires, Manantial/Universidad Nacional de General Sarmiento).

—— (2003) *¿Prevenir el delito más allá de la pena? Evaluando el Plan Nacional de Prevención del Delito* (Buenos Aires, Ministerio de Justicia, Seguridad y Derechos Humanos).

—— (2004) 'Institución policial y prevención del delito. Apuntes para una "historia del presente"' in JS Pegoraro & I Muñagorri (eds) *La Relación seguridad/inseguridad en los centros urbanos de América Latina y Europa* (Madrid, Dykinson).

Sparks, R (2001) 'Degrees of Estrangement. The Cultural Theory of Risk and Comparative Penology' *Theoretical Criminology*, 5, 159–176 [DOI: 10.1177/1362480601005002002].

Tiscornia, S & Oliveira, A (1998) 'Estructura y prácticas de las policías en la Argentina: Las redes de la ilegalidad' in H Fruhling & S de Chile (eds) *Control democrático en el mantenimiento de la seguridad interior* (CED).

Tiscornia, S (2000) 'Violencia policial, derechos humanos y reformas policiales' *Delito y sociedad*, 14, 9–20.

Tonry, M & Farrington, D (eds) (1995a) *Building a Safer Society. Strategic Approaches to Crime Prevention* (Chicago, University of Chicago Press).

—— (1995b) 'Strategic Approaches to Crime Prevention' in M Tonry & D Farrington (eds) *Building a Safer Society* (Chicago, University of Chicago Press).

Tremblay, RE & Craig, W (1995) 'Developmental Crime Prevention' in M Tonry & D Farrington (eds) *Building a Safer Society* (Chicago, University of Chicago Press).

Van Zyl Smit, D (1989) 'Adopting and Adapting Criminological Ideas: Criminology and Afrikanner Nationalism in South Africa' *Contemporary Crises*, 13, 227–251 [DOI: 10.1007/BF00729342].

Wacquant, L (2000) *Las cárceles de la miseria* (Buenos Aires, Manantial).

Zaffaroni, E (1989) *En busca de las penas perdidas* (Buenos Aires, Ediar).

—— (1993) *Criminología, aproximación desde un margen* (Bogota, Temis).

Index